Trust in Theological Education

Trust in Theological Education

Deconstructing 'Trustworthiness' for a Pedagogy of Liberation

Eve Parker

scm press

© Eve Parker 2022

Published in 2022 by SCM Press
Editorial office
3rd Floor, Invicta House,
108–114 Golden Lane,
London EC1Y 0TG, UK

www.scmpress.co.uk

SCM Press is an imprint of Hymns Ancient & Modern Ltd
(a registered charity)

Hymns Ancient & Modern

Hymns Ancient & Modern® is a registered trademark of
Hymns Ancient & Modern Ltd
13A Hellesdon Park Road, Norwich,
Norfolk NR6 5DR, UK

All rights reserved. No part of this publication may be reproduced,
stored in a retrieval system, or transmitted,
in any form or by any means, electronic, mechanical,
photocopying or otherwise, without the prior permission of
the publisher, SCM Press.

The Author has asserted her right under the Copyright, Designs and
Patents Act 1988 to be identified as the Author of this Work

Scripture quotations are from New Revised Standard Version Bible:
Anglicized Edition, copyright © 1989, 1995 National Council of
the Churches of Christ in the United States of America. Used by
permission. All rights reserved worldwide.

British Library Cataloguing in Publication data
A catalogue record for this book is available
from the British Library

ISBN: 978-0-334-06144-1

Typeset by Regent Typesetting
Printed and bound by
CPI Group (UK) Ltd

Contents

Introduction vii

1. Trusting in Theological Knowledge   1
2. Bodies Tell Stories   29
3. Being Seen as 'Trustworthy': The Gaze in Theological Education   54
4. The Priest and the Temptress: Engendering Theological Education   85
5. Distrusting Whiteness in Theological Education   120
6. Towards a Pedagogy of Trust   163

Index of Bible References   201
Index of Names and Subjects   203

Introduction

In the struggle for change, we must be neither solely patient nor solely impatient, but patiently impatient.
Paulo Freire[1]

Every truth, it seems, has its time.
Njabulo Ndebele[2]

In 1894 Bishop Macrorie of the Church of England described the need to be cautious over trusting in the motives and faith of the 'heathen' in the missionary efforts of the Church. He stated:

> We must recognize the fact that there are often mixed motives that bring the heathen to us. And while we must not altogether despise mixed motives, we are bound to watch their working ... we must expect to find, among those who come to the missionary, some who, so far from having a good report of them that are without, have lost their position among their old neighbours, and are outcasts or refugees from their tribe, and thus calculated to bring some discredit upon those to whom they attach themselves.[3]

The bishop's words show no trust in the sentiments, actions, intent and beliefs of the so-called 'heathen'. The bishop holds the position of authority and therefore assumes that his words and acts are to be trusted, maintaining that his trustworthiness is God-given. In contrast, the colonialized – whose land has been taken, religion dismissed, community pillaged and social structures mocked, labelled a 'tribal', 'heathen' – is described as having 'mixed motives', in other words, not to be trusted. In this narrative, trustworthiness is a social construct influenced by power and privilege, where the preconceived judgements of the religious leader shame and condemn the colonialized. The gaze of the ruling class, in this case the missionary, is that of white supremacy, which fixes the *other* into a state of distrust, and it becomes clear that trust is political. Trustworthiness is complex – it is dependent and influenced by one's socio-economic class status, religion, ethnicity and sexuality, it is gendered and is often manipulated. This is evident throughout the history of the Church and society, where 'trustworthiness' has been used as a social mechanism of control. In the medieval Church:

> The effect that the ideology of ecclesiastical trustworthiness had upon the distribution of economic resources was considerable, but it was arguably even more significant in entrenching assumptions about masculinity and femininity, hardening attitudes against female participation in public life, and projecting the alliance between patriarchal institutions and male heads of household far into the future.[4]

Through Eurocentric paradigms the boundaries of trust have become even more rigid: modernity, colonialism, capitalism and patriarchy have valued individuals differently, creating a hierarchy and enforcing differing standards of humanity and worth.[5] Theological education in the Western world has been complicit in validating such hierarchies, being dominated by educational models shaped by white supremacy, colonialism, patriarchy and heteronormativity. To quote Willie James Jennings: 'Theological education in the West was born in white hegemony and homogeneity, and it continues to baptize homogeneity, making it holy and right and efficient – when it is none of these things.'[6] Such an education has not adequately addressed its colonial past, racist histories and narratives of oppression. After all, 'It was in academic spaces of theological training that ideas of Christian supremacy were manufactured as knowledge, to be put to the project of conquest, colonization, conversion as they made their way from lecture hall, to pulpit, to legislative assemblies.'⁷ How can those of us involved in such a theological education be trusted in the process of learning and formation if we are not honest about our history or if we are ignorant or indifferent to the struggles of those who have been, and continue to be, marginalized by such an education? The bishop's words in the opening quote capture the misuse of power and the ingrained notions of trust that have been normalized and ingrained within the Church and theological education institutes. Polarized notions of trust and decency shaped by cultural ignorance and Eurocentric rationality shape our ways of knowing and being. Ignorance and a culture of deference permeate British society, enabling the 'knowledge' of the white ruling classes to remain dominant. In the words of Charles Mills:

> Imagine an ignorance militant, aggressive, not to be intimidated, an ignorance that is active, dynamic, that refuses to go quietly – not at all confined to the illiterate and uneducated but propagated at the highest levels of the land, indeed presenting itself unblushingly as knowledge.⁸

Such ignorance has consciously concealed its own geo-historical and socio-political locations, thereby creating the idea of universal knowledge, the only knowledge to be trusted. As Walter Mignolo remarks, 'The colonial matrix of power, put in place in the sixteenth and seventeenth centuries, was framed in and by Christian theology. Christian theology was the ultimate horizon of knowledge – since and after the Renaissance – that incorporated Greek rationality.'⁹ The theology of the Church in the context of the UK continues to be rooted in the norms that such knowledge has dictated, inclusive of patriarchy, heterosexuality and capitalism and grounded in binary notions of decency and indecency. Oppression and marginalization are maintained through the rigidity of these norms that preserve the privileges of the white, male, heterosexual ruling classes. Trust is maintained by controlling the boundaries of such norms. The means by which the mechanisms of trust have been imposed have been determined by systems of power that include the processes of globalization, such as colonial Christianity from the West, which has been driven by the 'desire to transform "the other" and thus undertaken with a spirit of mission and conversion, of exclusivism and superiority'.[10] During the colonial period great efforts were made by the colonizers to eradicate indigenous beliefs, languages and cultures, in order to control and colonialize the minds of the people. Consequently, Western beliefs, practices, theories, philosophies and theologies dominated the world practically and intellectually. Through a process of normalization, trust was granted – and internalized – to the hegemonic knowledge of the West that formulated a grand narrative in which the epistemologies of the colonized were marginalized and mocked. According to Mhango, 'since the inception of Western colonised and hegemonic education as espoused by the current dominant Western grand narrative, almost all fields of education have been hugely held and totally dominated by Western intellectualism which ignores other cultures by relegating them to the peripheries.'[11] Ignorance of such peripheral knowledge equates to distrust in the powerful, because the world views, knowledge, value systems, philosophy and theologies that have been at the underside of modernity have been shamefully silenced by those with power. Trust therefore requires power, because we are told to trust in other humans, but certain humans have been disqualified from 'full humanity', some throughout history have only been considered 'partially human'. Smith notes that 'Ideas about what counted as human in association with the power to define people as human or not human were already encoded in imperial and colonial discourses prior to the period of imperialism.'[12] Take, for example, portrayals of the incarnate Christ: for the missionaries he had to be reimagined as a white European man in order for him to be fully human. To the colonialized subject, the God of Christianity then appeared as the White man, and the White man demanded that the people put all their trust in God, the same God made in their mirror image. Through the polarized imagery of the White male gaze, Christ was conveyed in opposition to the woman, the 'heathen' and the 'whore', and theology was used to establish such models of 'decency' and divinity. Consequently, women in particular were portrayed as untrustworthy, the original sinners, temptresses and 'gateways to hell', and the theologies surrounding portrayals of the incarnate Christ, despite being inherently inaccurate, racist and patriarchal, dominated and continue to dominate in large parts of theological education.

Situating the context of theological education today

Theological education involves the shaping of our minds through what constitutes worthwhile knowledge of God and the Christian faith. To quote Rowan Williams, 'in the broadest possible sense, theological education is learning more about the world that faith creates, or the world that faith trains you to inhabit.'[13] This places emphasis on faith, character, spirituality, action and formational growth. Trust in such 'shaping of the minds' is therefore vital, particularly given the complexities of the age in which theological formation is taking place. In the context of the UK, and in many other parts of the world, theological education is being taught at a time when it would seem that there is more distrust than trust, when the masses are disillusioned by the hope and security the Church once promised them, and when neo-liberal capitalism has fuelled a world of inequality and greed. Racism and xenophobia are on the rise, gender-based violence has surged, wars are being fought, extremist religious ideologies are mobilizing and socio-economic structures are geared in favour of the rich. What role can and should theological education play at such a time as this? To ignore such realities is to participate in the oppression of the marginalized, because ignorance is complicity.

The theological relevance of societal structures of oppression has a significant impact on the Church's teaching, preaching and purpose today, and therefore directly impacts theological formation for those in education. The shaping of minds and knowledge of God should not accommodate the culture of the oppressor or simply accept unjust orders that deny the fullness of life for all. The role of the Church is to be prophetic in contexts of oppression, and yet the Church in the UK appears at times to have lost its prophetic voice. It often appears confused about its purpose within society and anxious over losing power and relevance, and so it often stays silent in situations of oppression. Such silence and neutrality come at the expense of allowing space for 'prophetic theology' to speak truth to power and be heard by those who are most downtrodden. Likewise, dominant discourses of theological education have favoured neutrality in the face of inequality: teaching that God is 'love', the greatest truth of all, comes without situating such love in the context of the oppressed. An education that permits greater self-awareness is needed, because 'Self-awareness is a significant factor for a person to deepen the relationship with Christ and realize the knowledge about God in daily life.'[14] Yet theological education does not always allow the space for students to have the freedom to be themselves, because students who challenge the norm of the white, male, heterosexual middle class are often condemned, silenced, marginalized and distrusted for doing so. Theological education could offer the space to empower those in formational training with the knowledge, passion and skills to struggle alongside the marginalized, while becoming critically aware of their own place and complicity in society and spaces of struggle.

Offering such theological education would challenge the Eurocentric epistemology that has focused on 'rational' ways of knowing without a critique of theological rationality that enables global majority voices to present diverse knowledge of God. This would cause the dominant discourse of European theology knowledge to self-destruct. The subject of trust and trustworthiness is becoming increasingly relevant to the

INTRODUCTION

Church in the UK today. The *Church Times* recently reported on a study that found increasing distrust of clergy:

> A little more than half the respondents (54 per cent) trusted the clergy to tell the truth – a drop of nine percentage points in the past year alone, and 29 percentage points since 1983, representing the biggest negative difference of the dozens of professions included in the questionnaire in this period.[15]

Trust in the Church and clergy has been in decline for a number of years, and yet the role of trust has not been given the attention it demands in theological efforts in the UK. In agreement, Trudy Govier suggests that 'One reason that we underrate the significance of trust is our strong tendency not to notice it until it breaks down.'[16] The breakdown in trust has wider implications for the Church, society and theological education; an exploration of trust in relation to the Church and theology enables critical contemplation of how and why there has been this breakdown.

The decline of trust in the established Church and its clergy impacts the role and purpose of theological education in the UK; theological education is finding itself vulnerable to societal shifts that have resulted in fewer applicants to many theological colleges. The Church is also experiencing what Christine Hong refers to as 'a crisis in conscience'. Hong is speaking about theological education in the USA but the same can be said for theological education in the UK, because 'institutions of theological education are still ultimately colonial and Christian enterprises.'[17] Through the systematic teaching of certain theologies that dominate the theological curricula, entire communities, people and truth claims have been erased from the process of learning. It is only in the last 100 years that women have been permitted into theological classrooms, LGBTQI+ voices are for the most part still marginalized, and black theology and theologies from the majority world have been silenced, pigeon-holed or mocked in theological education institutions. Hong rightly remarks that 'On the one hand, theological education hopes to change the world for the better, and on the other hand, it has difficulty holding a mirror up to its white supremacist, settler-colonial, and Christian hegemonic histories and practices.'[18] How then can such institutions be trusted if they have not come to terms with their colonial past or their complex histories? This book will therefore look at how we might trust in theological education, with an understanding that 'To trust people is to expect that they will act well, that they will take our interests into account and not harm us.'[19] The question of how theological education can become trustworthy is then central to the aims of this book, which seeks to address the ways in which environments of distrust have been created – particularly for the oppressed and marginalized. It will address how an environment of learning can be created that is sensitive to the needs and particularities of the less dominant groups – including women, LGBTQI+, disabled, and black and ethnic minority students. In doing so, it aims to recognize the need to be trustworthy to the oppressed. For the English philosopher John Locke, 'the vision of politics and of human life as resting upon trust needs to include the reverse of trust – betrayal; "and the remedy for the betrayal of trust was the right of revolution".'[20] If the people feel betrayed by theological education and the Church as a whole can no longer be trusted, then perhaps it is time for a theological revolution.

Exposing trust

Defining trust is no simple task. According to Fukuyama, trust is:

> the expectation that arises within a community of regular, honest and cooperative behaviour, based on commonly shared norms, on the part of other members of that community. Those norms can be about deep 'value' questions like the nature of God or justice, but they also encompass secular norms like professional standards and codes of behaviour.[21]

INTRODUCTION

In his exploration of the role of 'trustworthy men' in the medieval Church in Britain, Ian Forrest notes that 'Asked what a trustworthy man was, a late medieval bishop might have answered that it was someone whose standing in his community was a guarantee of the information he provided. It was a man who knew what was required of him.'[22] Forrest outlines the way in which bishops were able to manipulate parishes and communities by giving certain men the status of being trustworthy. These men were responsible for reporting on the 'sins' of the people in their communities and their trust status was often determined by their socio-economic privileges.

Women were relegated both socially and institutionally to the margins of the realm of trustworthiness, a space in which they have existed throughout the history of the Church. The belief that women are unworthy of trust is captured in the words of the Church Father Epiphanius, who wrote that 'women are a feeble race, untrustworthy and of mediocre intelligence. Once again we see that the Devil knows how to make women spew forth ridiculous teachings.'[23] The implications of such beliefs have been damaging for women throughout history, because such thinking has led to the justification of violence against them. It has enabled dichotomies in the depiction of women as either 'virgins' or 'whores' to be used to stigmatize and shame the bodies of women into silence. Trust is therefore a socio-political tool; Forrest notes that 'trust between equals may also depend upon mistrust of those people not considered equals, which has often led to marginalization of women, the poor, and people categorized as ethnic minorities.'[24] Trust has also been described as being 'the glue of society, a substance supporting social cohesion and the functioning of institutions – particularly important under the conditions of modernity, which is characterized by a reliance on externalized expert systems beyond the reach of most'.[25]

Discussions on the topic of trust are not new. There has been a great deal of attention paid to trust in psychology, philosophy and sociology, as well as in theology, where Aquinas recognized the need to give focus to notions of trust in God. Plato's

Republic relies on trust in the wisdom of the philosopher kings. Locke and Dunn infamously wrote on trust in state and governments, and more recently it appears in the work of the moral philosophers Annette Baier,[26] Nancy Nyquist Potter[27] and in Trudy Govier, who notes how 'attitudes of trust and distrust have a profound effect on our relationships, influencing almost every dimension of them.'[28] The collection of contextual explorations in *Trust and Trustworthiness across Cultures*, edited by Catherine T. Kwantes and Ben C. H. Kuo,[29] has exposed the cultural beliefs of trust and distrust. Erhabor Idemudia and Babatola Olawa's chapter notes that 'In many African languages, trust connotes "dependability", "hope", "expectation" and "faith".'[30] Such sentiments resonate with much of Christian theological discourse on trust that focuses on the importance of trust, hope and faith in God. However, Christian theological discourse has not sufficiently grappled with the role of trust in our relationships with each other. Nor has there been much work on the impact of trusting in God when God has been portrayed in the image of a white man throughout the missionary history of the British and European empires. Such an image has had significant implications for Christian theology and missiology, where trust in white, middle-class European men has often been assumed, to the detriment of all those who do not fit such a mould.

Trust is a mechanism of power that fundamentally affects our relationships with others because it involves what we have come to know and believe about other people, including their actions, beliefs and intentions. As Govier remarks, 'Our attitudes of trust and distrust affect our outlook on the world and our sense of ourselves and others.'[31] Trust has often been granted to the hegemonic structures of power that have sought to undermine, patronize and control those who have not dominated society, those on the periphery of society – those who the powerful have depicted as untrustworthy and undeserving. Therefore trust is not always equally distributed in terms of social and political relationships, because oppressed persons are often not granted the power to be trusted in their wisdom, knowledge, insights and experiences. Trust can therefore be learnt and unlearnt. This book will focus on challenging the power dynamics of trust in theological education; it will seek to work towards a model of trustworthiness that is described in African philosophy as 'Ubuntu', where the focus is on interconnectedness. Here trust is a communal act as opposed to an individual power that can be abused and misused, and 'society puts stress on the group rather than on the individual, more on solidarity than on the activity and needs of the individual, more on the communion of persons than on their autonomy.'[32] As Desmond Tutu expounded, 'We say, "a person is a person through other persons". It is not, "I think therefore I am." It says rather: "I am human because I belong. I participate, I share." A person with *Ubuntu* is open and available to others.'[33] The centrality of interpersonal trust and faith in God is found in the theology of Augustine, who wrote:

> For the truth is that from your heart you trust a heart other than your own ... with your mind you can see your own trust, but the trust of your friend cannot be the object of your love if no such mutual trust is found in you, a trust which enables you to believe something you cannot actually see in your friend.[34]

Situating the author

I have had the privilege of listening to the black theologian Anthony Reddie speak on a number of occasions, and in all the papers he has delivered that I have heard, he begins by situating himself, naming his context and identity as a 'black theologian from Yorkshire'. This is important for many reasons: Reddie situates his knowledge, noting that 'all knowledges are situated and every knowledge is constructed'; he does not conceal the 'geo-historical and bio-historical' location in which he contemplates God and therefore does not mimic the colonial way of theologizing that suggests some form of universality. Such theology is honest in its embodied and situated reality. Which raises the question of why Eurocentric epistemic feels the need to conceal its locations. For example, how many white, male, middle-class lecturers feel the need to situate themselves before delivering a paper? Do theological educators introducing the work of Torrance or Barth, for example, in a class on Doctrine, begin by locating the theologian's whiteness and class privilege? To do so would be 'epistemic disobedience' according to Mignolo, because it would allow for the 'illusion of the zero point epistemology' to be challenged.[35] It is the ego politics of knowledge, as Frantz Fanon has remarked, that 'permits scholars to work in the guise of disembodied, unlocated neutrality and presumed objectivity'.[36]

So before I continue, let me situate myself and the context from which I 'speak', thereby declaring my biases and geopolitics as a white, British, Anglican, northern woman. One's geographic location within the UK also matters, given that even the mastery of the English language determines one's social positioning in a classist context, and so a northern accent is often looked down upon as uncivilized.[37] My own situated theology has been shaped by my experiences of working for the Council for World Mission on theology programmes in India, Jamaica, South Africa, Guyana, Zambia and the Philippines, as well as by my experience of working for the United Reformed Church in global and intercultural ministries and for the Church of England, training ordinands and readers, and now being at Durham University. I believe that I learnt more about God in the slums of Chennai, the Smokey Mountains of Manila and the brothels of Delhi than I did in the comfort of a classroom in St Andrews, although I had been conditioned to think that such learning was not intellectual knowledge.

I share my 'roots' as a means of declaring where my knowledge has been constructed and is located. I am also aware of my complicity in the 'system', the same system that this book seeks to critique. In agreement with Hong, 'if you take a paycheck from an institution that behaves in white and Christian supremacist ways, you are complicit ... only in admitting to the systems and structures in which we too are entrapped can we begin to disrupt them effectively.'[38] I therefore confess my own complicity and intention to disrupt.

This book

In the past 100 years the context in which theological education takes place in the UK has shifted dramatically. There has been an increase in the number of women students entering theological education, partly as a result of mainstream Christian denominations now permitting the ordination of women; the number of students from black and ethnic minority backgrounds has also risen significantly. We need therefore to be asking the question of whether our vision for theological education has been sufficiently transformed. Has theological education been engendered or are women just being modelled to fit into the theological cassocks of men? Have we done enough to reformulate our theology and offer theological curricula that are both relevant and life affirming to men and women? And have we deconstructed the dominating colonial theologies? Learning and knowing in theology hold the risk of becoming epistemologically flawed if they are guilty of reproducing and perpetuating exclusive ideologies that could create cultures of un-belonging in our theological education institutes. The premise of this book acknowledges that theological education in the UK remains predominantly white, patriarchal and Christian. At the heart of this book is the question: does theological education have the capacity to help the Church bring an end to racism, sexism and classism, abolish socio-economic inequality, gender violence and environmental degradation? It can of course be argued that this is not the purpose of theological education, but then what is its purpose if not to enable students with the skills to bring about God's kin-dom on earth? The book aims to make a contribution to the growing literature in the area of postcolonial and liberationist works that seek to challenge dominant models of theological formation. As Hong remarks, 'What theological education needs is not more minoritized scholars who can code-switch, but new frameworks of theological education altogether.'[39] It seeks therefore to challenge theologies that have been trusted and yet are shaped by individualistic ideologies that have enabled unjust structures of oppression and denied the truth claims of the oppressed. It will focus on the notion of 'trust' in order to explore the power dynamics of education and learning and address the issues of inequality and marginalization apparent within dominant pedagogies and curricula. It calls for critical thinking and demands a rebellion, an uprising that challenges our ways of knowing – which have systematically wiped out minoritized voices and communities – by asking how spaces of theological formation can enable all students to feel that they 'belong', that they can safely engage and are free to be themselves in their fullness.

Chapter 1 will situate the notion of trust in knowledge and the theological implications of unequal distributions of epistemological power that prevent life-flourishing curricula. Chapter 2 explores the role of bodies in pedagogies of theological education, highlighting the need to centre the testimonies of the oppressed. Chapter 3 considers the dominant gaze in theological education that defines who is deemed trustworthy and through Scripture identifies what it means to 'be seen' before the powerful and 'be seen' by God. Chapters 4, 5 and 6 offer means by which theological education can be transformed in order to be trusted by the oppressed and marginalized. Chapter 4 notes the need to engender the curriculum and the role of feminist pedagogy in formation. Chapter 5 suggests that the teaching of World Christianity offers a potential means of dismantling whiteness in theological education. Chapter 6 calls for an interconnected pedagogy of trust and solidarity to shape a theology of Ubuntu. Each chapter relies on feminist, postcolonial and liberative hermeneutics in order to engage with the biblical relevance of a pedagogy of liberation for theological education. In doing so, dominant Western, patriarchal interpretations and theologies are challenged throughout.

INTRODUCTION

Notes

1 Paulo Freire, *Pedagogy of the Heart*, trans. D. Macedo and A. Oliveira (London: Bloomsbury, 2016), p. 64.
2 Njabulo Ndebele, 'Foreword', in Steve Biko, *I Write What I Like, Steve Biko: A Selection of His Writings* (Johannesburg: Picardo Press, 2017), p. xi.
3 Bishop Macrorie, in *Missionary Conference of the Anglican Communion 1894*, ed. George A. Spottiswoode (London: SPCK, 1894), p. 141.
4 Ian Forrest, *Trustworthy Men: How Inequality and Faith Made the Medieval Church* (Princeton, NJ: Princeton University Press, 2018), p. 351.
5 See Otrude Nontobeko Moyo, *Africanity and Ubuntu as Decolonising Discourse* (Cham, Switzerland: Palgrave Macmillan, 2021), p. 4
6 Willie James Jennings, *After Whiteness: An Education in Belonging* (Grand Rapids, MI: Wm. B. Eerdmans, 2020), p. 6.
7 Jeannine Hill Fletcher, *The Sin of White Supremacy: Christianity, Racism, and Religious Diversity in America* (Maryknoll, NY: Orbis, 2017), p. 9.
8 Charles W. Mills, *Black Rights/ White Wrongs: The Critique of Racial Liberalism* (New York: Oxford University Press, 2017), p. 49.
9 Walter Mignolo, 'Decolonizing Western Epistemology', in Ada María Isasi-Díaz and Eduardo Mendieta (eds), *Decolonizing Epistemologies: Latina/o Theology and Philosophy* (New York: Fordham University Press, 2012), p. 29.
10 Fernando F. Segovia (ed.), *Interpreting Beyond Borders* (Sheffield: Sheffield Academic Press, 2000), pp. 19–20.
11 Nkwazi Nkuzi Mhango, *Decolonising Colonial Education: Doing Away with Relics and Toxicity Embedded in the Racist Dominant Grand Narrative* (Mankon, Bamenda: Langaa Research & Publishing CIG, 2018), p. xiii.
12 Linda T. Smith, *Decolonizing Methodologies, Research and Indigenous Peoples* (London: Zed Books, 1999), p. 25.
13 Rowan Williams quoted in Benjamin Wayman, 'Rowan Williams: Theological Education is For Everyone', 19 August 2020, available at: https://www.christianitytoday.com/ct/2020/august-web-only/rowan-williams-theological-education-for-everyone.html (accessed 1.12.2021).
14 Jane I. Lu, 'Educational Models of Spiritual Formation in Theological Education: Introspection-based Spiritual Formation', *Teaching Theology & Religion* 24:1 (2021): 28–41, 28.
15 See Hattie Williams, 'Public trust in the clergy has dramatically decreased in recent years, survey finds', *Church Times* (4 December 2020),

available at: https://www.churchtimes.co.uk/articles/2020/4-december/news/uk/public-trust-in-the-clergy-has-dramatically-decreased-in-recent-years-survey-finds (accessed 1.12.2021).

16 Trudy Govier, *Dilemmas of Trust* (Quebec: McGill-Queen's University Press, 1998), p. 5.

17 See Christine J. Hong, *Decolonial Futures: Intercultural and Interreligious Intelligence for Theological Education* (Maryland, NY: Lexington Books, 2021), p. 1.

18 Ibid.

19 Govier, *Dilemmas of Trust*, p. 6.

20 Barbara A. Misztal, 'The Notion of Trust in Social Theory', in *Policy, Organisation and Society* 5:1 (1992): 6–15, 7.

21 F. Fukuyama, *Trust: Social Virtues and the Creation of Prosperity* (New York: Free Press, 1995), p. 26.

22 Forrest, *Trustworthy Men*, p. 127.

23 See Ruth A. Tucker and Walter Liefeld (eds), *Daughters of the Church: Women and Ministry from New Testament Times to the Present* (Grand Rapids, MI: Zondervan Publishing House, 1987), pp. 116, 148.

24 Forrest, *Trustworthy Men*, p. 162.

25 Florian Mühlfried, 'Introduction: Approximating Mistrust', in Florian Mühlfried (ed.), *Mistrust: Ethnographic Approximations* (Bielefeld: Transcript Verlag, 2017), p. 7.

26 See Annette Baier, 'Trust and Antitrust', *Ethics* 96:2 (1986): 231–60.

27 See Nancy Nyquist Potter, *How Can I Be Trusted? A Virtue Theory of Trustworthiness* (Oxford: Rowman & Littlefield Publishers, 2002).

28 See Govier, *Dilemmas of Trust*, p. 3.

29 See Catherine T. Kwantes and Ben C. H. Kuo (eds), *Trust and Trustworthiness Across Cultures: Implications for Societies and Workplaces* (Geneva: Springer Nature, 2021).

30 See Erhabor S. Idemudia and Babatola D. Olawa, 'Once Bitten, Twice Shy: Trust and Trustworthiness from an African Perspective', in Kwantes and Kuo (eds), *Trust and Trustworthiness*, pp. 33–40.

31 Govier, *Dilemmas of Trust*, p. 4.

32 See Idemudia and Olawa, 'Once Bitten, Twice Shy', in Kwantes and Kuo (eds), *Trust and Trustworthiness*, p. 36.

33 See Maduabuchi Leo Muoneme, S. J., *The Hermeneutics of Jesuit Leadership in Higher Education: The Meaning and Culture of Jesuit-Catholic Presidents* (London: Routledge, 2017), p. 158.

34 See Augustine of Hippo, *De fide rerum invisibilium*, ed. M. P. J. van den Hout, CCSL 46 (Turnhout: Brepols, 1969), pp. 1–19, trans. Michael G. Campbell in *The Works of Saint Augustine: On Christian*

Belief, ed. Boniface Ramsey (New York: New City Press, 2005), pp. 183–6.

35 See Walter D. Mignolo, 'Epistemic Disobedience, Independent Thought and Decolonial Freedom', in *Theory, Culture & Society*, 26:7–8 (2009), 159–81, 160.

36 See Frantz Fanon, *The Wretched of the Earth* (New York: Grove Press, 1963), quoted in Moyo, *Africanity and Ubuntu*, p. 51.

37 Frantz Fanon offers a profound exploration of the role of language in how colonialism and whiteness operates; see *Black Skin, White Masks* (London: Penguin, 1967), pp. 17–18.

38 Hong, *Decolonial Futures*, p. 43.

39 Ibid., p. 6.

I

Trusting in Theological Knowledge

Freedom is always and exclusively freedom for the one who thinks differently.[1]
Rosa Luxemburg

Teacher, we know that you are sincere, and teach the way of God in accordance with truth, and show deference to no one; for you do not regard people with partiality.
(Matthew 22.16)

Theological education remains dominated by Eurocentrism and white male middle-class heteronormativity. As a result, a small number of theologians have been asking critical questions about the existing inequalities that dominate academic spaces of theological discourse, with some calling for a (de)colonizing of the curriculum. Yet, for the most part, theological education in the UK remains Eurocentric and the norms of colonial Christianity remain ingrained in the academy. This is in part a consequence of the Mission Christianity of Western imperialism, which has had a lasting impact on theological education, where, as John Gascoigne has remarked, 'the English drew on their deep reserves of Christian thought and tradition to explain to themselves why they were entitled to have an empire.'[2] After all, empires need creeds as they seek to conquer and control the land of others, in order to sustain and justify their acts of violence and control, and the British did so in the name of God. Under the guise of a discourse of respectability and morality, the British developed a Christian theological narrative that, as in previous empires, used Christendom to attempt to theologically ground its colonial conquests. In so doing it created boundaries and barriers of belonging shaped by social and moral acceptability and decency, and those who violated them were condemned as heathens, dogs, harlots and sluts. The boundaries enabled the sustaining of the orders of power that were fundamentally white and patriarchal and were embodied in dichotomies that gave a simplistic understanding of good and bad: being Christian or heathen, virgin or whore, gay or straight, black or white.

The Bible has been used to justify such dichotomous thinking, as have the dominant discourses of theology, because, as the sociologist of education Paulo Freire remarks, education enables 'the transference of power and privileges'.[3] By applying such theory to theological education institutes (TEIs) we can witness how social structures such as racism, patriarchy and sexism are reproduced and have enabled theological curricula that have allowed the impression of universal theological truths to dominate. We see this in the curricula, the reading lists, the staff representation and the methodologies of teaching. The Victorian-era paradigm of discipline, obedience and deference has enabled such systems to go unchallenged and to dominate our TEIs while being further instilled in and by church bodies. The question then is how to go about deconstructing the ingrained notions of belonging, inequality and domination that are fundamentally life-denying to those who have existed and continue to exist on the margins. This is not, however, about simply creating environments of integration within the current systems that have enabled and justified oppression. It is about the need for transformation of the education systems so that students and staff can become 'beings for themselves'.[4]

In defining a curriculum, Denis Lawton argues that rather than it being 'that which is taught in classrooms', it is 'essentially a selection from the culture of society ... certain aspects of our way of life, certain kinds of knowledge, certain attitudes and values are regarded as so important that their transmission to the next generation is not left to chance'.[5] It is therefore no accident that the voices of women, the working class, the disabled, the queer and ethnic minorities are missing from curricula, as Jannette Elwood points out: 'the selection from the culture is not neutral and is dominated by particular, powerful groups who dictate what is taught, how it is taught and also how it is assessed.'[6] In order to create life-flourishing and life-affirming curricula in theological education, therefore, it will not be enough to go about a process of diversification of reading lists and staff bodies – this is too often a superficial process used to give an impression of transformation. This has been made apparent by the many education institutes that are going through processes of curriculum development where liberal efforts are being made to diversify reading lists and include more black scholars and women on the list, yet the systematic injustices of existing inequalities remain intact. There has to be an acknowledgement that theological knowledge and power have been historically imposed through the violence of racism, sexism, heteronormativity and classism. Consequently, the issue of inequality is systemic and deeply rooted, and failing to address these realities will offer little transformation for those who have been marginalized by the dominant concepts, norms and values that have prevailed from the norms of empire to the pedagogies of theological education institutes in the UK.

This can be captured in the words of a black student I interviewed, who stated:

> 'My tutor said to me that he was surprised I made it to class on time because people like me are always late. I knew what he meant by "people like me". He would always ask me to run the errands in the class, the comments on my papers were always patronizing. He wasn't the only person who made me feel out of place and like I shouldn't be there. When it came to group work I was often left alone.'[7]

Racist stereotypes have become ingrained in institutional spaces and normalized by those who students are expected to trust. Such experiences are often met with a deafening silence when reported to those within the institutions or churches, and such silence masks consent to racism. Exploring such realities requires a conscious awakening and interrogation of our own complicit selves, because in order to create life-flourishing curricula and learning environments, staff and students must become conscious of the life-denying aspects of theological education. To become conscious is to become aware of the unequal power dynamics that exist both within and outside of the classroom, and to recognize one's own complicity in the systems of inequality in order to challenge the unequal relationships of dominance. The black womanist writer Toni Morrison makes the point that we need to 'take away the gaze of the white male' and notes that 'Once you take that out, the whole world opens up.'[8] This is about addressing the imbalance of power and not seeking to theologically define who we are before God in ways that have been normalized by white, male, middle-class heteronormativity. It also requires a profound questioning of in what or whose world theological questioning and formation are being developed. Any serious efforts to address the imbalances of power cannot simply be a process of adding books to reading lists written by black and ethnic minority theologians and women, or adding modules to the existing arrangements of knowledge that leave the existing power dynamics intact. Though this is needed, change also requires deconstructing systemic injustices through education and action by critically examining existing presuppositions of knowledge and theological thought. This means becoming conscious of and rejecting those aspects of our theologies and institutions that maintain power and use such power to oppress and silence those who may challenge such social structures.

Theological education and consciousness

Theological education institutes and universities in the UK remain uncontested sites of power, places in which social and societal norms are being reproduced. As such we are often not given the spaces or even the tools to contemplate God in ways that might help us to challenge systemic injustices. Questioning the politics of Church and society is often not encouraged, because theological education has been dominated by what Freire has referred to as a 'banking system' of education, where 'knowledge is a gift bestowed by those who consider themselves knowledgeable upon those whom they consider to know nothing.'[9] Ignorance is most commonly bestowed on the students and scholars who are black, women and working class, as there exists a hierarchy of opinion, knowledge, theory and critique in which the ruling classes are deemed the most trusted in their insights. This can lead those at the bottom of the hierarchies to internalize feelings of inadequacy, un-belonging and unworthiness. And this remains the case despite the rise in diversity of students studying theology in the UK, because the social powers remain intact and have not been critically challenged, thereby perpetuating existing inequalities. Those in power therefore retain control over not just theological education but also mission, because they perpetuate their understandings of God's will, which can enable them to both justify their own social positioning and profess exclusive or patronizing theologies to the detriment of those without power – the LGBTQI+ communities, women, the working class and people of colour.

Consciousness demands an awareness of the systems of oppression, including racism, sexism and patriarchy, that have forced people into the margins. This requires what Anthony Reddie has referred to as:

> serious analysis of the wider socio-cultural and political construction of Empire and the ways in which the embedded nature of Whiteness has formed a world in which notions of manifest destiny and White exceptionalism have given rise to a toxic reality built on White supremacy.[10]

Such analysis requires an exploration of Britain's colonial past that has impacted theological education not just in the UK but around the world. As the South African theologian Marilyn Naidoo has remarked: 'The lens of colonial difference in institutions has not always been named or given the attention it deserves. Colonial difference is a reference to the spaces – the borders and peripheries of empire that have suffered the negative consequences of modernity.'[11] Colonialism has not only impacted the structures of power in nation states but also the minds of the people, and the colonized mind is 'more subtle and more difficult to identify, resist and transform'.[12] Colonialism has dehumanized indigenous communities, stereotyped people and disregarded their beliefs and religiosities as mere superstition and irrational thought. Through the process of 'othering', the colonial gaze distinguishes humanity into hierarchies of worth; the same process is used within the Bible to condemn other nation states and religious groups as deserving of the wrath of God for believing in other gods. Education has been used to legitimize such processes of dehumanization and control and oppress the colonized through the mind. This has produced dominant ideologies such as racism, patriarchy and classism that have been adopted into the structures of oppression and remain ingrained in former colonies of the British Empire and within the structures of power in British society.

Because there has been no process of reckoning for the atrocities of empire and the complicity of the Church in the UK, therefore there has been no reconciliation or forgiveness because the past has been suppressed to meet the needs of the present for those who maintain power and privilege. British society is very good at brushing things under the carpet, keeping a stiff upper lip and masking its sins and failures. For the British elites and establishments to critically address British imperialism and confess to its atrocities would lead to critical questions about those who maintain the power in this nation, and it is much easier to live in denial, excuse slavery, racism and exploitation, and suggest that it is simply a thing of the past, despite the current Prime Minister openly rejoicing in its glory and society becoming increasingly intolerant. Consequently the legacy of theological education remains Eurocentric and rooted in the imperial idealism of the empire and its Church, meaning that the ways in which we have historically contemplated God and reasoned with our place and purpose on earth have been understood through the lens of the white ruling class in this country and this too often remains unchallenged.

It is also the case that not all theological educators and students are content with discussions on identity, racism and patriarchy in theology. Some ridicule theologies of liberation, including feminist and black theologies, and others more subtly choose to keep such discourses off reading lists and modules. The Mud Flower Collective of theological educators in the USA, a group of feminist and womanist scholars, argued that those who ridicule such theologies, 'are those who have sizable investment in holding the power in place in prevailing patterns of social organization – often those who are already holders in institutional power'.[13] This argument can also be applied in the context of the UK, where theologies and methodologies are determined by the custodians of knowledge and the views of those on the periphery are not trusted or respected. This epistemic struggle therefore demands a rethinking of theological education in the shadow of empire and in the midst of patriarchy, racism, classism and heteronormativity, in order to gather the untrusted insights of the oppressed and contemplate God in resistance and solidarity. To do so requires a conscious awakening to the interrelated narratives of struggle – where theological education must situate itself in the histories of racial violence, interreligious intolerance, sexism and LGTBQI+ hatred and abuse. Awakening to such struggles enables a challenging of the systems of knowledge that have enabled such violence and subjugation to occur, the systems that have said 'trust in the white, straight, middle-class priest' but not in the *othered*. The systems that have enabled and justified centuries of theological oppression and abuse.

As Freire says, 'There's no such thing as neutral education. Education either functions as an instrument to bring about conformity or freedom.'[14] For the theological educator who does not seek social transformation for the oppressed, their interest lies in 'changing the consciousness of the oppressed, not the situation which oppresses them';[15] in other words, 'educating' the oppressed to accept the white, heterosexual, patriarchal, middle-class way of thinking and being, a tool used by the missionaries during colonial rule in order to infiltrate the colonized mind with Victorian norms and ideals. As for the liberal theological educator, they give the impression of promoting diversity, adding a seat at the table for one scholar of colour and a few spaces for white middle-class women, in order to suggest that transformation has occurred. Yet in reality this is tokenism in diversity, used to appease the conscience of the liberal educator while maintaining the status quo. This way, trust in the knowledge that they profess and their social status remain intact within the system that granted them their powers. The theological educator who believes in a life-flourishing and life-affirming education believes in emancipatory education, a theological education that is in itself an act of liberation – not oppression and control; a theological education where the theological educator enters into affirmative spaces of dialogue and enables transformative contemplation of God, and where students are able to be truly critical and conscious of their own identities and being. In doing so, such educators are committed to structural analysis and institutional change.

'Bollocks' theologies and power in theological education

Theological education institutes and colleges in the UK are finding themselves vulnerable to societal shifts because theology and the Church no longer occupy the societal position of relevance that they once held. There is also a certain amount of vulnerability being exposed by those who have held the power, and we are seeing this being played out in public forums such as Twitter. For example, the theologian John Milbank, Professor Emeritus at the University of Nottingham, tweeted in 2020: 'Of course, the themed identity theology you mention (liberation, local, "practice based" black, feminist, queer, trans, disability etc etc), is tiresome careerist and naturally elitist bollocks. But no one serious takes it seriously. Or if they do that is utterly tragic.'¹⁶ There is a fear on behalf of those who have possessed the power and upheld the norms that with the questioning of trust in dominant theological discourses, and the uncertainty of the place and role of theology in the academy, the power dynamics will shift – and that the epistemologies that the dominant white middle-class scholars have upheld, that have enabled the cultural norms that marginalize the exact voices that Milbank mocks, will be challenged by these so-called 'bollocks' theologies. Milbank's fears may well be justified, because it appears that we are potentially on the brink of a Kairos moment in theological education, where the collective solidarity that is apparent in liberation theologies is beginning to have an increasing impact by entering the academies of the UK and refusing to be silenced.¹⁷ This may be too optimistic, but the truth is that views such as those declared by Milbank need to be collectively resisted because he is not alone in his mocking and patronizing attacks on theologies of the body and liberation. This is made apparent in the epistemic injustice committed by academics who silence such voices by refusing to include such theologies in reading lists and modules. At the root of Milbank's condemnation of black, feminist, queer and disabled theologies is disdain and distrust. In the mind of those privileged scholars such as Milbank, their word and their word alone should be trusted, because society has accommodated the bodies of the privileged to the extent that they do not even need to be aware of their own bodies. They are the norm, their opinions have been deemed valid from birth as a result of their gender, ethnicity, sexuality and class. They do not have to worry about being spoken over in meetings, asked to fetch the water jugs, asked what their credentials are, because British society is structured in such a way that these people expect deference and take it for granted.

James Baldwin calls out such behaviour as that of whiteness, commenting that 'Whiteness is a metaphor for power.'¹⁸ It is Whiteness that argues that the theologies of the marginalized are 'bollocks' theologies when they are shaped by the lived experiences of the oppressed, because the theologies of whiteness refuse to see themselves as the oppressor. Hegemonic forms of knowing have determined that the foundations of knowledge are Western and patriarchal, and the body-politics of knowledge have been racialized and institutionalized. Theological students are for the most part taught to adopt the perspectives of the privileged because knowledge production is not neutral and is determined by those who hold the power. Students who fall into the categories that Milbank refers to as 'bollocks' must then attempt to contemplate God guided by scholars who do not trust that their bodies can be the producers of knowledge or, rather, that they matter in knowledge production. Such a theological education system can itself not be trusted because the ruling elites holding the epistemic privilege have the power to control the perspectives through which those in formational training reflect on God, ministry and mission. This is potentially oppressive to women, disabled people, people of colour and LGBTQI+ people, as well as all students who must be free to contemplate God through the multiple lenses of God's people. Denying, dismissing or silencing such voices in theological education not only displays Eurocentric, patriarchal and heteronormative bias; it also enables the complicity of institutional marginalization. So-called 'bollocks theologies' challenge such power dynamics because they make visible the invisible and relocate theological thinking from the epicentre of imperial Christianity to the oppressed, marginalized and subjugated experiences of lived Christianity.[19]

The curricula of whiteness and the power dynamics within theological education must therefore be deconstructed in order to expose the injustice of systems of education that deny the voices of the marginalized. Then we can journey towards a theological education that can be trusted. This will demand a process of consciousness in the minds of both the oppressed and the oppressors, in which Eurocentric theology is dislodged from the centre in order to engage in an open dialogue with global and indigenous theologies as well as other disciplines. At present, modules on Black Theology, Feminist Theology and other Liberation Theologies too often remain on the periphery of theological education, often getting separate labels, an approach Thia Cooper has described as 'a sort of touristic attraction deprived of the power of articulation of a new theological discourse which could radically challenge the Western white and male discourse'.[20] In keeping such epistemologies on the periphery or missing altogether from courses on theological education, the dominant epistemologies remain undisturbed and the dominant White, middle-class, male theologies are left unchallenged.

Those who possess the power have come to assume that they possess all truths and that their truths are the only ones that are trustworthy. A culture of deference has enabled such a system of knowledge and education to continue. Yet the truth is that everyone holds part of the truth. As Freire remarks:

> I believe that those who are weak are those who think they possess the truth and are thus intolerant; those who are strong are those who say: 'Perhaps I have part of the truth, but I don't have the whole truth. You have part of the truth. Let's seek it together.'[21]

A theological education that 'seeks truths' together would be a theological education that is shaped by a dialogue of mutual respect, where a curriculum is developed that enables multiple truths to be heard. Such a process is vital if theological education is to enable students to flourish. However, teaching different knowledge will not be enough. There must also be an acknowledgement of the exclusionary framework that dominates theological formation in the UK. This requires looking at the credentials demanded of students before entering, the costs of studying where relevant, and the reporting structures that apply in particular to those studying for ministry, as well as addressing embedded classist structures. Until the 1960s, 'less than 5 percent of the population went to university and they were bastions of white, male privilege',[22] and for the most part they continue to be, thereby maintaining the class structure of society. In the context of formation, theological education operates in such unequal power structures that it has failed to address what centuries of missing voices in education means for the academy and formation today.

It was such institutional inequality and oppression that famously led Audre Lorde to warn against using the master's tools to dismantle their house. In other words, replicating dominant pedagogies and adding occasional diverse voices to the curriculum will leave the master's house intact. As Kehinde Andrews says, 'The struggle becomes how to subvert the tools, not how to abandon them.'[23] The Bible is a perfect example of how the master's tools can be subverted, as opposed to rejected, in order to bring down the master's house. The endeavours of Sam Sharpe in Jamaica offer an example of how the Bible was used in such a way. An enslaved person and preacher, whose enslavement was justified with the Bible by the missionaries and colonialists, fought for freedom and used the Bible as a tool to bring about an insurrection. Academics have the ability to use such tools to dismantle the academy, and the Bible offers a means by which we can contemplate how to do it. Using the decolonial methodology of storytelling and re-storytelling, the story of the Canaanite woman in Matthew 15 will be reread as an example of subverting power structures in order to bring about change in systems of knowledge.

When the Messiah calls you a dog ...

In the Gospel of Matthew we hear of how a nameless Canaanite woman comes to Jesus 'shouting', because she is in need of help for her daughter who is 'tormented by a demon'. However, Jesus seemingly ignores her, and his disciples tell him to 'Send her away, for she keeps shouting after us' (15.23). Jesus answers, 'I was sent only to the lost sheep of the house of Israel' (15.24). But the woman is persistent, and she comes and kneels before him saying, 'Lord, help me' (15.25). Jesus answers in a seemingly rude manner, saying: 'It is not fair to take the children's food and throw it to the dogs' (15.26). But the woman is quick in her response, 'Yes, Lord, yet even the dogs eat the crumbs that fall from their masters' table' (15.27). The story concludes with Jesus acknowledging the great faith of the woman and healing her daughter.

Many interpretations declare that this passage speaks of the importance of faith, but if we look at this text again, taking into consideration the dynamics of power, privilege and prejudice, the text appears to offer some significant challenges, especially when we consider how the dialoguing takes place within the narrative. We note that the author gives a great deal of attention to the interventions of the woman in the narrative and offers fascinating insights into power dynamics, gender, ethnicity and agency. As the Canaanite woman is instantly positioned as an 'outsider', we note 'the specific reference to the place as Tyre, the Gentile territories and the designation of the woman as Canaanite, the indigenous people of Canaan and ancient enemies of Israel'.[24]

The unnamed Canaanite woman appears on the scene in this narrative as someone who has been marginalized in the public sphere. As woman, foreigner and gentile, there are expected social, cultural, religious and political norms that she should adhere to. The marginalization of women's bodies within theological education in the UK is a common experience, as one student I interviewed shared:

'I am a working-class woman who has given up so much to be here and follow my calling to serve Jesus, but I constantly feel like I don't fit in. I can't relate to the books I read, I feel uncomfortable speaking out when I don't agree, I don't want to say when I can't make it to something because I have to look after my family member – because this just makes me look weak, and every doubt that the BAP had in me will be shown to be true.'[25]

The student is made to feel irrelevant, her bodily experiences have not been taken into consideration in the structures of the education system, and the reporting mechanisms of the Church have left her feeling inadequate. The theological education systems for formation were not made to accommodate working-class women with carer responsibilities; they have been structured in such a way that your worth is measured by the extent to which you can adapt to the dominant structures of power. Classism, sexism and racism shape the structures of learning institutes; as bell hooks says, they create 'a lived reality of insider versus outsider that is predetermined'[26] and the outsiders are often made to feel like they do not belong. For the most part pedagogies and curricula have not been shaped to respond to this reality. Those students who do not comfortably adapt to the power dynamics of theological education are often deemed an inconvenience to those who determine the boundaries of belonging, particularly when theological education is designed to maintain the existing structures, values and cultures of those with power.

The positioning of the woman's body in the biblical narrative is also important. The men mock her, they depict her as angry and annoying. The Canaanite woman is aware of her body and social positioning, yet 'she as an anonymous woman had to approach a distinguished man with her problem'.[27] The body is central to dialogue; how we witness, understand and comprehend our own body and the bodies of others determines how we are positioned and how we position others in conversation and in relationships. When the Canaanite woman puts her body before Jesus and the disciples, she makes herself visible but vulnerable, she raises her voice to Jesus yet she is ignored and the disciples tell Jesus to send her away. The silencing and sending away of women who seek to express their experiences and challenge imposed norms is a common occurrence. The false characterization of women, particularly women from minority faiths or women of colour, is often used as a mechanism for silencing, shaming and denying the truth of their religious, cultural, social and political experiences. Those who hold the power often hold little interest in the experiences or insights of the oppressed.

When the Canaanite woman falls to the floor, she communicates her passion, desire, need and vulnerability, she puts herself forward in her entirety before Jesus. She displays trust in Jesus and yet initially this trust is not reciprocated. According to Michelle Voss Roberts, this is because Jesus 'perceives the markers of her dress, facial features, and comportment as code for "Canaanite", and by extension, someone to be ignored and despised'.[28] Comparisons can be made with the judgements imposed on students of colour in theological education institutes in the UK. Take, for example, the words of a Black student training for ordination:

> 'I remember a tutor referring to James Cone as an angry black man who failed to understand Christology. As the only black man in the classroom I felt angry but knew then what that tutor thought of me, and suddenly all of his patronizing comments made sense. He was racist, but he had the power, so what was I supposed to do ...'[29]

What is made apparent is the extent to which the power dynamics of theological education and learning can reinforce oppressive values and beliefs, such as racism, sexism, homophobia, religious marginalization and classism. This is particularly the case when theological education takes place in a context or manner in which the power dynamics are unequal and where sexist, racist, homophobic or classist assumptions and prejudices are not addressed, leading to exacerbated intolerance and further injustice and oppression. By referring to James Cone as an 'angry black man' the tutor, who holds the position of authority, defines the body and knowledge of a black man as inferior and dangerous. According to Miguel De La Torre:

> White Christians understand who they are when they tell themselves *who they are not*. They self-define as subjects by contrasting themselves with the object they see, and the object that defines what it means to be white by emphasizing the difference with the other.[30]

The tutor seemingly defines himself as rational, knowledgeable and trustworthy by projecting upon the body of Cone and the student an image of angry, ignorant and unknowing.

Jesus does not appear to reject the woman in the narrative directly, but seemingly dismisses her plea, and responds to her by saying: 'it is not fair to take the children's food and throw it to the dogs' (Matt. 15.26). Jesus' actions towards the woman display the power dynamics apparent in the context. He determines that her place is equal to that of the dogs and therefore her word and knowledge are not to be taken seriously. Jesus and the Canaanite woman appear to be situated in 'a struggle of engagement'.[31] In order to progress they will have to become critically aware of their own social positioning, and the person with power, in this case Jesus, must choose either to continue to act in an oppressive manner or respond to the needs of the woman. The power imbalances are also clearly visible in the narrative, particularly when Jesus insults the woman, seemingly referring to her as a 'dog'. The woman responds by saying, 'even the dogs eat the crumbs that fall from their masters' table.' The woman uses her words, experiences and wit in order to respond, and does so in a space where she has not been made to feel welcome but knows she must speak out if transformation is to occur. She appears to shame the culture of impunity that has marginalized her by using the same words, or rather the same tools, but subverting them.

Consequently, Jesus is transformed through his interaction with the woman. In order to change his behaviour towards the woman, Jesus must examine existing presuppositions of knowledge and thought, in this case racism and sexism towards the Canaanite woman, and in doing so risks his own reputation and social positioning of power. According to Christine Hong, part of the process of anticolonial teaching is about those with power acknowledging the harm that they have caused, 'quickly acknowledging harm and admitting failures in the ongoing process of teaching and learning works to actively reverse the instructor and learner roles in the classroom, facilitating creative spaces for the nurturing of intelligence in both individuals and the community'.³² Jesus goes from being dismissive to ultimately acknowledging the importance of the woman's experience and insights, as Surekha Nelavala highlights, 'without his transformation the woman's situation would have remained unchanged, her bold protests against injustice in vain.'³³ Jesus' acknowledgment of the woman and her faith comes after the woman has corrected his positioning through her response. The woman appears to enable Jesus to become aware that his behaviour has dehumanized her. What is visible within the text is that Jesus becomes conscious of the woman's experiences and his own prejudices; the woman is vocal in challenging the system that dehumanizes her, and ultimately this leads to social transformation and the 'healing' of the woman's daughter. The woman had to enter the space and share her truth in order to transform it, and later in Matthew's Gospel we read of how Jesus, as a teacher, is sincere, and teaches 'the way of God in accordance with truth, and show[s] deference to no one; [and does] not regard people with partiality' (Matt. 22.16). What we are not reminded of is that it took a marginalized woman to voice her truth in her master's house or space in order to transform a culture of deference to one of equality and impartiality.

Trust in the consciousness of the *othered*

The woman in Matthew's Gospel has been defined as a 'Canaanite', and a 'dog', but like many of the unnamed women within and outside of Scripture, she has not been given the opportunity to define herself. She is the 'other', while Jesus holds the position of 'power' and is depicted as the teacher who is trusted and knowledgeable.³⁴ The unnamed woman in the text exists outside of the realm of power. She is part of the human struggle, she is different, untrusted, unequal, and her words and experience deemed irrelevant, and comparable to that of a dog. Both Jesus and the unnamed woman must become conscious of the injustice of the existent power dynamics in order to bring about change. Jesus must learn to distrust the normative consciousness that *others* the woman, and the woman must become aware that her *othering* is unjust and therefore struggle against it. Both have to learn to distrust the order of consciousness that has determined that the experiences of the woman are not rational. In the context of theological education in the UK, middle-class European men represent the trusted embodiment of rationality. When women, particularly women of colour, queer women and working-class women, enter into spaces such as the theological education institutes, spaces that were not until recently intended for them, the women are misplaced. Like the woman in Matthew, they are often reported as disruptive trespassers, made to feel like they do not belong and forced to negotiate their place and purpose in a hostile context.

The implications of such an environment of theological formation have been outlined by Willie James Jennings. With a particular focus on whiteness, he notes that theological education in the Western world is haunted by the image of 'a plantation at worship and an enslaved preacher'. Jennings describes how:

> Even places and settings and people involved in theological education far removed from the history of the slaveholding United States are implicated in this scene … an ecclesial reality inside a white patriarchal domesticity, shaped by an overwhelming white masculinist presence that always aims to build a national and global future that we should inhabit.[35]

Theological education in the UK is haunted by this same image and yet often refuses to acknowledge its part in forming and maintaining it. The experiences of marginalization and isolation of students of colour in theological education in the UK and in the Church of England narrate the extent to which racism continues to be a lived reality for many. As one student noted, 'I am frequently told that I should not bring my own experiences of how I have experienced racial abuse into the classroom ... that it doesn't matter, and it will only make people feel uncomfortable.'³⁶ The personhood of the student is not taken seriously, their presence is not affirmed, and through a misuse of power the student is unable to engage or relate their experiences to their theological learning in the classroom. The voices of black, women, queer and disabled students are often constrained. The question therefore must be asked, 'How can educators and students who want to share personal experience in the classroom do so in a way that is situated within a theory of learning and a safe space for the student?' In agreement with Henry Giroux:

> You can't deny that students have experiences and you can't deny that these experiences are relevant to the learning process even though you might say these experiences are limited, raw, unfruitful, or whatever. Students have memories, families, religions, feelings, languages and cultures that give them a distinctive voice. We can critically engage that experience and we can move beyond it. But we can't deny it.³⁷

The struggles apparent in the student's experiences are relevant ways of knowing that impact theological knowledge and learning and yet the authority of their experience is often disregarded as inauthentic knowledge production in the classroom.

A. D. A. France-Williams' profound exploration in *Ghost Ship* of institutional racism in the Church of England also captures the embedded racism and the lasting impact of colonialism on the Church and theology. He notes that 'The church may claim to want more black and brown recruits, but the message within black and brown communities is that these are not safe or welcome spaces.'³⁸ The Church of England has created an environment of un-belonging for people of colour. It is for this reason that in the recent report commissioned by the Church of England, entitled *From Lament to Action*, there is a sense of immediacy to act on systemic racial injustice. It states: 'Decades of inaction carry consequences, and this inaction must be owned by the whole Church. A failure to act now will be seen as another indication, potentially a last straw for many, that the Church is not serious about racial sin.'[39] As Jennings says, 'The Church and the academy, theological or otherwise, have been bound to the same whiteness since the advent of colonialism.'[40] Theological education in the UK has been dominated by white privilege, which has led to formation for ordination and lay ministry taking place in contexts of whiteness.

According to Anthony Reddie, what we see in Britain today is an embedded 'otherness' where 'full belonging in Britain has always been connected with the normative power of Whiteness'. He argues that to belong in Britain is to be white, Anglican and male.[41] Such notions of belonging affect people's embodied experience of their religious identity and belief because they are faced with the fear of hate crimes, intolerance and 'otherness' as they exist outside of such fixed boundaries. Theological education in such a context must consider the ways in which these boundaries are implemented and maintained. Those who practise border or boundary maintenance 'from the standpoint of a majority mostly seek to define others from an imagined superior positioning that necessarily places others in an inferior position'.[42] This is particularly the case when considering the relationship between 'the British Empire, colonialism, and Christianity', where, as Reddie remarks: 'Empire and colonialism found much of its intellectual underscoring based on white, Eurocentric supremacy, infused within the theological import of Christianity, which marked the clear binary between notions of civilised, acceptable and saved against uncivilised, transgressive and heathen.'[43] Before deliberating on a theological response it is vital to situate the context for trusting in theological education, because religion has played a significant role in the current situation of British politics. Despite the fact that on the surface secularism continues to be on the rise in Britain, with the number of people proclaiming no faith now at approximately 52 per cent of the population[44], this did not prevent far-right populist politics manipulating notions of Christian identity and 'values' in their political messaging as a means of propagating an exclusive vision for Britain.

Nigel Farage, the former leader of UKIP, called for a 'muscular defence' of British Christian heritage, arguing that 'Christian values and traditions have been marginalized.'[45] The narrative of 'persecuted' Christians was used by conservative Christian evangelicals as a means of intensifying the battle cry for Christian nationalism, while leaders of the extremist group Britain First stated that 'Christianity in Britain is under ferocious assault', arguing that 'many Christians now face discrimination and persecution because of their beliefs in many areas such as employment, business, and adoption.' The Conservative Party talked of 'the spirit of Protestantism as the inspiration for Britain to go at it alone and leave the EU'.[46] The messaging was simple: 'Get Brexit done' and restore Britain back to an age of Empire, Christian traditionalism and white national pride. The US Republican pundit Ed Martin spouted the same propaganda when speaking at a conservative Christian conference in Verona, stating that 'The Bible, borders, and Brexit, will make Europe great again',[47] thus suggesting that the greatness of a nation or continent is determined by its ability to exclude all others, where only Christianity prospers, and where strength is realized in a national pride shaped by racism, xenophobia and empire. The socio-religious and political narratives that shaped the Brexit campaign and the rise of the far right in Britain and the rest of Europe involved political and religious campaigns that have played on 'the conflation of notions of white entitlement and ... the demonization of black and other visible minorities'.[48]

In the context of Britain today, we are witnessing a rise of the far right (as is the case across much of Europe) and a political leadership where whiteness is very much allied with 'notions of nationalism, buttressed by empire, colonialism and mission Christianity'.[49] Since the Brexit referendum in Britain, racism and race-related hate crimes have risen dramatically, political discourse that is anti-immigrant, racist, xenophobic and Islamophobic has not only become mainstream, but has been legitimized by the Prime Minister, Boris Johnson. His significant majority in Parliament following the results of the

General Election in 2019 came despite the public being aware of his racist, classist, misogynistic, interreligiously intolerant rhetoric. He has previously compared Muslim women to letter boxes,[50] used racial slurs against black people and argued that Islam has caused the 'Muslim world to be literally centuries behind the West'.[51] And has further argued that single mothers are guilty of 'producing a generation of ill-raised, ignorant, aggressive and illegitimate children'.[52]

The Church of England as an institutional church therefore has an increasingly important role to play in responding to the rise of such extreme classist, racist and religiously intolerant beliefs. Yet my fear is that the Church in Britain has no theological understanding of its current social role or the positioning that is required in order to adequately respond. It does not appear to have come to terms with the fact that rather being a persecuted Church, a context in which the Christian Church was born, it is a Church guilty of enabling the persecution of others. Notably, that it has not owned its atrocities rooted in empire, whiteness and nationalism. In agreement with Reddie, this is because the Church of England in particular operates through the ideology of 'whiteness', where it holds a 'pivotal central place for that which is considered normative' because 'Whiteness has become the ontological and epistemological grounding on which White, English and British Christianity is operated and on which matters of doctrine, mission and pastoral practice has been predicated.'[53] Consequently, White English Anglicanism becomes the embodied ideal, where the boundaries of belonging in Britain are maintained through a politicized, Anglicized Christianity. This is the form of Christianity that is being deliberately used in the current political climate, where the 'Jesus of history' 'who comes to us as the radical ethnic other living as he did as a Galilean Jew' is being whitewashed in the UK as a Christ who continues to be contextualized as a White man, and a Jesus who 'becomes a symbolic Englishman who reaffirms empire, colonialism and British superiority'.[54] This comes at the expense of those who exist outside such fixed boundaries and notions of Britishness.

In order to challenge such fixed notions of belonging, theological education in the context of Britain must promote an understanding of self and other, noting that 'Being embodied and embedded, *all* human persons are unavoidably prejudiced; the challenge is not to let those prejudices get the upper hand.'[55] This requires an acknowledgment of the Church's embedded 'whiteness', its role in Empire, and its continued racism and fear of other religions, apparent, for example, in its approaches to interfaith dialoguing, where other religions are seen as objects for conversion as opposed to true learning. It demands an interrogation of our theological learning processes and pedagogies that are too often dominated by white, male, heterosexual theologians and deny the experiences of people of colour, women, disabled people and LGBTQI+ communities as being valid sources of knowledge. We need to be asking how we can challenge embedded and embodied prejudices that consider diversity to be a problem as opposed to an opportunity to build bridges and cross boundaries. At the same time we need to reflect on our social and political location, agreeing with Marianne Moyaert that 'To live one's life as a human person is to be involved in a never-ending hermeneutical process.'[56] This demands of Christians in Britain that they ask the question 'Where do we speak from?' For the most part, we speak from a position of privilege, of racism, of xenophobia, of hatred of 'otherness'; we speak as though we occupy a moral platform, when instead we are at times guilty of being an echo chamber of abuse – for example by seeking to control the bodies of believers and non-believers and making exclusivist statements on sexuality and women. A Church that is not under oppression risks becoming the oppressor unless its theology is rooted in liberation for the oppressed, and this is what we are seeing in Britain. The Church is predominantly indifferent to the Windrush scandal, to neo-liberal capitalist ideology, to the refugee crisis, to the plight of the Palestinians, to the outrage of a far-right nationalist uprising.

When we expose the injustices of theological education we are left with the question of how we can teach theology in a way that is not about disseminating dominant and accepted knowledge that has controlled and silenced the oppressed. How can we instead shape our theologies and knowledge together, so that we take an active lead in finding ways that help students to develop the knowledge and insights to change the systems and structures that oppress? Christianity is a radical faith, its Scriptures speak of resistance and revolution, and its disciples are called to be countercultural, to take up the cross and resist the oppressive systems that killed their Messiah. So our theological education must be radical if it is to be Christ-like and life-flourishing. To be radical is to be committed to human liberation, which requires a curriculum and pedagogies that are not afraid to confront, to listen, and to see the world unveiled. That are not afraid to meet the people or enter into dialogue with them and that must be aware of the context in which they seek to form people in their education and ministry. In the context of the UK this means acknowledging that our missional and theological history has been rooted in the complexities of the legacies of war, slavery and occupation. It requires acknowledging the context of today, one of global inequality in which we are at times capable of drowning out the cries of the poor, the plight of the refugees and those who suffer the most from climate change – another link on the shackle of colonization. I write today during a global pandemic that is fuelling existing inequalities. Alongside Covid-19, what rampages around the world is a virus of inequality that plunders our planet for profit in the guise of a lobbyist calling for tax cuts for the rich and the privatization of healthcare for the poor. A virus that violates a person's right to fullness of life, denies reparations for slavery and colonialism, and manipulates the spread of a global pandemic to fill the pockets of billionaires.

Such realities matter as we look at how we might trust in theological education, because education should be designed in a way that seeks to liberate people and enable students to be 'critical, creative, free, active and responsible members of society'.[57] Unfortunately, however, the varied experiences, cultures, theologies and knowledge(s) of students have not always been taken into consideration in theological curricula. A theological curriculum that is life flourishing is therefore dialogical, because it involves addressing the history of colonialism while acknowledging embedded colonial norms in which whiteness and patriarchy continue to oppress the colonialized. It challenges cultures of dehumanization and impunity and gives focus to the indigenous theology and theologies of liberation born out of struggle and resistance. It is a theological education that focuses on being life-flourishing and, like the Canaanite woman, subverts the master's tools and by addressing such power dynamics challenges notions of theology and mission that are imposed from a position of privilege, power and possession. Also, it must resist the temptation to embed itself in the safety of the academy and in doing so distance itself from the reality of the struggles of the people.

Notes

1 Rosa Luxemburg, in Peter Hudis and Kevin B. Anderson (eds), *The Rosa Luxemburg Reader* (New York: Monthly Review Press, 2004), p. 304.

2 John Gascoigne, 'Introduction: Religion and Empire, an Historiographical Perspective', *Journal of Religious History* 32:2 (2008): 159–78, 164.

3 See Dirk Michel-Schertges, 'Free Choice of Education? Capabilities, Possibility Spaces, and Incapabilities of Education, Labour, and the Way of Living One Values', in Roland Atzmüller et al. (eds), *Facing Trajectories from School to Work: Towards a Capability-Friendly Youth Policy in Europe* (Switzerland: Springer, 2015), p. 77.

4 Paulo Freire, *Pedagogy of the Oppressed* (New York: Continuum, 2000), p. 47.

5 Denis Lawton, *Class, Culture and the Curriculum* (London: Routledge, 1975), p. 6.

6 Jannette Elwood, 'Gender and the Curriculum', in D. Wyse, L. Hayward and J. Pandya, *The SAGE Handbook of Curriculum, Pedagogy and Assessment* (Thousand Oaks, CA: SAGE, 2016), p. 8.

7 Interview 8, author, 2020.

8 Toni Morrison, quoted in Ariel Leve, 'Toni Morrison on love, loss and modernity', *The Telegraph* (17 July 2012), available at: https://

www.telegraph.co.uk/culture/books/authorinterviews/9395051/Toni-Morrison-on-love-loss-and-modernity.html (accessed 16.2.2022).

9 Freire, *Pedagogy of the Oppressed*, p. 45.

10 See Anthony Reddie, 'Reassessing the Inculcation of an Anti-Racist Ethic for Christian Ministry: From Racism Awareness to Deconstructing Whiteness', *Religions* 11:497 (2020): 1–17, 6.

11 Marilyn Naidoo, 'Racism, Whiteness and Transformation: Reforming the Space of Theological Education in South Africa', *International Academy of Practical Theology Conference Series* (2019): 168–75, 169.

12 Ibid.

13 Katie G. Cannon et al., *God's Fierce Whimsy: Christian Feminism and Theological Education* (New York: The Pilgrim Press, 1985), p. 12.

14 Freire, *Pedagogy of the Oppressed*, p. 34.

15 Simone de Beauvoir, *La Pensée de Droite, Aujord'hui* (Paris); Spanish translation, *El Pensamiento politico de la Derecha* (Buenos Aires, 1963), p. 34.

16 https://twtext.com/article/1282213955688071168.

17 See for example the ongoing work on decolonizing the curriculum with Common Awards at Durham University, and the ongoing work at SOAS, as well as Oxford University's appointment of Prof. Anthony Reddie.

18 See Akala, *Natives: Race and Class in the Ruins of Empire* (London: Two Roads, 2018), p. 42.

19 See Raimundo Barreto and Roberto Sirvent (eds), *Decolonial Christianities: Latinx and Latin American Perspectives* (Cham, Switzerland: Palgrave Macmillan, 2019), p. 12.

20 Thia Cooper, *Queer and Indecent: An Introduction to Marcella Althaus-Reid* (London: SCM Press, 2021), p. 14.

21 Antonio Faundez and Paulo Freire, *Learning to Question: A Pedagogy of Liberation* (Geneva: WCC Publications, 1989), p. 20.

22 Kehinde Andrews, 'The Challenge for Black Studies in the Neoliberal University', in Gurminder K. Bhambra et al. (eds), *Decolonising the University* (London: Pluto Press, 2018), p. 139.

23 Ibid.

24 Mookgo S. Kgatle, 'Crossing Boundaries: Social-scientific Reading of the Faith of a Canaanite Woman (Mt 15:21–28)', *Stellenbosch Theological Journal* 4:2 (2018): 595–613, 596.

25 Interviews were conducted with women ordinands training at theological education institutes across the UK; all ordinands remain anonymous. Women Ordinand Interview 3, interview by author, Manchester, January 2020.

26 See bell hooks, *Teaching to Transgress: Education as the Practice of Freedom* (London: Routledge, 1994), p. 83.

27 S. K. Saga, 'Theology for the Dogs? An Intersectional and Contextual Analysis of Interpretation of Matthew 15:21–29 "The Canaanite Woman"'. Unpublished Master's thesis (2009), p. 34.

28 Michelle Voss Roberts, 'Discerning Doctrine: Interreligious Dialogue as Experiential Source of Theology', in Terrence Merrigan and John Friday (eds), *The Past, Present and Future of Theologies of Interreligious Dialogue* (Oxford: Oxford University Press, 2017), p. 137.

29 Interview 6, interview by author, online, February 2020.

30 See Miguel De La Torre, *Burying White Privilege: Resurrecting a Badass Christianity* (Grand Rapids, MI: Wm. B. Eerdmans, 2019), p. 102. Emphasis original.

31 Michael Atkinson, 'Interfaith Dialogue and Comparative Theology: A Theoretical Approach to a Practical Dilemma', *The Journal of Social Encounters* 3:1 (2019): 47–57, 49.

32 Christine J. Hong, *Decolonial Futures: Intercultural and Interreligious Intelligence for Theological Education* (Maryland, NY: Lexington Books, 2021), p. 31.

33 Surekha Nelavala, 'Smart Syrophoenician Woman: A Dalit Feminist Reading of Mark 7:24–31', *The Expository Times* 118:2 (2006): 64–9, 64.

34 Sylvia Wynter has argued that 'our present struggles with respect to race, class, gender, sexual orientation, ethnicity, struggles over the environment, global warming, severe climate change, and the sharply unequal distribution of the earth resources ... are all different facets of the central ethnoclass Man vs. Human struggle.' See Sylvia Wynter, 'Unsettling the Coloniality of Being/Power/Truth/Freedom: Towards the Human, After Man, Its Overrepresentation – An Argument', *The New Centennial Review* 3:3 (2003): 257–337, 261.

35 Willie James Jennings, *After Whiteness: An Education in Belonging* (Grand Rapids, MI: Wm. B. Eerdmans, 2020), p. 82.

36 Interview 5, author, 2020.

37 Henry A. Giroux, 'The Hope of Radical Education: A Conversation with Henry Giroux', *The Journal of Education* 170:2 (1988): 91–101, 99.

38 A. D. A. France-Williams, *Ghost Ship: Institutional Racism and the Church of England* (London: SCM Press, 2020), pp. 92–3.

39 https://www.churchofengland.org/sites/default/files/2021-04/FromLamentToAction-report.pdf, p. 17.

40 Jennings, *After Whiteness*, p. 83.

41 Anthony Reddie, *Theologising Brexit: A Liberationist and Postcolonial Critique* (London: Routledge, 2019).

42 Kathryn Cassidy, Perla Innocenti and Hans-Joachim Burkner,

'Brexit and New Autochthonic Politics of Belonging', *Space and Polity* 22:2 (2018): 188–204, 191.

43 Reddie, *Theologising Brexit*.

44 See Polly Toynbee, 'Faith in religion is dwindling, but when will British politics reflect that?', available at: https://www.theguardian.com/commentisfree/2019/jul/11/faith-religion-politics-british-attitudes-survey (accessed 11.2.2020).

45 See Kiran Moodley, 'Nigel Farage says Britain needs to stand up for its Judeo-Christian values to combat homegrown terrorists', available at: https://www.independent.co.uk/news/uk/nigel-farage-says-britain-needs-to-stand-up-for-its-judeo-christian-values-to-combat-homegrown-9708082.html (accessed 11.2.2020).

46 Maria Exall, 'Brexit and Christian Identity: A Challenge for Political Theology', available at: http://ccstp.org.uk/articles/2019/10/22/brexit-and-christian-identity-a-challenge-for-political-theology (accessed 9.2.2022).

47 Mary Fitzgerald, 'What the far-right really mean when they talk of "taking back Christian Europe"', available at: https://www.independent.co.uk/voices/european-elections-far-right-christian-europe-religious-us-hungary-italy-spain-a8928376.html (accessed 9.2.2022).

48 See Anthony Reddie, 'The wounded psyche of white privilege', *Church Times*, available at: https://www.churchtimes.co.uk/articles/2018/21-september/comment/opinion/the-wounded-psyche-of-white-privilege (accessed 11.2.2020).

49 Ibid.

50 It is worth highlighting that in this same week Islamophobic incidents rose by 375%. See https://www.independent.co.uk/news/uk/home-news/boris-johnson-muslim-women-letterboxes-burqa-islamophobia-rise-a9088476.html (accessed 9.2.2022).

51 Frances Perraudin, 'New Controversial Quotes from Boris Johnson Uncovered', available at: https://www.theguardian.com/politics/2019/dec/09/new-controversial-comments-uncovered-in-historical-boris-johnson-articles (accessed 7.1.2020).

52 Ibid.

53 Ibid.

54 Ibid.

55 Marianne Moyaert, 'Interreligious Hermeneutics, Prejudice, and the Problem of Testimonial Injustice', *Religious Education* 114:5, (2019): 609–23, 609. Emphasis original.

56 Ibid., 612.

57 Anne Hope and Sally Timmel, *Training for Transformation: A Handbook for Community Workers* (Gweru, Zimbabwe: Mambo Press, 1999), p. 8.

2

Bodies Tell Stories

In a previous role of mine, I spent some time working in the Pacific. One of the islands I got to spend time on was Samoa, where theology is dialogical not just between individuals but also with the land, communities, ocean, animals and the ancestors. Within such dialoguing, the oral traditions are a means by which the bodies of the ancestors come to life in the storytelling passed on through the generations – this is known as *Fāgogo*. *Fāgogo* is a pedagogical process that involves elders performing stories in the evening as a means of sharing cultural wisdom and knowledge. The storyteller 'is careful and intentional in her use of language to weave together a magical description of the world of the story, not only to tell the story but to be persuasive in doing so'.[1] There was one *Fāgogo* I recall that involved a goddess who had taken on the form of a human person but had supernatural powers; she was known as a sacred woman who could both bless and curse. The goddess could also take on the form of a stingray. One day she was in the ocean and the ocean washed up over the land. The goddess was still in the body of a stingray, but she became stuck on the land and the villagers did not know the stingray was the goddess and so they caught her and ate her. The story narrated the consequences of human actions as well as the relationship between the land, the ocean and the spiritual world, all of which have become central themes in Pacific Christian theology. Many of the *Fāgogos* were demonized through colonialism, in the process of Christianization whereby goddesses and spirits became depicted as demonic forces. Consequently, you will not read about the *Fāgogos* in the missionary histories of Samoa, or the of the spirits that live on in the Christian communities of the Pacific.

Bodies tell stories – they tell stories of love and passion, birth and death, abuse and rape, land and corruption, as well as sickness and grief. The stories of our bodies are often exposed by the scars left behind by the systems of hate that have sought to shame certain bodies and inflict violence on bodies with their ideologies of oppression – ideologies that want to kill black bodies, convert queer bodies, slut-shame women's bodies, deprive poor bodies, silence colonialized bodies, degrade so-called 'disabled bodies', mock working-class bodies, bleach brown bodies and subjugate Dalit bodies. Bodies tell stories of genocide, infanticide, eugenics, trafficking and slavery – they expose the stains of human history. But they also tell tales of resistance and protest, of spiritualities, civil rights movements, miners strikes, pride, and the collective calls for indigenous rights. They capture the hypocrisy of the privileged bodies calling for the idolized steel statues of the bodies of dead slave traders to stay standing, meanwhile staying silent when the living body of a black child in Birmingham is chased and murdered by white men hurling vile racist abuse.

It is the broken bodies that often have the most important stories to tell, and yet those same bodies often cannot breathe to tell their stories. In May 2021, 215 bodies of Indigenous children were discovered in an unmarked mass grave underneath what was a Roman Catholic school in British Columbia.[2] In Ghana, Elmina Castle still stands where the first Catholic church built by the Portuguese in Africa tortured and sold the bodies of enslaved Africans in the chambers underneath the table on which the colonialists distributed the body of Christ in the Eucharist. These bodies tell the stories of the sins of the Church and her missions; they tell the tales of theologies of violence and racism, where white bodies dominate and where the God of white Christianity has been used to justify heinous crimes against the bodies of the colonialized. And the pedagogies of whiteness have silenced the stories of these bodies from entering our curricula, challenging our presuppositions and exposing the weaknesses of dominant epistemologies. Bodies tell stories, they carry with them wisdom, knowledge and experiences that matter greatly to our pedagogies in theological education, particularly when we are made aware of the extent to which theologies have been used to subjugate the bodies of the oppressed and enable the silence and complicity of the Church.

Bodies as sources of subjugated knowledges

Knowledge begins in the body, and just as certain bodies have been subjugated, so too have certain knowledges. Some bodies are deemed problems, inconveniences, irrelevant, indecent and therefore incapable of being producers of knowledge – their experiences are often reduced to 'anecdotes', while the bodies of the privileged elites are the knowledge holders and truth bearers who shape and determine what should be deemed 'real theology'. The bodies who have been marginalized by the dominant epistemologies are often forced to disown their bodies as sources of knowledge and become instead passive bodies in an education system that denies people their rights to be free or rather to think and contemplate God in and of themselves. Those of us involved in theological education are often pressured to operate within the confines of these normalized power dynamics, in which there exists a network of relationships, and those with the most power are often incapable of decentring themselves, or rather their bodies, in order to welcome the voices of others. So bodies are often sites of subjugated knowledges, where the experiences of certain bodies have been erased from our epistemologies. This creates dis-embodied pedagogies. However, as Lorraine Code writes: 'No longer is "the knower" imaginable as a self-contained, infinitely replicable "individual" making universally valid knowledge claims from a "god's eye" position removed from the incidental features and the power and privilege structures of the physical-social world.'[3] Rather, such universal notions of knowledge are being challenged by marginalized epistemologies that highlight that it is possible for knowledge to be produced in subordinated groups that exist outside the powerful and privileged structures, and yet those who produce such knowledge are too often rejected in institutional spaces. Social and political epistemic marginalization has determined that knowledge and theologies produced by women, people of colour, the LGTBQI+ community and the working classes can be sidelined, labelled as niche hermeneutics or simply rejected.

Certain bodily ideals are taken for granted in theological thought, and human experiences are often disregarded as superficial or irrelevant in our contemplation of God. It is not by accident that our sources of knowledge in, for example, our theological reading lists are predominantly white, heterosexual, able-bodied, European, middle class and male. This is because our loci of knowledge are predominantly from the bodies of the privileged. Epistemic hegemony 'makes it possible for those in the dominant group to ignore or disavow their epistemic privilege'.[4] The bodies at the centre therefore dominate in pedagogies that fail to recognize the bodily narratives of those who have been marginalized. In other words, theological education is capable of housing oppression if it fails to reflect on the theological insights of the oppressed. Pedagogical methods that are disconnected from the bodily realities of racial injustice, socio-economic inequality, disability, LGTBQI+ persecution and gender division lack the critical consciousness that is demanded of honest and formative theological education. Students will be conditioned to adapt themselves to learning environments where they are made to feel as if they do not truly belong, and therefore will be rendered unable to ask critical questions and will instead surrender to dominant discourses of theology just as the indigenous communities were forced to do under the Christian education systems of colonialism.

Contemplating bodies and pedagogies therefore calls on theological educators to surrender certain cultural and social privileges that they have perhaps grown accustomed to, or themselves been silenced by, in order to enter into a dialogical community of learning where the bodies and experiences of students and the marginalized are taken seriously. Because, as Paulo Freire writes: 'Any situation in which some individuals prevent others from engaging in the process of inquiry is one of violence ... to alienate humans from their own decision making is to change them into objects.'[5] Students cannot flourish if they are mere objects in a classroom that imposes set norms and fails to recognize how the silenced bodies of the oppressed, and the existential experiences of the student, may challenge the epistemologies that we deem infallible. Such systems of education only serve to silence theological reflections and experiences that may help us to better contemplate God more truthfully. It is therefore essential to enable marginalized epistemologies to be heard in order to resist Eurocentrism and challenge the injustices of colonial domination that have impacted not just the bodies of the colonialized but also the minds.

Such systems of theological knowledge continue to enslave and disempower the colonialized by denying people their world views, their histories, cultures and identities both in theory and pedagogical practices. The knowledge of white, middle-class, male theologians has been deemed superior in Eurocentric rationality, and has been presented as universal, legitimate and authoritative. In contrast, the theologies of the majority world, indigenous communities, women, the poor and queer theologies, have been condemned as irrational, emotive, illegitimate and have therefore been silenced. However, Eurocentric theologies are not superior in their rationality, although modernity and imperialism have created a theological framework that has set up boundaries of belonging for certain bodies, theologies and epistemologies. In doing so, the theologies that emerge from those that exist outside such fixed boundaries have not been trusted. Colonialism, classism and patriarchy have not only destroyed bodies physically and emotionally through the process of colonialization and modernity, they have also murdered knowledge. The Portuguese sociologist Boaventura de Sousa Santos has called this process 'epistemicide':

Unequal exchanges among cultures have always implied the death of the knowledge of the subordinated culture, hence the death of the social groups that possessed it. In the most extreme cases, such as that of European expansion, epistemicide was one of the conditions of genocide. The loss of epistemological confidence that currently afflicts modern science has facilitated the identification of the scope and gravity of the epistemicides perpetrated by hegemonic Eurocentric modernity.[6]

Theological education in the UK has for the most part been grounded in the dominant discourses of knowledge and has relied upon the subjugation of theological discourses from the majority world, indigenous theologies and other marginalized voices that could challenge colonial norms. Santos' notion of epistemicide can be applied to the world views that dominant discourses of theology have attempted to 'murder'. Take for example storytelling as a theological pedagogy used in indigenous and liberationist theologies, where the lived experiences of the marginalized people and communities are emphasized as a means of contemplating God. The womanist theologian Renita J. Weems has highlighted this point, noting that African American women are drawn to the world of the Bible, which has a great part to do with the 'insatiable appetite readers have for stories. Through stories grassroots African Americans communicated their understanding of life, love, suffering, and god(s), and their vision for freedom and liberation.'[7] Yet storytelling and personal narratives are often disregarded as 'subjective' and therefore unreliable or untrustworthy in research and theology. The legitimacy of storytelling has often been denied, forcing such discourse to the periphery as subjugated knowledge. This is because certain power relations have determined what constitutes worthy knowledge, and certain bodies have been deemed unworthy of thinking and producing meaning; furthermore, 'the mind/body, spirit/matter dualisms pervasive in Western epistemologies' dominate in theological learning in the UK.[8] Students are therefore 'educated' under normative ways of knowing, as the hegemony of white, heterosexual patriarchy has silenced the lived experiences of the marginalized in spaces of learning. This is made apparent in the words of one student who was training for ordination:

> 'I wrote about my experiences of sexual harassment in a reflective assignment on the suffering of Christ on the cross, my tutor suggested that this was not suitable for an assignment. I was embarrassed, humiliated, I was being honest about how I understood the text and how it related to me and my understanding of God.'

When women are prevented from bringing their stories to their theologizing and interpretations of Scripture they are forced to remain dependent upon patriarchal and androcentric theologies that have historically dismissed the worth of women's bodies. Womanist theology enables such experiences to be brought to the forefront of theological discourse, because womanist theory maintains the right to make claims about experience and ways of knowing that are shaped by bodies.[9] Such interpretation is intersectional as it encourages reflection on racism, classism, sexism and casteism. Allowing the space for bodies to tell stories in theological discourse enables the complex social dynamics of certain bodies to unearth hidden truths and aspects to theology and Scripture that we may not have seen. Womanist theology enables storytelling, autobiography and testimony to enter theological spaces in order to transgress normative academic theology. Storytelling is of course not a new concept in theology; the parables as stories are central to the Christian faith. Which raises the question, at what point did storytelling become deemed irrational in theological education? And would the stories told by Jesus, the Palestinian anti-imperialist radical, be accepted as knowledge if he spoke them today?

In agreement with Lisa Bergin, it appears 'Some knowers (or would-be knowers) will be listened to, heard and taken seriously, some will not; some are in positions that privilege us as knowledge gainers and producers, some are not so positioned.'¹⁰ How then do we decide whose bodies we trust to be producers of knowledge in theological education? Such questioning is vital, especially as we take into consideration the experience of the student whose story of sexual harassment in relation to biblical hermeneutics was silenced. Her bodily story of abuse was not considered to be relevant, trusted or knowledgeable. Such pedagogy contradicts what womanist scholarship has contended, that the Bible holds significant relevance for the experiences of oppressed women today, and that personal perspectives and bodily stories of oppression enable profound reflections on texts. The womanist theologian Wilda Gafney, for example, suggests that women's experiences, 'the social location of the reader/interpreter; efforts toward the eradication of human oppression; and making scholarship accessible to a "wider non-specialist worshipping community" are central aspects of a womanist approach.' She therefore argues that 'womanist hermeneutics should seek to retell the stories of the "silenced", "unknown" and "erased".'[11] The retelling of silenced stories is a powerful act of resistance used in order to give voice to bodies of the 'silenced' and 'erased', especially when applied in theological education today, because listening to the stories of the bodies of the oppressed forces us to witness uncomfortable truths. However, it is one thing to witness and another to trust in the testimony of such embodied narratives of oppression. If we are to trust in the bodies of the oppressed we must act, otherwise we are complicit in their torture. Let me once again look to Scripture to situate this argument and retell the story of the silenced, abused and erased, in order to contemplate how such narratives impact theological education today.

A chopped up woman on a donkey – the politics of body, trust and testimony

In Judges 19 we read of how a Levite residing in a remote part of Ephraim 'took to himself a concubine from Bethlehem in Judah' (19.1). The story that unravels ends horrifically for the concubine. She attempts to escape from the Levite man and goes to her father's house, but the Levite who has claimed ownership of her body speaks 'tenderly to her' (19.3) in order to persuade her to come back to him. We are to assume that she accepts; however, given her father so willingly welcomes the man into his home, the woman's choice in the matter seems of little consequence. The father of the concubine makes the Levite man feel very welcome in light of whatever difficulties the man and his daughter had been going through, and together the men go on to eat and drink over a number of days (19.4–9). Eventually the man leaves with the woman, his servant and donkeys and they seek shelter on their travels in Gibeah (19.15). However, as no one will take them in, they rely on the hospitality of a 'foreign' man from Ephraim who was residing in Gibeah (19.21). The stranger welcomes them and feeds them, but 'While they were enjoying themselves, the men of the city, a depraved lot, surrounded the house, and started pounding on the door' (19.22). The men threaten to rape the Levite, but the owner of the house refuses to allow this to happen and says, 'Here are my virgin daughter and his concubine; let me bring them out now. Ravish them and do whatever you want to them; but against this man do not do such a vile thing' (19.24). The men grab the concubine, gang-rape her and abuse her body all through the night until the morning (19.25). However, her body could not take any more pain and suffering and she dies on the doorstep of the house that her master had been welcomed into – she is murdered in the most violent of ways. The Levite man throws her corpse on to the back of his donkey and when he reaches his home, he takes a knife, dismembers her, chopping up her tortured corpse into 'twelve pieces, limb by limb and [sending] her throughout all the territory of Israel' (19.29).

In Judges 19 we read a horror story, a narrative of gendered violence, torture, abuse, xenophobia and gang-rape. As Sheila Delany puts it, this is a narrative describing 'a father's treacherous offer of his virgin daughter to gang-rape; actual gang-rape of a woman who even as a concubine is protected under Mosaic law from: assault and murder; dismemberment; the massacre of innocent people'.[12] This text has traditionally not been read as a narrative of sexual oppression or a 'rape text', but instead as a text about the transgression of ownership of a man's possessions – as the concubine is portrayed as his 'secondary wife';[13] others suggest it is a narrative focused on kingship and chaos.[14] For others this is a story about a man's rights being violated, made apparent when the author insinuates that the woman had committed the offence of sexual infidelity that caused her to flee to her father,[15] and later when the man's property – the concubine – is 'destroyed'. Consequently, this is a story told by male bodies that appears to be intended as a lesson for male bodies; women are a silent prop in the narrative.[16] For Phyllis Trible, it is a tale of contrast between male 'power, brutality, and triumphalism' and female 'helplessness, abuse, and annihilation'.[17] Whereas Cherly Exum has commented that 'the fear of female sexuality' and the 'need of patriarchy to control women' runs throughout the narrative.[18] The testimony of the raped and tortured concubine is silenced. Sex in this narrative is under the control of the men. Yet retelling this story with a focus on the dismembered concubine challenges the ways in which her narrative of sexual oppression has been dismissed, and enables wider discussions about the role and place of women, as well as the erased stories of bodily abuse, that have the potential to offer profound insights in theological education, because 'the namelessness of the characters in the text is central to its ability to reach far beyond itself for both victims and those who think they never would be participants in oppression.'[19]

From the portrayal of the Levite man in the text we can assume that he is a man of wealth and means, apparent in his ownership of servants and donkeys and his ability to travel independently, noted also in his title 'master'.[20] The man's needs are prioritized throughout the story, as he remains concerned about his own ill-treatment, the inhospitality he received, as opposed to the violent rape and murder of the woman. He even continues to violate the voiceless corpse of the dead woman:

> he put her on the donkey; and the man set out for his home. When he had entered his house, he took a knife, and grasping his concubine he cut her into twelve pieces, limb by limb, and sent her throughout all the territory of Israel. (Judges 19.28–29)

For Isabelle Hamley, 'The dismembering then becomes an attempt to erase her and the memory of a crime that was first directed against him.'[21] But it is the very fact that this story exists as a sacred text that makes it relevant to the sexual narratives of the oppressed and therefore to contemplating how this story influences theological education. As Hamley says, as a sacred text it:

> acknowledges rape and its social consequences, questions the narrative of abuse, and does so in a text that cannot be ignored precisely because it is sacred, but it also acknowledges the socially taboo possibility of male rape, in witness to voiceless male victims, who are so voiceless and invisible they only appear as a suppressed possibility in the text.[22]

Her body is therefore given a prophetic voice when contemplated through the critical lens of womanist discourse; as Koala Jones-Warsaw has remarked, it is through the dismembering of the concubine that similarities can be drawn to the experiences of Black women. Black women are:

> constantly being required to cut off pieces of ourselves – white feminists ask us to downplay our concerns for racism in order to support the battle for equality for women; black

men ask us downplay our concerns for sexism in order to support the battle of racial equality.²³

Her dismemberment can also be compared to the way in which students in theological education, particularly those who are in training for ordination, are forced to chop off aspects of themselves in order to 'fit in' and be accepted. Take, for example, the words of a gay student in training for ordination:

> 'It wasn't just the tutors who I hid my sexuality from, it was the students, many made it clear that they believed same-sex relationships to be a sin. One student when they found out I was gay offered to pray that I may be healed. I found myself "acting straight" in class, hiding aspects of myself, it was bad for my mental health. I had many, many dark thoughts.'

The body of the tortured and dismembered woman tells a story of abuse and trauma, a story that is never spoken and yet impacts the consciousness of the reader through her bodily oppression. The only act of struggle for liberation in the narrative is the woman's attempt to escape to her father's house, before all hope is lost when the Levite man collects her, leading to her eventual death. I would compare this narrative to a theological education that denies bodies that struggle for liberation, that refuses to unveil the truth of oppression and only seeks to maintain the systems that permit such violence to occur. As this is a narrative about power, the same power dynamics are apparent in theological institutes where colonial norms of sexual decency, gay oppression and patriarchy dominate and house oppression, cementing the boundaries of belonging and perpetuating systemic injustices through established rules and regulations that emotionally and physically destroy students and staff who do not fit the mould. Neither the woman in Judges 19 nor the gay man I quoted above are free; neither are given the chance to share their truth or their testimony. They are chopped up, made into examples, forced either to obey or be destroyed. The world in which the concubine woman is dismembered has not been denounced in our theological education institutes, in fact it has been affirmed through the androcentric, patriarchal theologies and practices that continue to dominate. The experiences of women in theological education often involve ridicule and mocking, sexist, patronizing, violent and abusive behaviour, and in order to truly 'fit in', they must learn to adapt to the middle-class, heterosexual, patriarchal norm as a means of survival.

How then can theological pedagogy offer space for the erased, unearth silenced oppressions, and allow the sexual narratives of the oppressed to be heard? Judges 19.1–29 is a tale of sexual violence, where rape is both used as a threat and violently enacted, to the extent that the woman's raped corpse is dismembered and then sent out to Israel as a means of signifying the need to reinforce social norms. Even in death the body of the woman is tortured as the integrity of her corpse is disregarded. The othering and objectification of the woman is required by the author because the process of othering epitomizes the patriarchal desire to possess and consume. The woman is under the control of the patriarchal forces and must never be given subjectivity or space to tell her story because in doing so she would disturb the ordering of society. The text presents a narrative that fundamentally lacks solidarity and compassion; instead it is shaped around an individualized theology, where the marginalized become non-beings. As a non-being the woman's body is still central to the text, but in her centrality she is dehumanized. This can be compared to the ways in which patriarchy and racism centralize the bodies of women, black people and queers, while at the same time turning them into non-beings. Such ideologies operate in this way as a means of systematic control over bodies that do not fit the heterosexual, patriarchal, Eurocentric norm. This is visible in the theological praxis of the Church and theological education institutes where the bodies of those who exist outside the norm are central to the agenda of enforced decency – apparent in homophobic practices such as 'conversion therapy', where bodies are central to the narrative but shamed and stigmatized and the experiences of the queer body are erased and silenced. Such a process of dehumanization is also apparent in capitalist models of Christian mission, where the colonized subject is central to the narrative but only as a means of converting the 'heathen', and the colonized subject is dehumanized in the process, reduced to the position of a non-being without a story, simply a product in a missionary narrative of 'salvation'.

Apparent within this narrative are the binaries of worthy/unworthy, man/woman, pure/impure, ruling class/working class, decent/indecent, virgin/whore. The Church continues to operate within the frameworks of such binaries – binaries that were further instilled by the constructs of the Christian empire, to the extent that good and evil were polarized as 'heathen' and 'whore' vs 'Christian' and 'virgin'. Education systems were shaped around such notions of being, and those who exist in the realms of the indecent, the working class, the 'whore', are the marginalized bodies made to feel as though they do not truly belong. Because even if the woman had survived, who is to say that her word would have been trusted, that her knowledge of the evils of societal violence and gendered persecution would have been heard, 'in places and circumstances where the putative "knower" can, for a range of personal and situational reasons, be discounted because of who he or she is'?[24] The author of the text attempts to dismiss her worth from the offset by presenting her as an adulteress who runs away from her forgiving master. This same technique continues to be used today to dismiss the experiences of rape and trauma victims, where the characters of the victims are assassinated, presented as 'indecent', 'whores', 'troublesome' or 'liars' in order to discount their worth before the courts and God. This is also apparent within the Church of England, as Canon Rosie Harper, Chaplain to the Bishop of Buckingham, noted in relation to the sexual abuse of women by male clergy: 'Survivors who have the courage to disclose their abuse routinely experience lack of compassion and a culture of silence.'[25] Another female cleric commented, 'We have clergy in our midst who prey upon women at vulnerable times in their life, luring them with their "best pastoral skills", and then using the opportunity to emotionally and sexually abuse.'[26]

Clergy, educators and church leaders hold a significant amount of power and yet in the formation process they are not adequately educated in ways that address how such power relates to sexual violence and abuse. Safeguarding training, though vital, is often not theologically grounded, the rape culture of Christianity is not adequately addressed, and the patriarchy that permits violence against women is not dismantled – because to do so would require critical questions about the dogmatics of the Church. Meanwhile the Church and Christian theology remain limited by their heterosexual, patriarchal gaze through which they have engaged with gender and sexuality throughout history. This has had an impact on the way in which bodies are judged and perceived. The abused body of the concubine is therefore prophetic because it speaks of sex as an act of dominion and control, and so challenges dogmatic norms that have silenced the sexual narratives of oppressed bodies and sustained patriarchal norms, because 'At the core of any discussion on sexuality lies the threat of destabilizing dogmas and ecclesiologies which have made God a resource of heterosexual authority.'[27] The body of the concubine can be compared to the colonial 'other', where the colonizer's power is realized in their assumed superiority to those they encounter in their conquests. To do theology in resistance to such power dynamics is to acknowledge the way in which colonial difference operates and instead allow for 'indigenous practices, values, and ideas that were targeted for eradication by colonizers, exploring ways of writing/thinking/practising theology that would begin deconstructing embedded power imbalances, and establishing decolonial methodologies'.[28] It also highlights the extent to which the oppressive frameworks must be exposed and how the narratives of the marginalized must be given the space to disrupt and dismantle.

Judges 19 is a sacred text of sexual violence, a story of an abused body, an indecent narrative of torture that enables us to ask critical questions about theology, pedagogy and God alongside rape, and in its sacred legitimacy offers a space for the women throughout history who have had their sexual narratives of oppression erased from theological discourse and the classrooms of institutes of learning, where they have not been given the space to tell their stories. Furthermore, 'Setting the story within a sacred text also makes the experience of divine silence and abandonment a theologically acknowledged experience.'[29] Elsa Tamez says that because

> women's bodies are not just any bodies but those that form both the object of and the conscious witness to systematic and fortuitous violence and discrimination, we also have to introduce qualification with regard to them. God's option for the excluded puts them in a special position.[30]

To deconstruct theological education as we know it requires asking critical questions about the stories of the bodies we put trust in. Who, for example, can be trusted in this narrative in Judges 19—21? The middle-class, wealthy Levite, the group of men (the rapists), the concubine (already labelled an adulteress), God? Hamley suggests that:

> To some degree, God is caught in the web of the logic and grammar of totalitarian male discourse, so that the only response possible is a negative one: either enter the male discourse or withdraw and be silenced, thereby identifying with the other silent members of the story.[31]

How has God been caught in the web of patriarchy that continues to erase the experience of women in theological education today? Take for example just some of the abuse addressed to ordained and ordinand women in the Church of England, which was shared on a piece of protest art at Ripon College, Cuddesdon:

> Liberal, Christian, Slut
> Should a lady vicar be wearing that?

You will burn in hell you fucking cunt
Women should not be priests ...[32]

Trust must be granted to the erased stories of oppression, so that they may become a source of knowledge that forces communities of faith to look upon themselves and their communities and ask what role we might play in this narrative. Imagine for a second that the concubine, the Levite and the rapists entered the theological education institute and offered to share their experience of that gruesome night – it is, after all, a sacred narrative. Whose version of events would we most likely accept? Whose truth, experiences and story would be given the space to be heard? The indecent concubine? The Levite? Or the group of men? The answer to this question is almost too difficult to accept and that is why it needs asking, because we have created a framework of decency within theological education that offers little or no room for the sexual narratives of the oppressed – narratives that force us to ask critical questions about society, faith, mission and justice. The importance of such stories must be acknowledged in the theological classroom if theological education is to be trusted, because avoiding such narratives only further silences the oppressed and imposes further violence and trauma on raped, abused and oppressed bodies. Judges 19.30 offers a poignant message that speaks prophetically to the importance of allowing such stories to be heard in theological formation today: 'Consider it, take counsel, and speak out.'

Struggling with bodies in theological education

Judges 19 has important pedagogical implications for theological education, because when we reread this text in the context of the missing testimony of the dismembered concubine, we are forced to ask critical questions about the testimonies that have been silenced in the classroom, and to what extent theological educators operate within the same binary frameworks apparent within this narrative. The power dynamics that are apparent within this text often remain unchallenged in theological education, as a consequence of male authorship and male audiences, and the desire for dominance. The matrix of power that is presented both within and outside of the text exposes the androcentric, patriarchal and classist structures of society that have silenced the struggles, dreams and hopes of women. Reading Scripture in the light of such realities is important if we are to undress the multiple layers of oppression that theology and Scripture have enabled and permitted. Musa Dube has situated the need for such critical analysis:

> Post-colonial and feminist subjects are confronted with the struggle against reading canons they did not write or select; against literary images that derogate their humanity and legitimize their oppression; and against institutions such as the school, the church and the government that they do not control, which exclude their texts and impose texts that baptize their oppression.[33]

As theological educators we must become conscious of the oppressive ways in which we operate that instil feelings of un-belonging, and make space for the lived experiences of stories of oppression to enter the classroom and risk shaming the theologies that have dominated. Willie James Jennings has noted that:

> The cultivation of belonging should be the goal of all education – not just any kind of belonging, but a profoundly creaturely belonging that performs the returning of the creator, and a returning to an intimate and erotic energy that drives life together with God.[34]

Such a belonging is shaped by a theology from the body, in particular excluded bodies, and as the body is central to the Christian faith that includes the incarnation, the crucifixion and the resurrection of the body of Christ, our theology should be expanded and destabilized by radical realities. Yet theological education has often overlooked bodies and experiences, when 'seeing real bodies and doing theology from these bodies should change our theology, which has tended to prioritize the spiritual over the material'.[35] Being theologically pedagogic in a way that centres on the experiences of oppressed bodies, inclusive of the oppressed body of Christ on the cross, offers hope in the midst of suffering bodily narratives in theological education. Marcella Althaus-Reid highlights this point, stating: 'the divine body holds a space of possibility to deconstrain the body from the ideologies that rule the body in society, politics and theology. It is the space to be able to re-imagine ourselves, away from heterosexuality and other political bodily narrowness.'[36] A theological education that is shaped by a pedagogy that offers the spaces to freely engage with the broken body of Christ in honesty with the bodies that have been dismembered by the ideologies of capitalism, patriarchy and racism is one that is life flourishing as oppose to life denying. Theological educators who refuse to enable such theologizing risk modelling the pedagogy of the Levite and allowing not just the bodies of the students to be dismembered but also their minds. Being theologically pedagogic demands of the educator the need to understand theology as an act – an act of remembering, reflecting, retelling and conversing. These are bodily acts that can destabilize systems of oppression with and through theological education, where pedagogy recognizes the interconnectedness of theology, society, politics and economy in a way that leads to praxis.

Bodies spill over into our pedagogies

It is my hope and prayer that bodies spill over into our pedagogies, so that dominant epistemologies that have dehumanized bodies and denied bodies their right to flourish may be challenged by the lived experiences of those who have been marginalized. When bodies spill over into our pedagogies we are forced to recognize how dehumanizing disembodied pedagogies can be. For example, when the Christian missionary schools refused to recognize the *Fāgogos* of the Samoan people, they did not just deprive people of their ancestral histories and spirituality, they dehumanized the Samoan people. They perceived the theological truth claims and worldly understandings of the colonialized to be irrelevant and those of so-called 'heathens', and consequently they refused to take the bodies of the Samoans seriously in their pedagogies. Instead, they presented the people with a God made in the image of the colonializers, supported by a pedagogy that left no room for critical thinking; and this was no doubt supported by the promise of Hell for those who dared to try to rebel or believe otherwise. A theological educator should make it possible for the 'student to become themselves', not shape the student in their image but instead enable the space for a dialogue where 'the oppressed themselves' become 'the agents of their own pastoral activity'.[37] There is a quote from the World Council of Churches published in a statement in 1970 that holds just as much relevance today: 'Everything we do and say should contribute towards that education which frees human beings from being domesticated into lives of repression or mere routine and which liberates them into living creatively and abundantly in societies whose structures support education for freedom.'[38]

Pedagogies that deny the freedom of students have an impact on those whom society has already marginalized the most, and it is for this reason that pedagogies must engage with issues of class, gender, climate justice, disability and racism. Such discourses are vital as we look at the subject of bodies and pedagogies because theological education has not been an innocent bystander in the persecution of the bodies of the subjugated – just as no body is neutral, education in itself is not neutral. So the hope is that reflecting on bodies and pedagogies will be an opportunity to reflect on the role of the student and the educator in their participatory presence in environments of learning, noting that each educator and learner 'brings into the classroom not only a body and a mind and set of experiences,

but also a spirit and a culture, a history and a community ...';
and when we begin to realize this, 'Suddenly the classroom is
crowded, overflowing with the essential joys and the pains of
being human, and while this can be overwhelming to some
teachers, it can also become an essential engine of inspired and
honest teaching.'[39]

The marginalization of bodies is relevant to developing theological pedagogies that can be trusted because such lived experiences enable us to question whose bodies shape our world views. What are the lenses being used to reinforce these views? How do bodies exist in theological education? Are all bodies even allowed to exist in these spaces of learning and formation? For theological educators, such questioning gives us an opportunity to reflect on the self, and to locate theological reflection in and about the human body. In doing so, it is possible to develop curricula and pedagogy that offer space for asking critical questions about how things have come to be, and 'how what is seen as normal can be challenged'. Through such a development students are not confined to homogenized processes of theological education but are free to relate the diversity of their daily lives to their thinking about God.[40] While it may not be an easy task to address the potentially damaging and exclusionary practices and pedagogies in theological education, it is nonetheless essential because, as Robert Anderson has pointed out in his research on theological education and disability, 'theological schools alike usually do not discern the level of exclusion that they present to people.'[41] Such exclusionary realities should help shape our theologies and pedagogies. Pedagogies that enable space for bodies are affirming as opposed to controlling and dehumanizing; they can destabilize existing structures that are exclusionary, because through dialogue they allow student, educator and class to engage in struggles together and for bodies to then be at the centre of our theological discourses.

It isn't 'woke', it's biblical

The importance of allowing the bodies of the oppressed to 'spill over' into our pedagogies is not about 'culture wars' or 'wokeness', as the right-wing rhetoric suggests, it is about human rights, it is about dignity, the fullness of life – all of which are at the root of the Christian Gospels. Jesus Christ presents us with pedagogical models throughout the Gospels, where the necessity to allow oppressed bodies to speak truth to power is made apparent. Take, for example, Christ choosing to listen to the silent actions of the sex worker at his feet instead of the critical Pharisee, and in doing so enabling her marginalized body to be a source of knowledge (Luke 7.36–50). As the woman enters before the Lord uninvited, in the home of the Pharisee, she cries at his feet, while the Pharisee grumbles to himself; meanwhile Christ listens to her story through her bodily actions, he gives her the space to be witnessed, and she is heard and forgiven. In doing so, Christ presents a pedagogy of hope, forgiveness, struggle and liberation. Or take, for example, another text that presents Christ's pedagogy of social transformation, where Christ chooses to feed the bodies of 5,000 people before the beginning of his lesson, so that all are fed equally in order to be better nourished by the word of God (Matthew 14.13–21). The pedagogical models presented by Jesus throughout the Gospels enable us to witness what it means to centre bodies in theological education, and to be the kind of teacher who would enter the wavy waters of a storm to be with their students and to know, understand and address their concerns no matter how difficult and different their bodily location may be (Matthew 14.22–36). The bodies of the oppressed, the marginalized, the silenced and the suffering are at the centre of the pedagogies of Jesus. It is therefore a theological imperative that as theological educators we take bodies seriously in our pedagogies.

Notes

1 Brian F. Kolia, 'Eve, the Serpent, and a Samoan Love Story: A Fāgogo Reading of Genesis 3:1–19 and its Implications for Animal Studies', *Books & Culture* 15:2 (2019): 156–63, 156.
2 See https://www.theguardian.com/world/2021/may/28/canada-remains-indigenous-children-mass-graves (accessed 9.2.2022).
3 Lorraine Code, 'Feminist Epistemology and the Politics of Knowledge: Questions of Marginality', in Mary Evans, Clare Hemmings and Marsha Henry (eds), *The SAGE Handbook of Feminist Theory* (London: SAGE, 2014), p. 10.
4 Ada María Isasi-Díaz and Eduardo Mendieta (eds), *Decolonizing Epistemologies: Latina/o Theology and Philosophy* (New York: Fordham University Press, 2012), p. 3.
5 Paulo Freire, *Pedagogy of the Oppressed, 30th Anniversary Edition* (New York: Continuum, 2005), p. 85.
6 Boaventura de Sousa Santos, *Epistemologies of the South: Justice Against Epistemicide* (Boulder, CO: Paradigm, 2014), p. 92.
7 Renita J. Weems, 'Re-Reading for Liberation: African American Women', in Katie Geneva Cannon, Emilie M. Townes and Angela D. Sims (eds), *Womanist Theological Ethics: A Reader* (Louisville, KY: Westminster John Knox Press, 2011), p. 58.
8 Mayra Rivera Rivera, 'Thinking Bodies: The Spirit of a Latina Incarnational Imagination', in Isasi-Díaz and Mendieta (eds), *Decolonizing Epistemologies*, p. 221.
9 See Pamela R. Lightsey, *Our Lives Matter: A Womanist Queer Theology* (Eugene, OR: Pickwick Publications, 2015), p. 1.
10 Lisa A. Bergin, 'Testimony, Epistemic Difference, and Privilege: How Feminist Epistemology can Improve our Understanding of the Communication of Knowledge', *Social Epistemology* 16:3 (2002): 197–213, 198.
11 See Nyasha Junior, *An Introduction to Womanist Biblical Interpretation* (Louisville, KY: Westminster John Knox Press, 2015), p. 109.
12 Sheila Delany, '"The Borrowed Language": Body Politic in Judges 19', *Shofar* 11:2 (1993): 97–109, 99.
13 See Koala Jones-Warsaw, 'Toward a Womanist Hermeneutic: A Reading of Judges 19–21,' in Athalya Brenner (ed.), *A Feminist Companion to Judges* (Sheffield: JSOT Press, 1993).
14 See Marc Zvi Brettler, *The Book of Judges* (London: Routledge, 2002).
15 See Phyllis A. Bird, *Missing Persons and Mistaken Identities: Women and Gender in Ancient Israel* (Minneapolis, MN: Fortress, 1997), p. 23.

16 Isabelle M. Hamley, *Unspeakable Things Unspoken: An Irigarayan Reading of Otherness and Victimization in Judges 19–21* (Eugene, OR: Pickwick Publications, 2019), p. 222.
17 Phyllis Trible, *Texts of Terror* (Philadelphia, PA: Fortress Press, 1984), p. 65.
18 See J. Cheryl Exum, *Fragmented Women: Feminist (Sub)versions of Biblical Narratives*; JSOT Supp. 163 (Sheffield: Sheffield Academic Press, 1993), p. 181.
19 Hamley, *Unspeakable Things*, p. 234.
20 See David Moster, 'The Levite of Judges 19–21', *Journal of Biblical Literature* 134:4 (2015): 721–730, 723–4.
21 Hamley, *Unspeakable Things*, p. 223.
22 Hamley, *Unspeakable Things*, p. 226.
23 Jones-Warsaw, 'Toward a Womanist Hermeneutic', p. 183.
24 Code, 'Feminist Epistemology', p. 18.
25 https://www.churchtimes.co.uk/articles/2017/10-november/news/uk/assault-and-abuse-are-rife-in-the-church-women-say (accessed 9.2.2022).
26 Ibid.
27 Marcella Althaus-Reid, *From Feminist Theology to Indecent Theology* (London: SCM Press, 2004), p. 102.
28 Oscar García-Johnson, *Spirit Outside the Gate: Decolonial Pneumatologies of the American Global South* (Downers Grove, IL: InterVarsity Press, 2019), p. 3.
29 Hamley, *Unspeakable Things*, p. 235.
30 Elsa Tamez, 'Women's Lives as Sacred Text', in Kwok Pui-Lan and Elisabeth Schüssler Fiorenza (eds), *Women's Sacred Scriptures* (London: SCM Press, 1998), p. 49.
31 Hamley, *Unspeakable Things*, pp. 223–4.
32 The community artwork 'Eva's Call' was put up as an act of lament for the prejudices experienced by women training for ministry and women ordained. See Alice Watson, https://artsrcc.wordpress.com/2018/03/02/evas-call/ (accessed 9.2.2022).
33 See Musa W. Dube Shomanah, 'Scripture, Feminism and Post-Colonial Contexts', in Pui-Lan and Schüssler Fiorenza (eds), *Women's Sacred Scriptures*, p. 49.
34 Willie James Jennings, *After Whiteness: An Education in Belonging* (Grand Rapids, MI: Wm. B. Eerdmans, 2020), p. 62.
35 Thia Cooper, *Queer and Indecent: An Introduction to Marcella Althaus-Reid* (London: SCM Press, 2021), p. 89.
36 Marcella Althaus-Reid, 'Pussy, Queen of Pirates: Acker, Isherwood and the Debate on the Body in Feminist Theology', *Feminist Theology* 12:2 (2004): 157–67, 159.

37 Gustavo Gutiérrez, *A Theology of Liberation: History, Politics, and Salvation*, trans. C. Inda and J. Eagleson (Maryknoll, NY: Orbis Books, 1988), pp. 154–5.

38 Quoted by Irwin Leopando in *A Pedagogy of Faith: The Theological Vision of Paulo Freire* (New York: Bloomsbury, 2017), p. 31.

39 Victoria F. Trinder, *Teaching Toward a Decolonizing Pedagogy: Critical Reflections Inside and Outside the Classroom* (New York: Routledge, 2020), p. ix.

40 See Cooper, *Queer and Indecent*, p. 12.

41 Robert C. Anderson, 'In Search of the Disabled Human Body in Theological Education: Critical Perspectives on the Construction of Normalcy – An Overview', *Journal of Religion, Disability & Health* 7:3 (2008): 33–55, 34.

3

Being Seen as 'Trustworthy': The Gaze in Theological Education

> I am being dissected under white eyes, the only real eyes, I am fixed. Having readjusted their microtomes, they objectively cut away slices of my reality. I am laid bare.[1]
> *Frantz Fanon*

Frantz Fanon's description of the white gaze addresses the ways in which white surveillance operates through its social structures, creating somatic norms where bodies that challenge such norms are dissected under the gaze of the powerful and 'laid bare'. The words of a theology student training for ordination in the Church of England narrate his sense of dissection under the dominant gaze of the theological education institute:

> 'I tried so hard to adapt to the environment, to fit in, but I was called a "sinner" for being gay, "blasphemous" for my understanding of the incarnation and "a token tick-box" by a fellow student. I felt so worthless and ashamed of who I was.'

Shame is often a feeling brought about by the external gaze that 'springs from perceiving oneself unworthy with respect to a pre-fixed model or standard'.[2] The gaze of the powerful situates the boundaries of belonging and acceptance, where those that look and act the same as the ones who hold the gaze are able to go about their daily business because they are the 'faithful flock', the 'decent ones'. Yet anyone who disrupts the gaze is considered a danger; they are forced to either adapt to the environment in the awareness that their bodies are not trusted in their entirety because they exist outside of the normalized gaze of the ruling class, or to attempt to remove themselves from the gaze altogether. Shame is a tool of the gaze because 'Even if shame does not actually lead to the physical death of individuals, its effects can be devastating in terms of lowering morale and inducing a sense of hopelessness and passivity.'[3] Therefore the dominant way of seeing and being seen impacts one's knowledge of oneself, as the dominant gaze controls the norm and shapes perceptions of our own bodies and the bodies of others. Eric Stoddart has described how 'Surveillance and human flourishing are interwoven in everyday life.' How one is seen, unseen and watched is therefore of significant theological concern because it involves personhood and flourishing.[4] Such surveillance is apparent within theological education and the process of formation for ordained ministry in particular operates in a way that regulates the bodies of those in training. In the context of the Church of England, such regulatory processes are apparent before the students enter the theological education institutes, because their bodies are watched from vocation to calling. This is visible in the selection process, in their church, by the diocese, in the theological education institute, by their theological educators, directors of study and fellow students, and throughout modules, training programmes, placements and assessments. Using the language of Foucault, we can witness how the bodies of those in theological education are 'manipulated, shaped, trained ... subjected, used, transformed and improved'[5] under the gaze of the Church, the institutions and the educators. It is those with the power who control the dominant gaze that determines who should flourish and how; as Miguel De La Torre says, 'Power is conveyed to the one who sees.'[6] Those who are given the space and ability to flourish are also the ones who those with power have determined are worthy of trust. The gaze of the powerful has deemed them 'trustworthy', as opposed to 'untrustworthy'. This is particularly relevant to theological formation in the light of the Church of England's new framework of assessment for candidates for ordained ministry, where 'trustworthiness' will now be 'tested' during training. The new framework for candidates has highlighted the need for the following qualities:

> Love for God; Call to Ministry; Love for People; Wisdom; Fruitfulness; Potential. During training, a seventh quality – 'trustworthiness' – will be tested, 'to reflect the commitments that ordained ministry requires of an individual in terms of safeguarding, professional conduct and living within the boundaries and values of the Church'.[7]

The testing of such 'trustworthiness' requires taking into account the relations of power because, as Trudy Govier writes, trust 'is an attitude that affects our emotions, beliefs, actions, and interpretations … based on the belief that the trusted person is competent and well motivated and therefore likely to live up to these positive expectations'.[8] The question then is who should be trusted, in what way and why? And how is such an attribute to be tested? One's social and political location impacts the amount of trust and consequently power that the person is capable of receiving, particularly in a society governed by patriarchal and heteronormative values. The global power structures of class, sexuality, gender, religion, ethnicity, language and geography impact the extent to which one is deemed trustworthy, and the gaze of the powerful, particularly in the context of Europe, is more fixed on the those who are working class, women, LGBTQI+, non-Christian and black and minority ethnic. Those being 'tested' as trustworthy must therefore negotiate their identity in the midst of such power dynamics in order to be 'seen' as trustworthy. The dominant gaze in theological education is that of the white, heterosexual, middle-class male. It manifests itself through curricula, structures, systems, pedagogies and procedures that systemically normalize their gaze while distorting perceptions of those who deviate from it. Therefore, in order to maintain the power and control of their watchful eye, they create a culture of belonging and un-belonging, where certain bodies are deemed acceptable and 'trustworthy' and others are portrayed as 'indecent', 'troublesome', 'uncontrollable' and 'untrustworthy'.

The bodies of students and staff are predominantly watched under such a gaze in theological education institutes, where perceptions of the individual are filtered through certain ideological lenses, including sexism, racism, classism and heterosexuality. We are led to assume that the system that 'tests' and 'monitors' is neutral and so it goes unchallenged, thereby maintaining a position of power and privilege. This chapter will address the issue of assessing 'trustworthiness' in theological education – noting the complexity of what it means to be trusted in contexts of inequality. At times the focus will be on trustworthiness in the context of formation in the Church of England; however, the themes of power, inequality and the dominant gaze are relevant to all mainstream denominations and institutes of learning. I will therefore consider the impact of the socio-political and economic structures that dominate and have the ability to deny those under the dominant gaze the right to move freely in the world. Thereby I will argue that social status, ethnicity, sexuality and gender impact the extent to which one is valued as trustworthy; in contrast, those with power often assume a trustworthy status that can be used to control and manipulate the 'distrusted'. Where, as Christine Hong remarks, 'The academy and its institutions are in the business of domesticating, civilizing, and disciplining, the minds, bodies, theologies, spiritualities, and identities of co-learners',[9] the gaze of those with power tends to point in one direction: away from the powerful towards the powerless. This chapter will therefore call on theological education to turn the gaze on to the oppressor by dissecting the powerful through queer, black and indecent lenses – in order to allow the marginalized to 'be seen', while noting that they have never not been seen by the God who is on the side of the oppressed.

The 'trustworthy' gaze of the Church

The Church of England's new criteria for ordained ministry have focused on the need for ordinands to be 'trustworthy', but this is not a new concept for the Church. Ian Forrest's brilliant book *Trustworthy Men: How Inequality and Faith Made the Medieval Church* exposes how the bishops of the medieval Church in Europe manipulated the inequalities of society in order to use so-called 'trustworthy men' as witnesses and informants. The men's trustworthy status was influenced by their social and economic status.[10] The system was structured in a way that 'trustworthiness was systematically gendered male',[11] and the ecclesiastical decision to trust one set of people – landowning, wealthy, socially 'decent' men – 'was predicated upon the disqualification of others, notably women, from consideration'. Consequently trust in one set of people equated to distrust in others, and this was sustained through multiple inequalities.[12] Trustworthiness determined greater socio-political and economic capital that exacerbated existing inequalities. As Forrest notes:

> The trust that the institutional church placed in select local men was a major component in the inequalities of life, and the church in turn depended upon the existence of those inequalities in order to identify trustworthy men … the trustworthiness of the trustworthy men was established by a combination of institutional rhetoric and their possession of a certain status in local society.[13]

Trustworthiness was then an act of discrimination used in order to control and oppress, in which 'The institutional church was located in the combination of respect, fear, deference, and envy … and this is also what kept women, the poor, and those without good *fama* out of the late medieval public sphere.'[14] Individuals would be watched and judged by the 'trusted', operating through social mechanisms of surveillance that are also apparent in models of theological education today.

BEING SEEN AS 'TRUSTWORTHY'

As the ACCM remarked in 1990, 'It is vital that in ministerial formation students live together for residential periods where they are vulnerable to one another's continued gaze and enquiry.'[15] Patriarchal assumptions also remain entrenched within the Church; female participation in the priesthood is a very new concept in the Church of England and most other mainstream denominations in the UK. Even now, the place of women is still the subject of great debate and contestation. Chapter 4 will discuss the gendered experiences of theological formation in greater detail; however, central to discussions on the topic of 'being seen' by the Church and institutions is the role of patriarchy. Take, for example, a case of distrust that dates back to 1340 but speaks to the distrust of women's testimonies in the Church today. A woman named Alice Kirkbride escaped the violence of her husband after he cut off her hair and her skin and hit her so hard she lost her unborn child; he also broke the back of another of her children. The domestic violence was historically recorded because the husband relied on canon law to take out a case of defamation against her. Alice Kirkbride went before a Bishop Kirkby, who did not trust her word but called upon so-called 'trustworthy persons' to tell their version of events. Having once again narrated the abuse she received, public pressure was no doubt put on Alice, with the backing of the Church, and for unknown reasons she later changed her story, 'confessing that accusations were false'. However, the incident did not end there; her situation was so bad that a court of appeal got involved upon discovering that Bishop Kirkby had worsened her situation. It was later discovered that this same bishop, who had little concern for the well-being of a beaten and tortured woman, threatened excommunication to the same wife beater when he was accused of stealing another man's falcon.[16]

One might think that a story such as this would not happen in the Church today, but this is not the case. One woman who went forward to the Bishops' Advisory Panel in the Church of England shared how, when she was asked why she had divorced her husband some twenty years before, she had informed the bishop that this was because he had beaten and abused her and she had at times feared for her life. However, the inquisitor (or rather the bishop) did not accept her word; he interviewed members of her family, 'trustworthy' people, in order to make sure she was telling the truth. Forrest writes, 'If bishops built the church upon trust, they also built it upon the inequalities that flowed from this.'[17]

These same inequalities penetrate the Church today. Women's experiences and stories often remain untrusted. It is therefore interesting to see that there is a new commitment by the Church of England to focus on 'the unseen-and-excluded called', those who have been excluded by the existing framework that they suggest 'favours middle-class candidates'.[18] The 'unseen-and-excluded called' should also include women, LGBTQI+ and black and ethnic minorities, who of course may also be working class. However, there is seemingly little awareness of the Church's role in forming such a framework that has created the 'unseen-and-excluded'. Nor has there been any engagement with the theological implications of the 'unseen' entering spaces of education, formation and clerical roles that were not designed for them, but rather designed to control them – places that enable 'the transference of power and privileges'.[19] A. D. A. France-Williams has narrated many such experiences of the misuse of power within the Church of England in his book *Ghost Ship*. One such story tells of his encounter with a vicar when he was a youth worker in 'a large multi-ethnic church' where he was asked to report back on the experiences of black women who felt marginalized in the parish. He writes:

> I presented my report to the vicar ... he perched on his swivel chair, accepted and held my document, which was teeming with comment, conversation, grief and expectation. The voices within the document were clearing their throats ready to sing out powerful possibility and purpose. He looked at me for a moment then spun round in his chair and in a single move dropped it onto the top his in-tray. He deftly spun back around to meet my gaze. I could feel a coolness in the air

as, in his rich baritone voice, he declared: 'The Spirit is saying now is not the time for diversity, now it is the time for unity.'[20]

The experiences of the black women in the church and the truth of their marginalization were met only with a superficial gaze of interest by the church leader who held the power, and in the name of the Spirit he declared them irrelevant. Even worse, he suggested that they would be responsible for disunity, despite their bodies seemingly not being welcome into the sacred space of the church. Such misuses of spiritual power are a recurrent theme throughout the history of the Church. As is the suggestion that challenging issues of abuse, barriers to belonging and misuses of power are acts of 'disunity' for the Church. The call for 'unity' in the face of injustice is often used as a weapon of imposed decency, used to mask the 'disunity' brought about through the persecution of the oppressed. Enforced silence for the sake of unity is a weapon too often wielded by the Church and the establishments. Professing that the Church should be 'united in Christ' too often equates to those who have been marginalized by the dominant structures being shamed or stigmatized into silence. This is abuse. It is unity in abuse – the same form of unity used to dismember the body of Christ itself. Powerful men determining what is and should be. When powerful bodies unite in their doctrines of hate we know from history that this does not end well for those who exist on the wrong side of the doctrines. The same battle cries for unity are rarely issued in the face of poverty, the refugee crisis, domestic violence, rape, wars and abuse. There were no statements issued from the Church of England calling for us to be united against the cuts to universal credit, the diminishing of legal funding for rape victims or the cuts to international aid; these issues, though vital to humanity, are met with an impotent silence. Yet when it comes to equal marriage or the place of women in the Church, the Church calls on us to be united in saying no to same-sex marriage and in gracefully accepting that some priests do not believe in a woman's right to the pulpit. One cannot always trust in the unity of the Church, because somewhere a body is being silenced, downtrodden and oppressed for the sake of such unity. Furthermore, for the most part theological education does not offer the space, resources or pedagogical methods to adequately contemplate both the silence of the Church in the face of oppression and what it means theologically for individuals to be 'united' in a Church where the bodies of women and LGBTQI+ people are in effect silenced and shamed.

Witnessing classism in the classroom

In order to resist oppression we have to name the oppression and how it operates and turn the oppressive gaze on to the oppressors themselves. One such system of oppression that continues to segregate Britain today is the class system, since Britain is a nation divided by class. This has been made visible during the Covid-19 pandemic, in which the working class have been the most affected, due in part to more working-class people being exposed to the virus as a result of the jobs they hold – jobs such as care workers, shop workers and taxi drivers. It has also been a consequence of poverty being a significant cause for underlying health issues such as malnutrition, heart disease and obesity. Consequently, 'those in the poorest English and Welsh communities were more than twice as likely to die as those in the most affluent.'[21] Globally those most affected by the continuing devastation of the climate crisis are the working class: pollution, flooding, droughts and destabilized food supplies disproportionately impact the poorest communities. Class in itself is difficult to define. Sociologically it is understood in terms that go beyond economic relationships, because class functions as an identity made visible by certain social signifiers including 'accent, proximity to manual labour, immigration status, education, race, consumer habits, geography'.[22] Class status is also dependent upon wealth and power. Understanding how class operates within British society requires witnessing class through an intersectional lens, because working-class black and ethnic minority people are more likely to suffer from extreme poverty and unemployment, as well as experience social persecution and racial injustice from institutions and authorities. When we consider the dominant gaze in theological education in relation to class, it is important to recognize that on the one hand the working class will be more visible as a result of stereotyping and the low expectations placed upon them by preconceived prejudices, and on the other hand, invisible and overlooked. The class system dominates British society and the divisions are visible within the Church and theological education, where class prejudice is rampant. As one student stated:

> 'I had a tutor who told me I could only serve on estates because of the way I spoke and how I dressed. He said I was exactly what the church needed though in reaching out to the "unchurched" and "illiterate". He said the working class, like me, need God urgently because there are so many single mums, hoodies and drugs that they need salvation and they need it fast.'

The tutor in the student's experience uses typical class stereotypes to stigmatize the working class, seemingly oblivious to or ignorant of the societal inequalities experienced by those he/she mocks through class prejudice. Educational systems, inclusive of theological education, mirror and reproduce class hierarchies and inequalities that are apparent in wider society. Interestingly, when it comes to the marginalization of the working class within the Church of England there have been recent efforts to address what one priest described as 'an ongoing spiral of middle-class leaders, leaving the working class out in the cold'.[23] However, there appears to be very little understanding of the role of class struggle in addressing the disparities faced by the working class in Church, society and education. Commitments from the Church of England have focused on addressing 'barriers' to the working class faced by those responding to vocational callings within the Church. Yet little has been done to address class disparities and the implications of class struggle in theological education and formation, noting that class is very much embedded within higher education as a whole within the UK, where working-class students experience 'hostile' and 'unfamiliar' environments that can be both physically and psychologically damaging.[24]

Efforts to address reaching out to the working class in the face of church decline have been ongoing within the Church. In 1985, the Archbishop of Canterbury's Commission on Urban Priority Areas issued the *Faith in the City* report, which noted that 'the Church of England's most enduring "problem of the city" has been its relationship with the urban working class.'[25] Perhaps, however, the problem is clearly stated here: the Church of England is not the Church that represents the interests of the working class, but rather it intends to be *in relationship* with the working class – a relationship blurred by complex power relations and significant issues of trust, in which the Church does not appear committed to the political struggles of the working class but instead is focused on bringing the working class into their flock without doing anything to address the classist structures and struggles. To do so would require addressing the role of capitalism in bringing about social inequalities, as well as looking to liberation theology in formation in order to greater understand the socio-political implications of the Christian faith in relation to class struggle and consciousness. In order to address the complexity of the Church of England's relationship with the working class there is also a need for the Church to take more responsibility for the classist history that continues to dominate its structures, systems and leadership today – a history that has given the working class little reason to trust in the Church. Take one of the most significant atrocities in working-class history in the UK, the Peterloo Massacre of 1819, where 60,000 people gathered at St Peter's Field in the centre of Manchester to attend a peaceful meeting calling for parliamentary reform. They were met with violence as a result of the ruling classes of Britain sending out the troops to disperse them; 18 working-class people were murdered and 650 were injured. The atrocity committed against the working class was met by the Church siding with the establishment, forbidding the gathering of more than 50 people on church land in order to prevent future protests or calls for political transformation and reform.

As we look to class consciousness in theological education, it is vital to understand that there is no such thing as a single working-class experience. As Owen Jones remarked in *Chavs*, 'All too often, the common image of a working-class Briton is someone who is male, middle-aged, straight, white, lives in a small town and holds socially conservative views.'[26] The white working-class middle-aged male does not embody the entirety of the working-class experience, as economic exploitation can intersect with gender, sexuality and ethnicity or a combination of such lived realities. Class stereotypes, prejudice and stigma therefore affect many students, because, for example, the class system has determined that a child from a private school is far more likely to be the Prime Minister of this country, or the Archbishop of Canterbury, than is a child from a local state comprehensive school. The system is geared against the working class and trust has been placed in the middle class and ruling elites. Take the words of one student who experienced distrust as a result of their class status:

> 'I have been called lazy because I wasn't able to make a deadline, they didn't believe me that I had finished a late shift at work, had to look after my mum and the kids and it was impossible to make the deadline they expected. I ended up having to have a meeting with someone high up the chain who explained to me that if I lied to get out of submitting work that was on me and my conscience. They even said that I had deliberately plagiarized. I didn't but they didn't believe me so I failed that assignment.'

The student who had to work unpredictable working hours due to shift work, and was responsible for multiple carer responsibilities, had burdens that the tutor clearly had no understanding of and was therefore not able to relate to. Furthermore, the student had limited education prior to entering theological education and the rules regarding plagiarism were not entirely understood. Class prejudice has determined that working-class people are often far more likely to be distrusted than middle-class people. Many theological educators, particularly in the university setting, are themselves privileged with a private school education that puts them at odds with the vast majority of the rest of the population and those who the Church of England now wishes to focus on putting forward for ordained ministry and theological formation. In the desire for more working-class people to enter ordained ministry there is seemingly little focus on transforming the working-class conditions in this country. Notably, the need for class consciousness does not appear to be taken into consideration in the formation process, pedagogical methodologies or theological curricula.

Yet the hierarchy of Church and society has had a direct impact on the classrooms of theological colleges because, as Marx says, the ruling elites maintain the authority: 'The bureaucracy is a circle from which no one can escape. Its hierarchy is a hierarchy of knowledge.'[27] The Church and theological education institutes have attempted to control the hierarchy of knowledge and in doing so have denied people certain truths. Marx and Engels famously stated that the bourgeois are the class of people who own the means of social production. The proletarians, for Marx and Engels, were the class of 'modern wage laborers, who having no means of production of their own, are reduced to selling their labour power in order to live'.[28] Knowledge can be considered a 'means of production'; in terms of theological knowledge it is not the working class who own the means of theological knowledge production but rather the privately educated middle class, whose knowledge gets unequally distributed and is therefore deemed more trustworthy. Consequently, the working class are forced to use the tools and lens of the middle class in their theological formation. There are then significant pedagogical implications with regard to the working class 'being seen' theologically and physically in theological education and formation. Having no means of knowledge production equates to potential spiritual and psychological damage in the formation process if people are forced to fall in line under the watchful eye of the normalized gaze that maintains its boundaries through a classist culture of deference; a formation process in which the powerful who have been granted trust remain unexposed behind the classist, white, male veil of ignorance.

When Hagar is 'seen' by God under the gaze of oppression

> The African people trusted the 'white man' who came in religious clothing but eventually carried out several outrageous and almost permanent damage on the people of Africa by pillaging their natural resources and engaging in inhuman degradation and many atrocities.[29]

Being deemed trustworthy does not always equate to righteous, worthy or just. Shame and trustworthiness were powerful tools of control and condemnation for the missionaries during colonial rule in Africa. Take for example the words of one English woman missionary:

> Weighed down with rough work – rather the slave than the wife to their husbands – ignorant beyond belief – their mouths full of vile words and their hearts filled with fears of witchcraft and evil spirits – there is yet in them much promise of good.[30]

The colonialized African women were described as 'ignorant', their beliefs were stigmatized as 'witchcraft' and therefore the preconceived racial prejudice of the missionaries determined that the African women were in need of 'saving' and until then could not be granted any trust. Under the dominant gaze of oppressive ideologies it is often women's bodies that are the most scrutinized. They are visible to the oppressor as an object to be controlled, but they are not truly 'seen' in their own being but rather dissected, labelled, policed and vilified. The story of Hagar in Genesis 16 is one of the most challenging texts that brings to light issues of trust, power, class, gender, ethnicity and control, and it is also a text in which God is named and 'sees' the oppressed for who they truly are. Hagar's story is one of struggle and liberation, in which an enslaved woman is denied agency, is sexually abused, vilified and distrusted, and consequently, as Phyllis Trible has noted, 'As a symbol of the oppressed, Hagar becomes many things to many people. Most especially, all sorts of rejected women used by the male and abused by the female of the ruling class.'[31] She is the *Shifhah* or *Amah*, meaning 'slave-girl', of Sarai, the wife of Abram, and her body is seemingly under the control of both, because Sarai tells Abram to impregnate Hagar in order that he might have a child to fulfil his legacy (Gen. 16.2), since Sarai assumes that she cannot carry a child herself (Gen. 16.1). Instantly, the class dynamics of the text are visible. Sarai and Abram, who have wealth, own a 'female slave' as property and they wish to 'use' her as a concubine surrogate – this was common practice in the ancient Israelite context. The economic class disparities also determine how the women perceive one another, as Renita Weems notes:

> The differences between the two women, therefore, went beyond their ethnic identities, beyond their reproductive capabilities. Their disparities were centered in their contrasting economic positions. And economic differences have, on more than one occasion, thwarted coalitions and frustrated friendships between women.[32]

Hagar is denied agency; her identity for the couple who hold the power is that of a womb, without name, voice, history or knowledge. Luke Hillier makes the point that 'a careful reading of Genesis 16 shows that whenever Hagar is described by Sarai or Abram, her name is never used.'[33] The attempt to erase her identity and see her as a mere object is apparent throughout the text. Under the gaze of the oppressor the oppressed are visible in ways that are useful to the oppressor; in the missionary context the colonized were useful as souls to be 'saved' or charitable causes to fuel the white saviour complex, but they were dehumanized in the process, hence why the colonized 'heathen' women are nameless in missionary narratives. Hagar, as an Egyptian slave, is the 'outsider' to Sarai and Abram, who are Hebrew. Consequently Renita Weems comments that this is also a 'story of ethnic prejudices exacerbated by economic and sexual exploitation'.[34] Hagar's narrative is therefore one of intersectional abuse as she is marginalized for her class, ethnicity and gender.

When Hagar conceives, Sarai seemingly responds in jealousy and suggests that Hagar is showing her 'contempt' (Gen. 16.4). Patriarchy and capitalism work in a way that pits women against each other as a means of preventing solidarity in resistance to systems that oppress. Both women in the text are victims of patriarchy; each is reliant on their womb in order to survive the system. Sarai, as a wealthy Hebrew, holds more power, just as white, middle-class women in capitalist societies hold more power, yet because she is 'barren' her socio-political positioning is at risk. In contrast, Hagar's narrative speaks to the experiences of black women, who face multiple oppressions and are forced to subvert the system as they struggle to survive within it. As Emily Peecook notes, 'Modern African American women identify with Hagar's transcendence of the biblical gender roles in their own history. Female slaves were often required to accept any role or task assigned to them.'[35] Both women are prevented from fully 'seeing' each other in their suffering as a result of the ideologies that dominate, thereby preventing solidarity or resistance. Bharti Mukherjee comments: 'I hope that Hagar smirked ... The smirk is the only way of dissenting that is allowed for a woman from a disempowered position.'[36] Hagar has no reason not to smirk at Sarai; why should she trust her or respect her? After all, Sarai demanded that her husband impregnate Hagar and in the process Hagar's agency was denied; furthermore, Sarai then 'dealt harshly with her' (16.6). It is as a result of patriarchy, capitalism, racism and gender violence that this whole narrative has come into being. It is in negotiating her identity in the midst of such ideologies that Hagar decides to escape: 'She cannot and will not endure such treatment from Sarah; she will be liberated from her, and she sees the only possibility of liberation in flight, even though it endangers her life and that of her unborn child.'[37] This leads Hagar into the wilderness, the space in which she is finally 'seen'.

The messenger of God says, 'Hagar, slave-girl of Sarai, where have you come from and where are you going?' (16.8) The question 'Where have you come from?' can be a loaded one, particularly for women of colour. URC Minister Karen Campbell's poem addresses her experience of such a question:

> 'Where do you come from?'
> It's buzzing round my mind;
> Such a heavy-loaded question I very often find:
> Referring not to who I am –
> The way that I see me –
> But laden with assumptions
> 'Bout what they think they see
>
> My skin, it seems, speaks loudly,
> But its message isn't clear;
> It depends on who is listening
> And what they want to hear;
> And because that is the way it is,
> Sometimes, without intent,
> I can't hear the simple question
> Without questioning what is meant ...[38]

Hagar does not answer the question of where she comes from, only that she is running away from her mistress Sarai. The narrative, however, suggests that the messenger already knows her story, history and embodied reality. Trustworthiness is a central theme here, Sarai does not trust Hagar, she sees her as an *outsider*, an Egyptian working-class woman who is now pregnant with her husband's child. Hagar does not trust Sarai, she is a rich woman who has vilified her and been violent against her. Abram puts some trust in his wife, in that he trusts her with her 'own property', but as a woman Hagar seemingly does not appear to truly enter Abram's gaze beyond that of being a womb (16.6). Yet in the wilderness Hagar shows trust in God and God in Hagar, as Hillier points out: 'it is precisely at the outskirts where Hagar experiences God most intimately and finds herself transformed and blessed.'[39] As an oppressed person, she is also the first person in the Bible to be visited by a divine messenger, and the only person to name God. The messenger of God is also the first person to name Hagar and speak *to* her, rather than *about* her. The messenger trusts in the narrative and embodied experience of Hagar, but also tells her to return to her oppressor. It takes an immense amount of trust on behalf of Hagar to accept that she must suffer more, but she is told that in doing so she will have innumerable descendants, and is given the promise of a son whose name shall be 'Ishmael', meaning 'God hears', because God has heard her affliction. Letty Russell comments that 'Ishmael will be a free man and a strong man ... he will live in perpetual strife with all his brothers ... Hagar and her son live on the boundary of affliction and release, a boundary decreed by God.'[40] Hagar responds prophetically to what the Lord has told her and names the Lord who spoke to her (Gen. 16.13). She calls God 'El-roi', meaning 'God of seeing'; in doing so, 'Uniting the God who sees and the God who is seen, Hagar's insights move from life under affliction to life after theophany.'[41] She puts trust in the God who sees her for who she truly is, the God who knows her narrative of struggle, understands her suffering and, for Delores Williams, is 'a God that provides insight and vision into one's social-historical and geographical situation. There is always a potential for despair, but the gift of vision allows for renewed hope in the midst of wilderness experiences.'[42] Trible concludes her reading of Hagar's narrative with a message to the reader: 'All we who are heirs of Sarah and Abraham, by flesh and spirit, must answer for the terror in Hagar's story. To neglect the theological challenge is to falsify faith.'[43] This same challenge applies in theological education, because when women or others on the margins attempt to theologize without being 'truly seen', they are denied a voice and identity and their narratives of oppression go ignored, to the detriment of the Christian faith. Becoming conscious of our role in Hagar's narrative is also critical, because it forces the reader to become aware of their own prejudices. It is not, therefore, about responding to Hagar's narrative as an individualized story of oppression, but rather about acknowledging that the issues of patriarchy, racism and classism, are systemic and structurally entrenched and bring about the silencing and distrust of those whose narratives must be witnessed. God sees Hagar, and joins her in the wilderness in her struggles, but what of those who do not see her, name her or hear her struggles? If we did not have Hagar's narrative in our Holy Scripture there would be no character who is trusted enough to name God, but we know from Hagar that the gaze of God looks on the oppressed and sees the struggles and knows those who exploit. Through the eyes of the oppressed God is then experienced as the God of solidarity, of love, truth, trust and justice.

'Seeing' ourselves through our own eyes in theological education

Allan Boesak has argued that God sees 'through the eyes of the oppressed, the despised, the outcasts, the ravaged, the powerless, and those whose imaginations and dreams of justice and peace are transformed by the imagination of God'.[44] Yet the God who has been constructed by Eurocentric patriarchal Christianity has appeared as a stranger to such 'outcasts'. The experiences of the powerless have not been granted space in theological thought, and consequently those who have been oppressed by dominant norms of Christianity have not always been able to contemplate God honestly and formatively through their 'own eyes' in theological education. Theologies of Hagar have been replaced by theologies of Abram, to the detriment of witnessing the God who 'sees' the oppressed. Jarel Robinson-Brown makes this point:

> You can see that as Black LGBTQ+ Christians we live with myriad ideas and images of God, and in that we are not alone. What makes our experience of God distinct is that our image of God is narrowed by the Church's historic and present-day overemphasis on LGBTQ+ sin, such that for us the last thing we often understand God to be is our friend, and if we come to that understanding we often enter into that friendship having left our sexuality behind.[45]

Such a narrowing understanding of Christ forces people into a state of distrust in their own embodied experiences of God and the world around them. In order to resist such dominant norms, the body must be taken seriously in theology. In order to better contemplate the human image of God, trust must be granted to the experiences of the flesh in order to grant truth not only to the systematic doctrines of the spirit but also to the knowledge that stems from the bodies of the powerless. What we 'know' of God is always dependent upon the conditions of how that 'knowing' came to be; in other words, how our consciousness has been constructed by certain factors. John Hull, who has written profoundly on blindness and theology, places the importance of consciousness of our situatedness in relation to theological contemplations, noting that the biblical image of God is representative of the 'domination of the normal'. He stated that

> The God of the Bible is the God of the able-bodied not of the disabled. Women were not permitted to be priests, and the God of the Bible is not a woman. Men with a physical defect were not permitted to be priests, and the God of the Bible does not possess physical defects.[46]

In order to challenge such dominant notions of the normal, Hull suggests that we need to become 'access aware' in our own ways of being and knowing. He writes:

> Only when the clock stops ticking do you realize that you have been hearing it. Only when you become blind do you realize that you were living in a sighted world. So it is that most sighted people, who have perhaps never experienced disability or had occasion to empathize with a disabled loved one, do not acknowledge a plurality of genuine human worlds. To them, there is the common-sense world to which some people do not have access. Thus there is the world of normality and there are disabled people who have the misfortune to be excluded from that world.[47]

For theological educators, being 'access aware' means being aware of who is being excluded from the 'world of normality', and becoming conscious of the silencing and marginalization in education of those who have not had access to education in the normalized 'common-sense' world. An education that is 'access aware' puts trust in the experiences and insights of disabled bodies and other bodies that have been excluded by the dominant gaze. Such an education becomes conscious of the ways in which dominant cultures of learning and dialogue have relied on knowledge that contradicts the ways the oppressed have existed in the world. In other words, theologies dominated by the white Christ and theologies of whiteness contradict the black Christ of liberation theology, and patriarchal theologies deny women their experiences in the world. In the world of the dominant 'able-bodied', white, middle-class, heterosexual male, the norm is the only world they know, and the world of the *other* is crushed, diminished and silenced, and their theologies too are denied authenticity. As Paulo Freire remarks, 'the person who is filled by another with "content" whose meaning s/he is not aware of, which contradict his or her way of being in the world, cannot learn because s/he is not challenged.'[48]

Theological education must therefore consider the 'content' being taught, the ways in which theology is taught, and the ways it enables the student to engage more deeply with the world that they know and the world that *others* have come to know. Such an education engages with different positions; it does not judge or deny differing theologies but enters into loving dialogue in order to enhance theory and practice and critically deconstruct structures of power that have been constructed by the world of normalcy to the detriment of disabled, black, women and LGBTQI+ bodies. Turning the gaze on to situations and structures of oppression therefore requires recognition of our own privileges and failures to recognize the experiences of others. It therefore demands profound humility because those of us with power are called on to own mistakes of the past and present. This is part of the process of anticolonial teaching, where 'acknowledging harm and admitting failures in the ongoing process of teaching and learning works to actively reverse the instructor and learner roles in the classroom, facilitating creative spaces for the nurturing of intelligence in both individuals and the community.'[49] Anticolonial teaching that is also 'access aware' makes visible the invisible, including the critical reflections of those who have been 'invisible' in the world of the powerful.

Beyond the 'trustworthy' gaze of the powerful

Trustworthiness as a personal trait is often granted to those who unquestionably obey the powerful at the expense of the oppressed, and it is often attributed to those who show deference to the ruling elites even in the face of injustice. Drawing once again on Ian Forrest's research on 'trustworthy men' in the medieval Church:

> Trust or faith was an inherently discriminating act, and in many cases discriminatory as well ... The institutional church was located in the combination of respect, fear,

deference, and envy with which the trustworthy men were viewed, for this was what made their testimony useful, and this is also what kept women, the poor, and those without good *fama* out of the late medieval public sphere. The effect that the ideology of ecclesiastical trustworthiness had upon the distribution of economic resources was considerable, but it was arguably even more significant in entrenching assumptions about masculinity and femininity, hardening attitudes against female participation in public life, and projecting the alliance between patriarchal institutions and male heads of household far into the future.[50]

The attribute of 'trustworthiness' has been used to systematically discriminate against those who the powerful, wealthy, ruling classes have determined are of less worth and who have been dehumanized in the process. Those who are 'untrustworthy' in the gaze of the powerful are predominantly women, the LGTBQI+, the working class, and people of colour. By designating these categories of people as untrustworthy they are often disempowered and stigmatized. Those who challenge the status quo are also instantly depicted as dangerous, troublemakers, 'harlots', 'whores' and 'heathens'. In the Bible, women's bodies in particular are polarized through notions of trust and distrust. Take Delilah, for example, who has been described as a 'Philistine prostitute' who could not be trusted. Judges 16 tells the story of how a woman named Delilah persuades Samson to reveal his weakness to her at the demand of the 'lords of the Philistines' (16.5), so that they can kill Samson. Josephus' introduction to her character states, 'nothing is more deceitful than a woman', in so doing 'setting the stage for the reader to distrust Delilah from the moment she enters the scene'.[51] She was known as a 'prostitute', a 'woman' and a 'foreigner'. Consequently, men throughout the ages, including Augustine, have, as Caroline Blyth notes, relentlessly portrayed her 'as a treacherous and licentious destroyer of godly men, whose uncanny narrative presence both electrifies and horrifies her audience'.[52] Judges 16 is an indecent narrative involving sex, power and control; embedded within the text are certain power dynamics and socio-political realities that in many exegeses go ignored, yet rendered women of this age powerless. However, it is the woman who has been blamed throughout history as the 'untrustworthy' one. Samson meanwhile, who was preoccupied with fulfilling his sexual desires, has been portrayed as the 'righteous' and 'loyal' man of God, seduced by the a non-Israelite 'harlot', as he was 'prone to sensual appetites and fleshy lusts'.[53] While Samson has been portrayed as 'strong', 'righteous' but 'weak', Delilah has been polarized against him as 'wicked', 'distrustful' and 'dangerous'. As Blyth comments, 'her attributes are identified as all that is considered unsafe and undesirable about women: their social and sexual autonomy, their negotiations of power and their encroachment upon traditionally masculine territories of authority, violence and sex.'[54] Gendered discourses of trust are apparent throughout the Bible, and the male lens has determined that the women's legacies within the text can be used to control women outside of the text, by presenting women as devious, untrustworthy, sinners. How then can the lens be distorted, so that we may instead see the world through the eyes of Delilah and all the other people who have been stigmatized as distrustful, and how might such a transformative way of seeing the world impact our pedagogies in theological education?

In Jarel Robinson-Brown's book *Black, Gay, British, Queer, Christian*, he discusses the precarious nature of what it means to 'live queerly', where LGBTQI+ people 'are at constant risk of theological violence as ecclesial terror …' as 'those who live somewhere between hope and faith in a world that requires daily courage and perseverance just in order for us to survive in our Queer Blackness'.[55] The theme of enforced bodily shame is apparent in the context of Delilah, where sexuality is deemed in need of controlling. In Robinson-Brown's experience, the gaze of the heterosexual norm has attempted to impose a moral order on to the queer bodies, forcing people to attempt to deny who they are, to the extent that queer bodies and all bodies that challenge the heterosexual, patriarchal norm experience feelings of blame, 'theological violence', and of being watched and condemned, as they are told repeatedly 'it's a sin'. This is how the gaze of judgement operates within neo-liberal capitalist societies shaped around patriarchal and heterosexual norms, where, as Eric Stoddart remarks, 'we encounter surveillance at numerous points in our everyday life but the intensity, fairness and consequences are not the same for all of us.' One's sexuality, ethnicity, religion, class and income level impact the way in which the gaze of these ideologies operate and discriminate.[56] Such a gaze is apparent within theological education, particularly in the process of formation for ministry – where students are watched, reported on, tested, judged and at times condemned as they occupy epistemological spaces of learning and formation, where they are often not given the freedom to be themselves in their fullness.

However, in the Gospels Jesus appears to challenge normative ways of seeing 'indecent' bodies. Take Luke 7.36–50 for example, the story of the so-called 'sinful woman' anointing the feet of Christ. What if that woman was like Delilah, a woman 'known for being sinful', on the margins of society, who walked into the house of the Pharisee unannounced and uninvited, to 'see' the son of God? Imagine a marginalized woman, condemned for her sexuality, entering the home of the religious elite, knowing how he would 'see' her but having the faith to know that Christ would not 'see' her through a lens that is shaped by exclusionary ideologies of decency. She walks into the house of the Pharisee, the religious elite – in accounts of this or similar events in the other Gospels, there were more of them than just Simon, whispering in the corner (Mark 14.3–9). She looks boldly past Simon, hiding the sense of shame he imposes on her with his cruel stare and judgemental gaze. She walks over to the Messiah; she does not appear to know what she is going to say, she just knows she needs to be near him and for him to see her as she is, before the God she loves. She stands behind Christ, she remains silent, but begins to cry (Luke 7.38). Imagine, having been 'seen' for so long through the eyes of the Pharisees, suddenly looking into the eyes of Jesus and being accepted. She is bold now, she declares her passion for Christ publicly, she strokes his feet, touches him, she feels safe because this is the man who understands her pain, isolation and grief. She is lost for words in her love for him. She uses her hair to wipe the feet of Christ and pulls out her perfume and pours it on to his feet (Luke 7.38). Meanwhile Simon says to himself: 'If this man were a prophet, he would have known who and what kind of woman this is who is touching him – that she is a sinner' (Luke 7.39). She looks down and weeps and her Lord says something in response to the judgemental man, but she has retreated into herself, until Christ looks directly into her eyes and says to Simon:

> Do you see this woman? I entered your house; you gave me no water for my feet, but she has bathed my feet with her tears and dried them with her hair. You gave me no kiss, but from the time I came in she has not stopped kissing my feet. You did not anoint my head with oil, but she has anointed my feet with ointment. Therefore, I tell you, her sins, which were many, have been forgiven; hence she has shown great love. But the one to whom little is forgiven, loves little. (Luke 7.44–47)

In that moment she is recognized for who she is, she is loved, her body that she has been told is unclean, unworthy, sinful, an abomination is looked upon with love, her indecency is rewarded. Jesus has turned the gaze of the oppressor on itself, and he has shamed him by narrating his love for her. He makes it known that the woman who Simon condemned as sinful and unworthy is a woman of faith who has shown 'great love'.

In this text we see Jesus challenging the normative, celebrating the love of a woman known to be 'sinful' and therefore a woman who is 'distrusted'. The religious elite, however, 'trusted in themselves that they were righteous and regarded others with contempt' (Luke 18.9). Yet Jesus is a radical who 'showed deference to no one' (Mark 12.13–17) and was not trusted by the powerful; in fact he was so distrusted by both the religious and political elites that he was crucified and his followers persecuted. As Frederick Herzog has remarked, Jesus was considered 'politically subversive' and suffered the consequences of his politics that spoke out for the poor and oppressed against the powerful (Luke 11.42).[57] Jesus challenges what the people know to be true, his actions oppose the so-called 'trustworthy men', and in so doing he presents a politics of truth and trust that enables a glimpse of the kin-dom to come. According to Foucault, societies sanction what is known to be 'true', noting that:

> Each society has its regime of truth, its 'general politics' of truth: that is, the types of discourse which it accepts and makes function as true; the mechanisms and instances which enable one to distinguish true and false statements, the means by which each is sanctioned: the techniques and procedures accorded value acquisition of truth; the status of those who are charged with saying what counts as true.[58]

The society that Jesus presents opposes the society constructed by the elites, because in the society of Christ truth and love comes from the bodies of the persecuted, as opposed to the laws and judgements of the ruling elites. This presents us with a way of knowing that transgresses normalized ways of knowing, because the truth is made apparent when the narratives of the indecent oppressed are listened to and 'seen'. James Cone argues that:

> our survival and liberation depend upon our recognition of the truth when it is spoken and lived by the people. If we cannot recognize the truth, then it cannot liberate us from untruth. To know the truth is to appropriate it, for it is not mainly reflection and theory. Truth is divine action entering our lives and creating the human action of liberation.[59]

Such truth requires putting trust in the narratives of the oppressed and this must translate into pedagogies of liberation in theological education if theological education is to be truthful and trusted.

Notes

1 Frantz Fanon, *Black Skin, White Masks* (New York, Grove Press, 1952), p. 116.
2 See Federica Bergamino, 'The Gaze of the Other: Emotion and Relation in the Brothers Karamazov', *Church, Communication and Culture* 2:3 (2017); 233–48, 235.
3 Stephen Pattison, *Shame: Theory, Therapy, Theology* (Cambridge: Cambridge University Press, 2000), p. 150.
4 Eric Stoddart, 'Reforming Bodies under Surveillance: An Urgent Task for Theological Education', in Auli Vähäkangas, Sivert Angel and Kirstine Helboe Johansen (eds), *Reforming Practical Theology: The Politics of Body and Space* (Oslo: International Academy of Practical Theology; Conference Series Volume 1, 2019), p. 176.
5 Michel Foucault, *Discipline and Punish: The Birth of the Prison* (Harmondsworth: Penguin, 1977), p. 136.
6 Miguel De La Torre, *Burying White Privilege: Resurrecting a Badass Christianity* (Grand Rapids, MI: Wm. B. Eerdmans, 2019), p. 102.
7 https://www.churchtimes.co.uk/articles/2021/25-june/news/uk/new-selection-framework-seeks-unseen-called (accessed 9.2.2022).
8 Trudy Govier, *Dilemmas of Trust* (Quebec: McGill-Queen's University Press, 1998), p. 9.
9 Christine J. Hong, *Decolonial Futures: Intercultural and Interreligious Intelligence for Theological Education* (Maryland, NY: Lexington Books, 2021), p. 9.
10 Ian Forrest, *Trustworthy Men: How Inequality and Faith Made the Medieval Church* (Princeton, NJ: Princeton University Press, 2018), p. 141.
11 Ibid., p. 133.
12 Ibid., p. 161.
13 Ibid., p. 162.
14 Ibid., p. 351.
15 ACCM Occasional Paper 38 (1990), quoted in Trevor Welland, 'Living in the "Empire of the Gaze": Time, Enclosure and Surveillance in a Theological College', *The Sociological Review* 49:1 (2001): 117–35, 123.
16 See Forrest, *Trustworthy Men*, pp. 126–7.
17 Ibid., p. 347.

18 https://www.churchtimes.co.uk/articles/2021/25-june/news/uk/new-selection-framework-seeks-unseen-called (accessed 9.2.2022).

19 See Dirk Michel-Schertges, 'Free Choice of Education? Capabilities, Possibility Spaces, and Incapabilities of Education, Labor, and the Way of Living One Values', in Roland Atzmüller et al. (eds), *Facing Trajectories from School to Work: Towards a Capability-Friendly Youth Policy in Europe* (Switzerland: Springer, 2015), p. 77.

20 A. D. A. France-Williams, *Ghost Ship: Institutional Racism and the Church of England* (London: SCM Press, 2020), pp. 122–3.

21 Owen Jones, *Chavs: The Demonization of the Working Class*, new edition (London: Verso, 2020), p. xix.

22 See Ash Sarkar, 'Everybody is doing identity politics, even if they think they are not', Novara Media, 10 May 2021, available at: https://novaramedia.com/2021/05/10/everybody-is-doing-identity-politics-even-if-they-think-theyre-not/ (accessed 9.2.2022).

23 See Lynne Cullens, 'A middle-class culture dominates the Church', *Church Times*, available at: https://www.churchtimes.co.uk/articles/2019/1-march/comment/opinion/a-middle-class-culture-dominates-the-church (accessed 9.2.2022).

24 See Diane Reay, *Miseducation: Inequality, Education and the Working Classes* (Bristol: Policy Press, 2017), p. 178.

25 See ACUPA, *Faith in the City* (London: Church House Publishing, 1985), p. 28.

26 Jones, *Chavs*, p. xii.

27 Karl Marx, *Critique of Hegel's Philosophy of Right* (Cambridge: Cambridge University Press, 1970), pp. 46–7.

28 Karl Marx and Friedrich Engels, *The Communist Manifesto* (New York: Simon & Schuster, 1964), p. 57.

29 Erhabor S. Idemudia and Babatola D. Olawa, 'Once Bitten, Twice Shy: Trust and Trustworthiness from an African Perspective', in Catherine T. Kwantes and Ben C. H. Kuo (eds), *Trust and Trustworthiness Across Cultures* (Geneva: Springer, 2021), p. 35.

30 Miss Ruth Berkeley, 'The Dangers and Difficulties of the Missionaries', in George A. Spottiswoode (ed), *Missionary Conference of the Anglican Communion 1894* (London: SPCK, 1894), p. 641.

31 Phyllis Trible, *Texts of Terror: Literary-Feminist Readings of Biblical Narratives* (Philadelphia, PA: Fortress Press, 1984), p. 26.

32 Renita Weems, 'Do you See What I see? Diversity in Interpretation', *Church and Society* 82 (1991): 28–43, 34.

33 Luke Hillier, 'Seeing and Being Seen at the Margins: Insight into God from the Wilderness', *Denison Journal of Religion* 14:6 (2015): 1–15, 4.

34 Renita J. Weems, *Just a Sister Away: Understanding the Timeless Connection Between Women's Relationships in the Bible* (San Diego, CA: LuraMedia, 1988), pp. 2–12.

35 Emily Peecook, 'Hagar: An African American Lens', *Denison Journal of Religion* 2:2 (2002): 1–13, 6.

36 Quoted in Bill Moyers, *Genesis: A Living Conversation* (New York: Broadway Books, 1996), p. 194.

37 Claus Westermann, *Genesis: A Practical Commentary* (Grand Rapids, MI: Wm. B. Eerdmans, 1987), pp. 241–2.

38 See Karen Campbell, 'They ask me where I come from', available at: https://urc.org.uk/images/mission/at_home_strange/They_Ask_Me_Where_I_Come_From_ by_Karen_Campbell.pdf (accessed 9.2.2022). Used with permission of the author.

39 Hillier, 'Seeing and Being Seen', 2.

40 Phyllis Trible and Letty M. Russell, *Hagar, Sarah, and their Children: Jewish, Christian, and Muslim Perspectives* (Louisville, KY: Westminster John Knox Press, 2006), p. 41.

41 Ibid.

42 See Karen Baker-Fletcher, *My Sister, My Brother: Womanist and Xodus God-Talk* (Eugene, OR: Orbis Books, 2002), p. 152.

43 Trible, *Texts of Terror*, pp. 28–9.

44 See Allan Aubrey Boesak, *Selfless Revolutionaries: Biko, Black Consciousness, Black Theology, and a Global Ethic of Solidarity and Resistance* (Eugene, OR: Cascade Books, 2021), p. xiv.

45 Jarel Robinson-Brown, *Black, Gay, British, Christian, Queer: The Church and the Famine of Grace* (London, SCM Press, 2021), ch. 2.

46 John M. Hull, *The Tactile Heart: Blindness and Faith* (London: SCM Press, 2013), p. 41.

47 Ibid., p. 49.

48 Paulo Freire, *Education for Critical Consciousness* (London: Bloomsbury, 2013), p. xvi.

49 Hong, *Decolonial Futures*, p. 31.

50 Forrest, *Trustworthy Men*, p. 351.

51 See Josey Bridges Snyder, 'Delilah and Her Interpreters', in Carol A. Newsom, Sharon H. Ringe and Jacqueline E. Lapsley (eds), *Women's Bible Commentary: Revised and Updated* (Louisville, KY: Westminster John Knox Press, 2012), p. 139.

52 See Caroline Blyth, *Reimagining Delilah's Afterlives as Femme Fatale: The Lost Seduction* (London: T&T Clark, 2017), p. 2.

53 See Burton D. Fisher, *Saint-Saens' Samson and Delilah* (London: Opera Journeys, 2001), p. 21.

54 See Blyth, *Reimagining Delilah's Afterlives*, p. 3.

55 Robinson-Brown, *Black, Gay, British, Christian, Queer*, p. 43.

56 See Eric Stoddart, *The Common Gaze: Surveillance and the Common Good* (London: SCM Press, 2021), p. xi.

57 William R. Herzog II, *Parables as Subversive Speech: Jesus as Pedagogue of the Oppressed* (Louisville, KY: Westminster John Knox Press, 1994), p. 27.

58 See Michel Foucault, 'Truth and Power', in Colin Gordon (ed.), trans. Colin Gordon, Leo Marshall, John Mepham and Kate Soper, *Power/Knowledge: Selected Interviews and Other Writings 1972–1977*, (New York: Pantheon Books, 1980), p. 131.

59 James Cone, *God of the Oppressed* (Maryknoll, NY: Orbis Books, 1997), pp. 56–7.

4

The Priest and the Temptress: Engendering Theological Education

Could it be that God who sent forth his Son born of a woman might once more use womankind to present his Son to a sadly broken world?[1]
John Neill, Church of Ireland, 1989

What would they say, these silenced and maligned vaginas that have borne the force of clerical and theological wrath for centuries?[2]
Lisa Isherwood

It remains the case that there exists a lacuna in many curricula and spaces of learning for women's contributions to theology. Male voices often dominate as a consequence of gendered spaces of learning that systematically protect patriarchal norms by creating exclusive cultures that do not enable women to flourish, or their perspectives to be heard, or even permit women to enter spaces in which they feel welcomed. Feminist and queer theologies are often met with indifference, or pigeon-holed as contextual theologies, where they become optional voices that can be silenced altogether. Theological colleges and institutes often operate within certain frameworks, where norms and practices that undermine the well-being and inclusion of women and LGBTQI+ people dominate and in the name of tradition enable patriarchal practices and pedagogies to create environments of un-belonging. The silencing of women's voices in theological education has been part of both a historical and a theological process of exclusion. Throughout the history of the Church, women have been domesticated to stay silent, they have been labelled as 'sinful' and 'deviant', and their bodies have been socially, theologically and economically marginalized. Engaging with women's bodies in theological education therefore calls for pedagogy that does not focus solely on academic achievement but enables students to become conscious of the world around them and empowers them in the process. According to Rowan Williams:

> To do theology is, in some ways, to be taken back to that moment of bewilderment about the newness or the distinctiveness or the strangeness of being in this new Christian framework. Theological education is familiarizing yourself with how people have found their way around that landscape with the perspectives they've occupied and then learning to pitch your own tent, as one might say, in that territory.[3]

However, the landscape of theological education has shifted in that women are now permitted to enter theological education institutes. The question then is whether space has been given to enable them to 'pitch their own tent' in the 'territory' of education and formation. Or are women entering territories that were not designed for them, where they are propping up the 'tents' of the same systems and theologies that have been used to silence them for centuries?

Since women have been 'permitted' to enter ordained ministry in the UK in mainstream denominations, there has been a significant rise in the number of women in theological education in the last 30 years, yet the patriarchal pedagogies and curricula have not been sufficiently interrogated. The experiences of women's bodies, which include the realities of being silenced, mocked, marginalized, abused, patronized and violated, have not, for the most part, been made relevant or given the space to be heard in dominant pedagogies and curricula. In other words, theological education has not been undressed in ways that enable the multiple patriarchal and misogynistic belief systems to be exposed, because misogyny that masks itself as tradition and hermeneutics has permitted and justified the silencing and shaming of the bodies of women, and taught women to 'know our place' and 'stay silent'. Therefore the question needs to be asked: Have theological education institutes enabled women to become speaking theological subjects, and to what extent have the lives of women and all other marginalized peoples been enabled to truly flourish?

This chapter will explore the theological and pedagogical implications of women being 'granted' more 'trust' in the Church and theological education, noting the shift from women being told to 'stay silent' and portrayed as 'temptresses' and 'harlots' to then being permitted into ordained ministry and theological education institutes. This transformation requires dismantling theologies and practices that have vilified the bodies of women, because such theologies are often not sufficiently addressed in theological education. As Elisabeth Schüssler Fiorenza remarks, 'consequently women … still have to adopt the language and discourse of those clerical and academic communities that have silenced us … marginalized us and relegated us to the status of social, religious, and intellectual nonpersons.'[4] This leads to the question: have theological education institutes enabled women to 'speak' theologically and be 'seen', and to what extent are the lives of women and all other marginalized peoples relevant in pedagogies and curriculums? In response, this chapter will look to transformative pedagogy, and engendering theological education in order to encourage pedagogies that enable the experiences of women to become 'a major resource for the hermeneutical process of doing theology and reading the Bible'.[5] Failure to do so means that women are in effect being moulded to fit into the theological cassocks of men. Focus will also be given to the role of shame in preventing women and all others who are castigated by the patriarchal norm from engaging critically and honestly in theological formation and learning, as the politics of shame and shaming is often gendered and involves the degradation of certain bodies in order to reinforce dominant norms.

Shameful women in formation

Recalling her time as a woman priest and theological educator in the Church of Ireland, Ginnie Kennerley writes:

> In my early days at the Theological College, I was very struck by the vehemence with which the Revd Noel Shortt, then serving in the Diocese of Derry, deplored the appearance of a woman cleric wearing a trouser suit! 'Trying to look like a man' seemed to be the problem, the idea that women trying to be priests were women denying their own femininity. I've no idea how representative his views were, but they influenced me greatly. For all my time at the college, I don't think I ever appeared in trousers, although I always wore a clerical collar as a matter of principle and favoured fairly sober colours and a sort of 'smart casual' look, which I was later told influenced some of our women ordinands when their time came.[6]

Kennerley narrates her experience of theological education as an educator, where even though she held a certain amount of power in comparison to a student, she was still shamed because of her gender, to the extent that she changed her clothing in order to be accepted by the critical lens of the male educators and clergy. Reflecting on my own experience as a theological educator, I recall that when I was teaching at my first summer school at All Saints Centre for Mission and Ministry in Manchester, a male theological educator and minister peered through the glass door as I was teaching a class. Following the class he walked over, laughing, and said, 'It is ok to smile when you are teaching.' I retorted, 'I was teaching on rape in Scripture so I am not really sure what you want me to smile about.' He walked away laughing. The same tutor made many remarks throughout my teaching time there – in the first staff meeting he asked, 'What are your credentials?' Later he informed me that I was 'hired to tick a gender box'. It did not matter what my experiences or qualifications were, or that there were others present during his 'questioning'; he wanted to make it clear that because I was a woman I ought to know my place, so at every opportunity he sought to patronize and shame me. Conversations around curricula often went down a similar path, with women scholars being referred to as 'overly sensitive' and 'theologically incapable'. He also had the audacity on a number of occasions to refer to himself as a feminist. Educators have the ability to reinforce the notion that women are inferior through what they teach, as well as how they teach and how they act towards both students and fellow educators. The impact of such cultures of patriarchy are of great significance to the well-being of students. As one student stated:

> 'I am a working-class woman who has given up so much to be here and follow my calling to serve Jesus, but I constantly feel like I don't fit in. I can't relate to the books I read, I feel uncomfortable speaking out when I don't agree, I don't want to say when I can't make it to something because I have to look after my family member – because this just makes me look weak, and every doubt that the BAP had in me will be shown to be true.'[7]

Women students are often forced to internalize their differences or individual needs as personal failures, and they often embed shame that has been imposed upon them. Women often describe feeling like 'imposters' within positions of authority, particularly within the Church and education systems, where rigid boundaries have been built to maintain patriarchal and heteronormative norms. When those boundaries are transgressed this can lead to feelings of isolation, guilt and shame on behalf of the 'transgressor'. Women have been theologically 'formed' to conform to patriarchy, as theological 'conformity' has been pedagogically embedded from childhood – where women have been educated to accept patriarchal norms. Those who do not conform to imposed norms can be considered a threat to the status quo. For this reason it is often women, LGBTQI+ people and people of colour within religious groups who remain silent in their feelings of non-belonging in order to be accepted. In their silencing the epistemologies of women and other marginalized groups are also silenced. Those in positions of power within faith communities often adapt to religiously and socially constructed norms, and this comes at the expense of those on the margins of their faith communities. This is particularly the case in the formation process, where ideal notions of priesthood are presented, and a 'sacramental shame dynamic grows out of and serves to protect theologies that ground recognition of personhood in a particular binary understanding of gender and sexuality.'[8] This is made apparent in the words of Ginnie Kennerley, for example. In describing a fellow clergywoman who she notes 'appealed to her', she writes:

> She showed herself to be everything one feels a clergywoman should be. Gentle and wise, strong but softly spoken, concerned for the women – and one man who had come to meet her, but equally concerned for their effectiveness in the church of the future ... A firm advocate in England's General Synod of women's contribution to the ordained ministry, she is markedly un-strident and no one's idea of a women's libber.[9]

The language is embedded in patriarchal norms, noting that a woman should be 'gentle', 'wise' and 'softly spoken' and not seek the liberation of women, but should instead accept the systemic patriarchy and their place within it. Kennerley appears to accept the polarization of women – where good women are the softly-spoken, 'decent', gentle ones, in contrast to the loud, confident, 'indecent' and liberated ones. As with many women who have felt/feel called to the priesthood, there is often a need to accept and embed certain patriarchal beliefs and practices in order to be accepted. In doing so, women who do not fit the mould of the so-called decent, godly, gentle and softly spoken clergywoman, are pushed further to the margins and their theologies are marginalized with them.

Shame is often used as a tool to keep women subordinate and prevent women and all others who do not fit the dominant gaze from 'acting out' and challenging the system. It is a mechanism by which boundaries of belonging can be maintained, particularly within faith communities. Sally Nash's research into shame in the context of Christianity has highlighted this – she notes that shame can be 'personal, relational, communal, structural, theological and historical'.[10] Shame is an embodied reality that is further impacted by one's socio-political and economic status and therefore can have a lasting effect upon the well-being and sense of worth of the individual, particularly if they feel shamed in the formation process to the priesthood – noting that 'Priesthood is not only about what a person does. Priesthood is about what a person is.'[11] One ordinand's narrative captures the extent to which power is abused within the structures and processes of the Church:

> 'Prior to going to BAP they asked me why I got divorced, I explained that we were married at 18, that he was violent with me and that I could no longer take the abuse and so I had to leave. They didn't take my word for it though, they had to interview members of my family and his to make sure I was telling the truth. I felt humiliated, I had to relive the abuse over again, it was 35 years ago that this happened and it was like another blow to my face. My confidence was shattered and so I decided not to carry on the process. I went back the following year because I still felt God's calling. Now in training I still feel ashamed of my past, even though I wasn't responsible for it.'[12]

The ordinand's reference to feeling 'ashamed' has implications for her 'feeling at home' or rather feeling a sense of belonging within her training for ordination, because shame directly impacts the body politics of the individual. Her experience also highlights the extent to which the power structures of the Church can instil shame, noting the questioning of her traumatic relationship, forcing her to relive her suffering in order to 'prove' herself worthy and suitable. The embodied sense of shame has theological consequences: 'Shame, dispensed unevenly and unjustly amid social hierarchies, often becomes an instrument of oppression, sometimes becoming instilled as a disposition in members of stigmatized social groups.'[13] Such 'shame' was dispensed through the discernment process to interrogate the ordinand's history of a violent relationship, domestic violence, abuse and divorce; whether it was done subconsciously or consciously, the power dynamics isolated and shamed the ordinand. Addressing the politics of shame involves addressing the emotions attached to the personhood of the individual, and ultimately their fears of being unworthy, defective and deserving of rejection, because 'shame indicates both a desire to hide or withdraw and a yearning for recognition and belonging.'[14] Sally Nash has written on the role of shame in theological formation, stating that 'Ministerial education was unlike anything I had experienced before because of the power of others to write not just about what you can do, but also, more significantly, about who you are as a potential priest.'[15] Power and shame are interrelated, as students often do not feel as though they can 'speak out', even when they experience prejudicial behaviour, because of the fear of being reported as a 'bad (potential) priest' or student. Students can therefore often feel powerless when resisting experiences of oppression.

A student who was openly gay, for example, expressed a fear of going on a placement as part of his formational journey and education at a church that explicitly preached against same-sex relationships; however, he was informed that such a placement was vital if he was to experience the diversity of the Church. The psychological implications of this decision, however, were not addressed, and this relates directly to what Moon and Tobin refer to as a form of toxic 'sacramental shame', which they argue is brought about by a religious community that 'unjustly stigmatizes and shames a group of people', creating a feeling of unworthiness and inequality for the stigmatized individual. The sacramental nature of the shame 'complicates this dynamic by both posing as love and locating the shame in the shamed person's own constant failures of will. It makes being recognized as a person – in the eyes of God and others –

contingent on constant displays of will to change things most LGBTI people cannot change, instilling shame as an enduring, conscious mental state.'[16] The ordinand expressed a feeling of 'fear' at the notion of going to a place of worship where he would feel 'despised' and 'dirty'. Such embodied emotions in the formation process are dangerous for the mental health of the ordinand if left ignored, as the individual is left feeling guilty for their very being and shamed from their cohort and community. The sacramental nature of shame can risk leaving people feeling isolated from God. If the theologies that underscore certain beliefs in regard to sexuality and women are not 'undressed', or rather, critically examined through a queer and feminist lens as part of theological formation, then they continue to control and destroy the bodies and epistemologies of those they have sought to condemn. Failure to do so denies flourishing on the part of the gay ordinand, and consequently shame can become 'instilled as an embodied disposition'.[17]

According to Rowan Williams, in theological education 'you're learning about the human as well as about God'[18] and learning about both requires contemplating the complexities of humanity and context. For Williams, 'It's very important that theology has a capacity for self-criticism, and for honesty.' He notes that there is a need 'to be honest about where you're coming from'. The difficultly, however, is when students feel too ashamed of who they are to be honest in their own situated identity. They are forced to learn about themselves and God while experiencing shame, distrust, un-belonging and disembodiment. In a patriarchal education, women are often forced to adapt to idealized notions of femininity, where they are quiet, respectful, obedient, decent good-wives. They must learn the way of the male theologians in order to know what counts as 'real theology', and learn about themselves and God through the dominant discourses of theology – without necessarily addressing the patriarchy and misogyny that is often apparent within the texts. Marcella Althaus-Reid describes how 'women become things to fit the androcentric illusion of the agency of women defined by community and patriarchal values, heavily invested in patterns of the most abstract and ideological classical theology of all times.'[19] There is a need to think critically and theologically about gender, sexuality, disability and ethnicity in theological education, because failure to do so results in continued and profound inequalities in the Church and theology. bell hooks makes this point in relation to teaching in a way that challenges the marginalization of black bodies: 'Without a counter-narrative ... children of color, black children internalize the belief that they are inferior. If they do not internalize the belief fully they may be consumed by doubt and fear. Wounded or fragile self-esteem leaves the psyche vulnerable – capable of being shamed.'[20] If theological education does not allow the space to transgress imposed norms, and think critically about dogmatic beliefs, then it simply accommodates patriarchal privileges and maintains fixed boundaries of belonging, while polarizing individuals – leaving feelings of un-belonging, isolation and sacramental shame to go unchallenged. Theological education holds the potential to challenge such binaries, if it can be transformed in order to enable those who have been excluded and marginalized to 'become speaking subjects and agents for systemic change'.[21] As we shall see, this requires an engendering process where the experiences of women and other marginalized communities enter into dialogue in theological education, in order to challenge imposed norms that prevent students from being themselves and contemplating God through their own embodied experiences.

From 'temptress' to priest 'for a time such as this'

> Men are afraid of any woman who makes poetry and dangerous portents. Unable to predict when, for what, and for whom she will open her mouth, unable to stitch up her lips, they silence her.
> Meena Kanadasamy[22]

The notion of a woman 'knowing one's place' is something that women have had to negotiate and navigate throughout history, particularly in the history of the Church – after the likes of Paul, as quoted in 1 Timothy 2.11–14, stated, 'Let a woman learn in silence with full submission. I permit no woman to teach or to have authority over a man; she is to keep silent.' It is only in the last ten years that all orders of the Church of England have been open to women, and this has not been an easy process, but rather a time of much hurt, contestation and debate. As Emma Percy remarks, following the vote to permit the ordination of women into the priesthood: 'Bishops told the women not to rejoice too much, not to appear triumphant and to be conscious of the pain they were causing to others ... many women, well socialized into this behaviour, duly conformed.'[23] Women ordinands in the Church of England often have to navigate their way through patriarchal structures while negotiating their belonging in the 'pathway' to priesthood in ordination training and beyond. When women are ordained this often does not equate to them being 'seen' as equal to their male counterparts. This is made apparent in the disproportionately high number of female clerics who remain unpaid in their ministry in non-stipendiary roles, while male clerics have the 'privilege' of being treated more humanely by receiving a stipend, or rather a pay cheque.[24] Therefore, while more women are being ordained than ever before in the Church of England, they are not always made to feel of equal worth. While there has been a clear desire and commitment within the Church of England to become more inclusive in regard to those who are put forward for ordination, the fact remains that both the discernment process and the theological educational 'pathway' to the priesthood remain for the most part embedded within patriarchal structures. Those who were previously not welcome are now entering territories that were not designed for them. Spaces where traditional, heteronormative, patriarchal theologies that have been used as a means of historically creating cultures of un-belonging for women, LGBTQI+ people and people of colour remain the norm for moulding priests in the formation process. As a result, theological education remains to a large degree responsible for the boundary maintenance of those in training, at the potential expense of ordinands' freedom to transgress so that they are free to contemplate themselves in their fullness before God. Consequently, women in the Church of England may be welcome in the priesthood, 'but the welcome can still feel provisional and it comes with an expectation of gracious tolerance towards those who strongly believe that they should not be there'.[25] Percy comments on how the Church of England 'has chosen pragmatic solutions rather than theological ones in the desire to keep a broad Church',[26] and this has come at the expense of personal notions of belonging for those in training for ordination and beyond.

Theological education has not for the most part taken seriously the transition from women being told for centuries to stay 'silent' in church, to being granted space in the pulpit, because what is also apparent is the sense of un-belonging that continues to be expressed by ordinands, clergy and theological students. As Jody Stowell, a clergywoman in the Church of England, stated:

> What is it like to live in this world? How do women survive and even perhaps thrive, as they seek to live out their calling? The truth is that some do manage to do this, and some will not. Imagine growing up in a church where you are told over and over again that there are some jobs that women simply do not do – not only that, but that God says it is sinful for women to do them, and sinful for men to 'let' them.[27]

Is theological education adequately preparing women with the skills to cope theologically with such experiences? This question is vital, because women are having to negotiate a patriarchal system that is dominated by men, where men hold the vast majority of power and where learning about God is dominated by male perspectives – where God has been made in their image. This reality is not only apparent within the experience of women clergy in the Church, because women lay theologians also narrate a constant sense of not being taken seriously, being alienated and rendered invisible – as noted by the Mud Flower Collective of women theologians, who state that:

> In our pain, diversity and struggle, we need and want to be taken seriously. The tales of our lives bear witness to this deep need. One of the few things we are confident in speaking of as a universal is the need common to us all to be the subjects of our own lives.[28]

Women's epistemology is challenging to patriarchal systems of power because of the ontological experiences of women that involve the struggle to be 'seen' and 'heard' within a system geared against them, and where their bodies encounter violence, subjugation and oppression through multiple systems and practices of patriarchy. Yet, as Althaus-Reid remarks, 'that epistemology has not informed pastoral reflections or ecclesiology or Christian ethics or church history … had it done so we might now be enjoying a theological revolution flourishing like the "Intergalactic Flowers" of the Zapatistas, who have made of sexual and gender transformations an issue of political revolution.'[29] Women in theology, the Church, and academic institutions often continue to be alienated, their personhood is denied, and they are often not able to speak their truth about the sexism they experience at the risk of being further marginalized. Consequently, women's epistemology is marginalized through ignorance disguised as knowledge that eliminates the truth claims of those whose knowledge has not been normalized by the dominant patriarchal, heteronormative gaze. This form of ignorance enables white, heterosexual, middle-class males to be ignorant of their own privilege, while sustaining the belief that they are superior, and rendering women, LGBTQI+ people and ethnic minorities inferior. Just as all 'knowledge practices are socially situated, motivated by, and grounded in our complex and concrete lives',[30] so too are theologies, inclusive of theologies that hold exclusive beliefs on 'male leadership and authority'.[31]

Nancy Nason-Clark conducted a study in 1987 focusing on the response of clergymen to the ordination of women in the Church of England. She found that 'there is a marked association between views on the priesthood of women and general attitudes toward female rights and responsibilities in society and within the family.'[32] In other words, those who hold patriarchal views regarding the role and place of women were far more likely to hold the belief that women should be not be ordained priests. She notes that patriarchal hermeneutics has played a significant role in situating the place of women in such thinking, noting that 'the symbols of women as "temptress" and "virgin" have in some measure contributed to the low status of women in Western church.'[33] Nason-Clark's research also found that 'many clergymen and clergy wives who rated their position on women's ordination as neither strong support nor strong opposition (4–7 on the scale), held the view that the time was not yet ripe for a vote in favour of women priests.'[34] The idea that the 'time was not yet ripe' for action is often professed by people within churches and institutions in order to prevent change and transformation, particularly when change involves the inclusion of those the powerful have marginalized. It also brings to mind a comment that Allan Boesak once said to me at an event for the World Communion of Reformed Churches on *Freedom of Religion and Belief*, in Frankfurt, Germany. He said, 'Every time I read the Bible I become even more radical, radical in my love of the poor and oppressed.' This statement is vital because the Bible is a radical book that enables the radicalization of our faith for the sake of the marginalized, which is needed when it comes to speaking truth to systems of power and oppression.

One of the texts that speaks directly to women's leadership and responds to the claim that 'now is not the time' for women's bodies to be in positions of power is the book of Esther. This is a story about 'a Jewish woman in diaspora who must hide her ethnicity and assimilate into Persian culture'.[35] The Jews who were in exile in Persia were vulnerable and persecuted to the extent that Esther had been forced to hide her ethnicity and identity. Esther, who is known to be beautiful, is to be married to King Xerxes as a replacement for Queen Vashti. Her Uncle Mordecai, who is in hiding with Esther, refuses to bow to the Persian King's adviser, Haman. Upon finding out about an edict to murder the Jewish people, Mordecai then publicly laments, and having just heard that the lives of her people were in danger, Esther must now decide what actions she must take ...

> Mordecai told them to reply to Esther, 'Do not think that in the king's palace you will escape any more than all the other Jews. For if you keep silence at such a time as this, relief and deliverance will rise for the Jews from another quarter, but you and your father's family will perish. Who knows? Perhaps you have come to royal dignity for just such a time as this.' Then Esther said in reply to Mordecai, 'Go, gather all the Jews to be found in Susa, and hold a fast on my behalf, and neither eat nor drink for three days, night or day. I and my maids will also fast as you do. After that I will go to the king, though it is against the law; and if I perish, I perish.' Mordecai then went away and did everything as Esther had ordered him. (Esther 4.13–17)

Mordecai's words, 'for such a time as this', are prophetically powerful as they call to account all who don't act in the face of injustice; they speak to the silence of the Church in the face of violence against women and to theologians who write as though context is irrelevant at such a time as this. Esther hears her uncle's words and shows immensely brave leadership; she commands her uncle to gather the persecuted, whose side she takes, and in the awareness that she must risk her own life to save them she says, 'if I perish, I perish'. Esther who, as Hatzaw remarks, 'is expected to be passive, submissive, obedient, and sexualized' as a result of her marginalized status as a Jewish woman in hiding, instead 'weaponizes her sexuality as she recognizes it as the only domain of power available'.³⁶ She goes before the King to save her people and 'As soon as the king saw Queen Esther standing in the court, she won his favour and he held out to her the golden sceptre that was in his hand' (5.2). Esther is able to subvert the systems of power through her womanhood, bravery and wisdom, and subsequently Haman's plot to kill the Jewish people is overthrown and the Jews are saved. Esther has the option of enjoying the comfort of the palace and ignoring the plight of the oppressed, but she chooses to risk her life for the well-being of others. As a woman she is sexualized and objectified but 'transforms her objectification from an oppressive tool into a weapon she can wield over the king'.³⁷ It is through a woman's leadership that shows resistance, bravery and subversion that the people are saved. Her story raises the question that is relevant to us all: What if I was called 'for a time such as this'? And it narrates the bravery of leadership that can be trusted, because *if I perish, I perish* for the sake of the oppressed.

When women become 'speaking subjects' – transforming patriarchal pedagogy

It is not without risk that women become 'speaking subjects' in the Church, society and theological education, as Musimbi Kanyoro remarks: 'when trained women theologians begin to make connections between what happens at home and in church with a view of suggesting change in the name of justice, they have to be cautious of disturbing the set order.'³⁸ Changing the established orders of education and pedagogy is often met with resistance, including the denial that things need to change. Resistance also takes the form of the belief that diversity and equality have been achieved because there may be one white woman tutor, or the suggestion that, due to the financial needs of the institution and concerns over fewer students opting to study theology, the time is not right to focus on transformative pedagogy and/or issues of equality. Resistance also appears in the form of uninterest and indifference to the situation of women in education who feel marginalized and silenced, as one anonymous woman theologian commented:

> This isn't the experience of men in the school, who seem to look about in confused wonder when the toxic experience of women is raised. The niche in this country for biblical studies is gendered and well-guarded. Certain men experience long tenures in theology at the institution. Their tenures end with handshakes, ceremony and adulation.[39]

There is often a desire to distrust the experiences of those who are marginalized and for the truth of such experiences to be rendered irrelevant in shaping curricula and pedagogies, as Miguel De La Torre comments: 'When repressive structures must be sustained, truth is always the first casualty. Truth must be crucified, ignorance and prejudices must be mobilized, and Christianity must be nullified.'[40] The question then is: How can we create pedagogies and curricula that enable the truth of those who are marginalized to be 'heard'? Feminist pedagogy enables an interrogation of patriarchal praxis and the empowerment of all people in order to enable social change and transformation. By addressing the marginalization of women, LGTBQI+, black and ethnic minority and working-class bodies in theological education, a critical feminist pedagogy offers an opportunity for educational, theological and social change. Critical feminist pedagogy encourages exposing existing structures that prevent people from belonging in institutes of learning by engaging with human struggles, including social, political and theological struggles. As bell hooks describes, 'We must envision the university as a central site for revolutionary struggle, a site where we can work to educate for critical consciousness, where we can have a pedagogy of liberation.'[41] This means a learning process that goes beyond that of academic learning and gives focus to social transformation and justice. The purpose of such pedagogy is to create a space that allows power structures to be examined while affirming those engaged; in other words, enabling theological students to examine structures and systems of power within the Church and society without the fear of repercussions for doing so. Such pedagogy enables dominant hegemonies, assumptions, ideas and beliefs to be challenged because narratives of struggle are given the space to be heard. However, such a pedagogy is not easy, as Debbie Ollis remarks: 'Developing an explorative, fluid, nuanced approach that explores multiple subject positions and "truths" remains a challenge.'[42] This is particularly the case in theological education, where reflections and beliefs about God are intertwined with embodied 'truths'. Such a challenge requires honesty and trust, and for the educators to be trustworthy they must acknowledge their own situated identity, 'so that they in turn can gift their own students with such power'. Kelly Morris Roberts makes this point: 'Teachers should be made aware – through readings, through intentional and targeted discussion, and through meaningful activities – that knowledge is not knowledge but has been selected, constructed, distributed, and legitimated.'[43] Once the educator becomes conscious of the unjust distribution of knowledge – that has led to the subjugation of women's knowledge – the educator is then responsible for challenging the hierarchal structures that enabled the delegitimization of subjugated knowledge of all who exist outside the dominant hegemony. Such exposure of power dynamics is critical for the educator themselves to be free, because:

> Failure to understand the social construction of knowledge not only divides teachers against themselves, devaluing part of their personhood; it also perpetuates hegemony of thought when this segment of knowledge is unquestionably passed to the next generation, denying them of authentic voice as well.[44]

In the quest to transform patriarchal pedagogy that has silenced the bodies of women, there is then a need to make safe spaces for personal and lived experiences while cultivating learning environments that allow for the diversity and fluidity of lived experience and faith understandings to be 'heard'.

A feminist pedagogy offers a means by which the personal experiences of students and educators can become the grounds for critical theological engagement:

> Feminists reject the idea that activities of the public arena should be the ones that are considered most valuable; they wish instead that everyone could value the power and potential of the lived experiences that people have claimed only in the private arena.[45]

For example, the narratives of women ordinands and clergy who openly declared their experiences of being marginalized and oppressed within formational training and the Church should not be lived experiences that are silenced in the classroom, but rather become testimonies of lived religiosity that encourage critical dialoguing in the areas of mission, hermeneutics, doctrine and pastoral care. In order for theological formation to be trustworthy, value must be given to the lived experiences of students and educators. Reflection on lived experiences in theological education is a 'transformative tool' used in feminist pedagogy, where educators must also reflect on their own experience, through the use of journals and other methods, so that they 'might realize their own biases and worldviews through a reflective and critical examination ... as well as their practices and interactions in the classroom'.[46] Keeping a teaching journal, where educators can take note of the resources, curriculum choices, assignment questions, dialogues and interactions, can enable educators to examine their own choices and methodologies and become conscious of potential biases. In doing so, educators may become aware of class, race and gender biases in their reading lists, as well as engaging more critically with methods used in the classroom.

This requires intentional action on behalf of the theological educator, noting that once the educator becomes conscious of class, race and gender disparities in curricula they must make a choice of whether to be indifferent to such disparities or become agents of change and be more inclusive and diverse in reading lists and methodologies of teaching. In doing so, the theological educator must come out of their comfort zone in order to consider intersectional issues of marginalization that have been theologically justified by totalitarian theologies that have dichotomized women in particular. Patriarchal pedagogies have enabled such theology to dominate by failing to allow for discussion or alternative theologies that offer different perspectives. Reflecting on the pedagogy of Jesus Christ, William Herzog outlines how Christ existed in a context of 'imperial situation', where there were systems of power that led to the degradation of the poor and marginalized. As a teacher, Herzog notes, Jesus' parables dealt with issues of interest to his 'students'. The parables function to 're-present a familiar or typified scene for the purpose of generating conversation about it and stimulating the kinds of reflection that expose contradictions in popularly held beliefs or traditional thinking'.[47] Take for example the parable of the widow in Luke 18.1–8, a narrative where a marginalized and nameless woman becomes the centre of Jesus' teaching. The widow, who would have been 'the prototype of the unprotected and unprivileged in Israel',[48] shapes Jesus' pedagogy as he enables her lived experience to shape his teaching, and in so doing the parable disturbs the status quo because her story is used to address power dynamics and stereotypes while reflecting on God.

The pedagogy of Jesus engages with the lived conditions of the 'students' in the same way in which feminist pedagogy encourages the relevance of lived experiences to be brought into dialogue in the classroom. Both the widow and the judge in the parable would have held particular socio-economic and political statuses that were relevant to Jesus' 'lesson'. Jesus directly addresses the power dynamics, noting that 'The judge is among the male urban elite, but still he is acting outside the bounds of society since he neither fears God nor has respect for women or men.'[49] Jesus' parable also appears to critique the systems of the temple that are dominated by greed and exploitation as opposed to justice. The widow is also made known within the text for having a voice of protest; as the judge says, 'because this widow keeps bothering me, I will grant her justice, so that she may not wear me out by continually coming' (18.5). Many traditional readings of this parable have sought to portray the widow as 'weak', but she is in no way a passive character in the parable. Although the system is geared against her, her narrative shapes the text and she resists the system from within. This has consequences for women outside of the parable who are empowered through reading or 'hearing' the text: because of her speaking out the woman gets justice and challenges the structures of power; she appears fearless before the powerful judge; and is deemed as worthy by God for doing so. Jesus' pedagogy is transformative because it enables dominant discourses of power to be dismantled while offering discourses of liberation for the marginalized. The parable also radically dismantles trust: the judge to whom society has granted trust, who has been deemed the trustworthy man and granted power to act justly, is portrayed as an unjust hypocrite; and the powerless widow highlights the failures of the judge through her protests and is consequently depicted as the trustworthy one before God. Through the pedagogy of Jesus, the gaze of the oppressor is turned on to the oppressor themselves, by centring the gaze of the oppressed, in this case the widow; and God appears to see through the eyes of the oppressed: 'And will not God grant justice to his chosen ones who cry to him day and night?' (18.7).

The theological educator can learn from the liberative pedagogy of Jesus, and be more intentional in seeking to empower students so that they also may become agents of social change. The subjugation of women's bodies within both Church and society requires such transformative pedagogy that enables praxis. Omiunota Ukpokodu outlines what is meant by transformative pedagogy:

> Transformative pedagogy is defined as an activist pedagogy combining the elements of constructivist and critical

pedagogy that empowers students to examine critically their beliefs, values, and knowledge with the goal of developing a reflective knowledge base, an appreciation for multiple perspectives, and a sense of critical consciousness and agency.[50]

Such pedagogy also requires those in positions of power who have become conscious of the lived experiences of women and other marginalized groups to be willing to be distrusted by those who seek to maintain the status quo, because transformation for oppressed and silenced bodies requires solidarity from those who have not been silenced. This is the case for white, heterosexual, middle-class males who become conscious of the oppression of women, LGBTQI+ and people of colour and seek to address such oppression within their teaching, curricula and pedagogies. They too will risk losing the trust of the establishments and institutions of power because they become a potential threat to the established order. The pedagogy of Jesus outlines how Jesus was willing to be distrusted by the ruling elites and establishments in order to highlight the plight of the widow and the injustice of the system and present a radical theology of liberation. The question for the theological educators who have not yet met the gaze of oppression is: Are you willing to be distrusted by the powerful, in order to be trusted in the eyes of the oppressed?

Engendering theological education

Engendering theological education involves integrating gendered content into the courses and giving focus to intersectional disparities in spaces of learning and formation. In doing so, women's voices, experiences and perspectives enable students and staff to challenge imposed norms and stereotypes that have been used to marginalize women's bodies and queer bodies. Focus is given to the curriculum as a means of encouraging transformative pedagogy in which students and staff can engage with embodied theologies and experiences in order to allow for critical dialogue that can empower students and enable social change and transformation. This enables a critique of the selective process of dominant curricula, where traditional, gendered, middle-class, ruling elite, white, Eurocentric influences have been 'selected' as that which should be known, at the expense of other knowledge. Gaby Weiner makes the point that a curriculum is 'socially constructed and as such is both a reflection of the dominant ideas and a place where these ideas are played out or restricted through practice ... as well as implicated in the definition and construction of gendered relations'.[51] Curricula that do not include the perspectives of women and other minority groups therefore reflect only the dominant ideas that are rooted in ideologies that silence marginalized epistemologies. Engendering theological education is therefore about developing environments of learning and formation that encourage social change and transformation for the betterment of all. It requires taking women's voices, writings and experiences seriously in education, noting that 'knowledge produced by women (Western or non-Western) are also regarded as inferior and outcast from the canon of thought. The foundational structures of knowledge of the Westernized university are simultaneously epistemically racist and sexist.'[52] A process of 'unlearning' is therefore required, in which women's anger, frustration and hurt are validated and the theologies of the dehumanized become central in theological discourses of formation. To quote the liberation theologian Gustavo Gutiérrez, 'The history of Christianity has ... been written by white, Western, bourgeois hands',[53] and the same can be said for the vast majority of our theological curricula and the dominant theologies that shape the academic formation process into the priesthood, because 'What is said in Manila is relevant for the Philippines. But what is said in ... Oxford or Yale is relevant for the entire church.'[54] This is about an unjust distribution of power in theological education.

It is for this reason that theological colleges around the world are doing theological education differently, as the Hispanic theologian Ada María Isasi-Díaz describes: 'To do theology is to free theology from the exclusive hold of academia; it is also a matter of denouncing the false dichotomy between thought and action so prevalent in Western culture.'[55] Such theologizing requires an understanding of context and the imbalances of power, where classist, racist, sexist, structures control resources and cultures of learning. Engendering theological education involves a recognition of such imbalances of power and seeks to find ways to transform them. Curriculum is therefore an important aspect of engendering because adding women theologians and other marginalized voices to reading lists enables students to be resourced with critical perspectives that challenge scholars who have dominated. In agreement with Musa Dube, failing to enable such voices leads to a sense of un-belonging. As she notes:

> Post-colonial and feminists subjects are confronted with the struggle against reading canons they did not write or select; against literary images that derogate their humanity and legitimize their oppression; and against institutions such as the school, the church and the government that they do not control, which exclude their texts and impose the texts that baptise their oppression.[56]

There is a need therefore for a pedagogy that is more inclusive, that recognizes that learning and knowledge take place 'in the context of people's lives and that people experience life differently',[57] while also acknowledging that theological education for the most part remains dominated by white male scholarship that, as Justo Gonzalez describes, 'is taken to be normative, universal theology, to which then women, other minorities ... may add their footnotes'.[58] If theological education is to deconstruct imposed norms and move beyond boundaries that seek to prevent us from realizing ourselves more fully in our contemplations of God, it must therefore be open to new possibilities. As bell hooks comments:

The classroom with all its limitations remains a location of possibility. In that field of possibility we have the opportunity to labour for freedom, to demand of ourselves and our comrades an openness of mind and heart that allows us to face reality even as we collectively imagine ways to move beyond boundaries, to transgress. This is education as the practice of freedom.[59]

For women and all students from minority backgrounds who have been held captive by male, Western, heteronormative epistemological scholarship, there is an opportunity for new and exciting ways of doing and living theology, as more diverse groups of people enter theological education institutes. Theological institutions both historically and today have, as Lester Edwin Ruiz notes, in many ways 're-presented society'. As such, it is 'more necessary than ever' to rethink the role of these institutions:

> because they are already implicated in society as sites for practices that shape human experience – for thinking, feeling, and indeed, acting – and, as sites of contestation, of contending perspectives, commitments, values, about the good, the true, and the beautiful which are necessary in the articulation of theological curricula adequate to the needs of the twenty-first century.[60]

If it is the task of theological education 'to motivate, equip and enable the people of God to develop their gifts'[61] then we need to be asking the question of how this is to be done.

In response to such lived realities of women clergy, Ellen Blue developed an engendered curriculum that included modules specifically for clergywomen in training, although open to all, in order 'to help women form their identity as women ministers'. She brought in ordained guest speakers who had worked in numerous church contexts, and 'Each began by recounting some of her journey in ministry.' The practice of storytelling is important in a feminist pedagogy because personal narratives 'give context, provide examples and public stories, and their use in education'.⁶² Blue taught her class the importance of a hermeneutics of suspicion, she offered space for student-led content, she used pastoral resources developed by other women, and highlighted that women's ministry is different as a result of their gender and centuries of patriarchal subjugation. Such experiences of patriarchy within ministry are outlined by Katherine Paisley when sharing her experiences in her first parish, stating: 'My very existence was confrontational to their understandings of life and the Church. I didn't actually have to do anything confrontational, just showing up on Sunday morning to preach did it.'⁶³ Theological education should prepare women for such experiences by wrestling with the realities of marginalization in the context of theological discourse so that feelings of un-belonging do not become all-consuming. Engaging with feminist scholarship will also resource both men and women with a deeper understanding of the need for resistance and solidarity in situations of patriarchal oppression.

The process of engendering education also offers the opportunity to explore the theological arguments and diversity of opinions over such things as the role of women in ministry that continue to impact the embodied religious and priestly belonging for women ministers – and therefore require greater dialoguing in theological formation. Such dialoguing involves ensuring that 'all voices are heard – particularly the whispering and silent voices'.⁶⁴ This necessitates transformative pedagogy that is inclusive of a diversity of opinions and allows the space for the stories, beliefs, experiences and theologies of all students to be 'heard'. There is freedom in difference when dialogue is shaped to enable for critical interrogation in order to allow biases to be challenged and changed by becoming conscious of the beliefs and experiences of others. bell hooks notes, 'The moment power differences are openly talked about where erotic desire surfaces, a space is created where choice is possible, where accountability can be clearly assessed.'⁶⁵ Each student and educator carries with them a personal narrative that cannot be separated from their contemplations on God; recognition of such narratives in pedagogies enables life to be brought into the classroom and such narratives can begin to shape the learning experience. Just as life is messy, the learning process may become messy when space is made for greater dialogue on the experiences of women and other marginalized groups, but it will enable a theologizing that walks with people through the journey of life, reflecting and acting in the process.

Trusting in engendered theological education

For too long Eurocentric patriarchal theologizing has treated theological education as though it were an 'objective science' controlled by the 'wisdom' of the male elites, when our theologizing, our contemplations on God, are born out of particular perspectives and contexts, and often shaped by the day-to-day needs and struggles of those engaged.[66] Theological education, particularly in formation for ministry, involves the individual contemplating 'their deep sense of an existential interconnection between themselves and the divine'.[67] Yet, as Anna Mercedes notes, 'There are too many examples of lives shattered by the teaching of the churches in combination with unjust situations. Christian rhetoric can be dangerous, and has been particularly for subjugated persons.'[68] An engaged pedagogy that takes seriously the lives, voices and experiences of women and other marginalized groups of people will enable a more critical engagement with such structures of injustice, because 'praxis-orientated education includes narrativity, human experience, critical thinking, interdisciplinary and non-hierarchal learning.'[69] Such dialoguing requires trust in *others* in order to create environments that can challenge power dynamics and enable transformative learning. Rowan Williams remarks:

> [W]hat I've seen of it working well is very often the kind of group where people feel they have permission to ask the real questions, where there's a degree of real trust and mutuality, where people don't feel obliged to come up with shortcuts but are able to take time.[70]

Asking real questions in environments of trust and mutuality is critical if theological education is to encourage students to understand their own situated reality while celebrating difference of opinion in a context of solidarity as opposed to hierarchy. Reflecting on excluded bodies and experiences also challenges the theologies that attempt to turn Christ into an un-dialogical figure by removing the messiness and marginality of the life and teachings of the Jesus of the Gospels. An engendered pedagogy enables passionate dialoguing, as Boaventura De Sousa Santos beautifully states: 'To think without passion is to make coffins for ideas; to act without passion is to fill the coffins.'[71]

Thinking with passion requires recognizing opinions we may not agree with and acknowledging that 'all members of the teaching/learning community bring experience, wisdom and pertinent questions to the table.'[72] It requires listening to the truths of others and allowing embodied truths to be brought into readings of Scripture and modules on pastoral care, doctrine and mission, as part of what Parker Palmer refers to as 'the community of truth'. Palmer describes how, in such a learning community,

> as in real life, there are no pristine objects of knowledge and no ultimate authorities. In the community of truth as in real life, truth does not reside primarily in propositions, and education is more than delivering propositions about objects to passive auditors.

Such a community of learning enables space for dialoguing on complex subject matters that offer divergent insights and experience and 'admits diversity, ambiguity, creative conflict, honesty and humility'.[73] In such 'communities of truth' all are able to learn together and become conscious of the truths of others. This may of course lead to conflict or consensus: 'far from being linear and static and hierarchal, [it] is circular, interactive, and dynamic.'[74] Knowledge, ideas, opinions, relationships and individuals are able to flourish in such a community because it enables honesty, humility, ambiguity and diversity. However, it is also vital to address the power dynamics in such communities of truth – noting that those whose voices have been marginalized and oppressed may not feel safe to be open about their beliefs and experiences. Teaching in a way that encourages people to speak their truth also requires the teacher to be vulnerable, as hooks notes: 'Professors who expect students to share confessional narratives but who are themselves unwilling to share are exercising power in a matter that could be coercive.'[75] It is therefore vital to address the power dynamics of learning environments and pedagogies, noting that pedagogies are lived, relational and embodied and therefore subject to hegemonic discourses of power that require honesty on behalf of the educator and students about their own situatedness. Communities of truth in theological education must therefore challenge dominant understandings of trust and ask whose truth is being silenced. What is my role in silencing such truth? How can I trust in those whose truth negatively impacts my own? And how can I act in solidarity with those whose truth is one of suffering?

Returning to the parable of the widow in Luke 18.1–8, Jesus offers a model of engendering the curriculum that engages with issues of trust and truth, noting that the parable puts trust in the experiences of the widow – her testimony of marginalization is at the centre of the theology that shapes the pedagogy for Jesus' teaching. Jesus uses storytelling as a means of communicating his message and in so doing enables critical conversations about power dynamics and socio-economic hierarchies and the relevance of such politics in contemplating God. He also makes himself vulnerable in that he is not afraid to be critical of the status quo and makes it known that God is the ultimate judge. In centralizing the experiences of the marginalized widow he engenders the parable, in the same way that adding the voices of women to the curriculum and engaging with the lived experiences of women and other marginalized people enables such voices to be taken seriously in theological education. Engendering theological education demands consciousness in the lived experiences of women; it requires of male educators and students the need to denounce systems of patriarchy that have marginalized and violated women and join them in acts of solidarity in their narratives. It is through consciousness and solidarity that transformation can happen. When the widow in Jesus' parable becomes conscious of the injustice of the judge in his failure to act, she protests and resists the system by calling for justice until she is 'heard'. When we become conscious of women's struggles against patriarchy, action is required in the light of such struggle. When people become conscious of the dehumanizing realities of patriarchy and misogyny, the contradictions of such systems become visible in the light of the promised Kingdom of God – which Jesus highlights. The incompetent judge is representative of the systems on earth that react unjustly to the plight of the marginalized.

The consciousness of women students and all other marginalized peoples must be liberated from dogmas that have throughout history degraded them. As Lavinia Byrne notes:

> I believe that the problem for women is that the Christian tradition has been less open to human differences than the Gospels are. The tradition has thought it necessary to set up half of the human family at the expense of the other ... one consequence is that, as women, we have been forced to define our identity in ways that lead us to deny that identity.[76]

Christian theology and tradition have the potential to exacerbate violence against women, and the psychological dimension of exclusion and feelings of non-belonging cannot be overlooked. It is for this reason that we must be free to explore the liberative narratives of our Scriptures, to witness where women have navigated their identities in Christ in cultures that have not necessarily been on the side of women. Because the issue here is that Christian theologizing has a history that spans over two thousand years, and missing from its chapters are the voices of women. So the question must be asked: Are we seeking greater participation in a patriarchal structure, and if so, how do women find space within a system? That is, in a theological education system that was not created for us? Or are we seeking liberation from within – so that we may theologize from our particular social locations, from our own bodies – bodies that Christian theologies have for centuries determined unworthy and 'refused to attribute the fullness of the *imago dei* ... noting that not only could women not represent God to the Christian community, they could not represent the generically human – before God or before the community'?[77] In doing so we may come to 'know our place' as one of struggle – but a struggle that will help shape a theological education that enables true flourishing.

Notes

1 Quoted in Ginnie Kennerley, *Embracing Women: Making History in the Church of Ireland* (Dublin: The Columba Press, 2008), p. 91.

2 Lisa Isherwood, 'Indecent Theology: What F–ing Difference Does it Make?' *Feminist Theology* 11:2 (2003): 141–47, 147.

3 Rowan Williams quoted in 'Rowan Williams: Theological Education is For Everyone' by Benjamin Wayman, 19 August 2020, available at: https://www.christianitytoday.com/ct/2020/august-web-only/rowan-williams-theological-education-for-everyone.html (accessed 9.2.2022).

4 Elisabeth Schüssler Fiorenza, *But She Said: Feminist Practices of Biblical Interpretation* (Boston: Beacon Press, 1992), p. 171.

5 Elsa Tamez, 'Women's Lives as Sacred Text', in Kwok Pui-Lan and Elisabeth Schüssler-Fiorenza (eds), *Women's Sacred Scriptures* (London: SCM Press, 1998), p. 57.

6 Kennerley, *Embracing Women*, p. 98.

7 Interviews were conducted with women ordinands training at theological education institutes across the UK; all ordinands remain anonymous. Women Ordinand Interview 3, interview by author, Manchester, January 2020.

8 Dawne Moon and Theresa W. Tobin, 'Sunsets and Solidarity: Overcoming Sacramental Shame in Conservative Christian Churches to Forge a Queer Vision of Love and Justice', *Hypatia* 33:3 (Summer 2018): 451–68, 453.

9 Kennerley, *Embracing Women*, p. 52.

10 Sally Nash, 'On Researching Shame in the Church', *Practical Theology* 10:4 (2017): 396–406, 399.
11 The Diocese of Salisbury, 'Your role ... Ordained Ministry', https://www.salisbury.anglican.org/ministry/vocations/your-role...-or dained-ministry (accessed 9.1.2022).
12 Women Ordinand Interview 6, interview by author, February 2020.
13 Moon and Tobin, 'Sunsets and Solidarity', 452.
14 Ibid., 455.
15 Nash, 'On Researching Shame', 401.
16 Moon and Tobin, 'Sunsets and Solidarity', 452.
17 Ibid., 457.
18 Williams quoted in Wayman, 'Rowan Williams: Theological Education is For Everyone'.
19 Marcella Althaus-Reid, *From Feminist Theology to Indecent Theology* (London: SCM Press, 2004), p. 71.
20 bell hooks, *Teaching Community: A Pedagogy of Hope* (New York: Routledge, 2003), pp. 95–6.
21 See Adesanya Ibiyinka Olusola, 'Exploring the Relevance of Feminist Leadership in Theological Education of Nigeria', *Khazar Journal of Humanities and Social Sciences* 16:4: 26–40, 30.
22 Meena Kandasamy. *Ms Militancy* (New Delhi: Navayana Pub, 2010), p. 12.
23 Emma Percy, 'Women, Ordination and the Church of England: An Ambiguous Welcome', *Feminist Theology* 26:1 (2017): 90–100, 92.
24 See Hattie Williams, 'Disproportionate number of women in unpaid ministry raises equality questions, says WATCH', *Church Times*, available at: https://www.churchtimes.co.uk/articles/2021/12-march/news/uk/disproportionate-number-of-women-in-unpaid-ministry-raises-equality-questions-says-watch?utm_term=Autofeed&utm_medium=Social&utm_source=Twitter#Echobox=1615594033 (accessed 9.1.2022).
25 Percy, 'Women, Ordination and the Church of England', 100.
26 Ibid., 98.
27 Jody Stowell, 'To women vicars like me, it's no surprise there are still people who believe we shouldn't exist', available at: https://www.independent.co.uk/voices/women-vicars-church-sexism-religion-a8782501.html (accessed 9.2.2022).
28 Katie G. Cannon et al., *God's Fierce Whimsy: Christian Feminism and Theological Education* (New York: The Pilgrim Press, 1985), p. 99.
29 Althaus-Reid, *From Feminist Theology to Indecent Theology*, p. 71.
30 See Cynthia Townley, *A Defense of Ignorance: Its Value for*

Knowers and Roles in Feminist and Social Epistemologies (New York: Lexington Books, 2011), p. xi.

31 Nancy Nason-Clark, 'Ordaining Women as Priests: Religious vs. Sexist Explanations for Clerical Attitudes', *Sociological Analysis* 48:3 (1987): 259–73, 267.

32 Ibid., 268.

33 Ibid.

34 Ibid., 263.

35 Cii Sian Siam Hatzaw, 'Reading Esther as a Postcolonial Feminist Icon for Asian Women in Diaspora', *Open Theology* 7:1 (2021): 1–34, 2.

36 Ibid., 3–4.

37 Ibid., 3.

38 Musimbi Kanyoro, 'Engendered Communal Theology: African Women's Contribution to Theology in the Twenty-First Century', *Feminist Theology* 9:27 (2001): 31–56, 38.

39 Anonymous author, 'An Epitaph for the feminist Biblical Scholar', https://www.shilohproject.blog/an-epitaph-for-the-feminist-biblical-scholar/ (accessed 13.8.2021).

40 Miguel De La Torre, *Burying White Privilege: Resurrecting a Badass Christianity* (Grand Rapids, MI: Wm. B. Eerdmans, 2019), p. 33.

41 bell hooks, *Talking Back: Thinking Feminist, Thinking Black* (Boston: South End Press, 1993), p. 31.

42 D. Ollis, 'The Power of Feminist Pedagogy in Australia: Vagina Shorts and the Primary Prevention of Violence against Women', *Gender and Education* 29:4 (2017), 461–75, 470.

43 Kelly Morris Roberts, 'Integrating Feminist Theory, Pedagogy, and Praxis into Teacher Education', *SAGE Open* 11:3 (2021): 1–16, 6.

44 Ibid.

45 Ibid., 7.

46 Ibid., 9.

47 William R. Herzog II, *Parables as Subversive Speech: Jesus as Pedagogue of the Oppressed* (Louisville, KY: Westminster John Knox Press, 1994), p. 26.

48 Marianne Bjelland Kartzow and Loreen Iminza Maseno, 'Widows, Intersectionality and the Parable in Luke 18', *International Journal of Sociology and Anthropology* 2:7 (2010): 140–48, 141.

49 Ibid., 142.

50 Omiunota Ukpokodu, 'The Practice of Transformative Pedagogy', *Journal on Excellence in College Teaching* 20:2 (2009): 43–67, 43.

51 Gaby Weiner, *Feminisms in Education* (London: Oxford University Press, 1994), p. 4.

52 Ramón Grosfoguel, 'Epistemic Racism/Sexism, Westernized Universities and the Four Genocides/Epistemicides of the Long 16th Century', *Human Architecture Journal of the Sociology of Self-Knowledge* XI:1 (2013): 77–90, 74.

53 Gustavo Gutiérrez, 'Two Theological Perspectives: Liberation Theology and Progressive Theology', in Sergio Torres and Virginia Fabella (eds), *The Emergent Gospel: Theology from the Underside of History* (Maryknoll, NY: Orbis Books, 1978), p. 248.

54 Justo L. Gonzalez, *Manana, Christian Theology from a Hispanic Perspective* (Nashville, TN: Abingdon Press, 1990), p. 52.

55 Ada María Isasi-Díaz and Yolanda Tarango, *Hispanic Women: Prophetic Voice in the Church* (San Francisco, CA: Harper & Row, 1988), p. 2.

56 Musa W. Dube Shomanah, 'Scripture, Feminism and Postcolonial Contexts', in Pui-Lan and Schüssler-Fiorenza (eds), *Women's Sacred Scriptures* (London: SCM Press, 1998), p. 49.

57 Cate Siejk, 'New Responses to Enduring Questions in Religious and Theological Education', *Religious Education* 106:2 (2011): 198–214, 202.

58 Gonzalez, *Manana*, p. 52.

59 hooks, *Talking Back*, p. 207.

60 Lester Edwin J. Ruiz, 'The Theological Curriculum in Accredited Graduate Theological Education: A Commentary on a North American Conversation', in Dietrich Werner et al. (eds), *Handbook of Theological Education in World Christianity* (Oxford: Regnum, 2010), p. 278.

61 Olusola, 'Exploring the Relevance of Feminist Leadership', 30.

62 Ellen Blue, 'Should Theological Education be Different for Clergywomen? Doing "Women's Work" in a Mainline Protestant Seminary', in Ian Jones et al. (eds), *Women and Ordination in the Christian Churches: International Perspectives* (London: T&T Clark), pp. 66–8.

63 Ibid.

64 See Nico A. Botha, 'Towards the En-Gendering of Missiology: The Life-Narrative of Mina Tembeka Soga', *Missionalia* 31:1 (2003): 105–16, 105.

65 hooks, *Teaching Community*, p. 155.

66 See Isasi-Díaz and Tarango, *Hispanic Women*, p. 2.

67 Ibid., p. 65.

68 Anna Mercedes, *Power for: Feminism and Christ's Self-Giving* (London: T&T Clark, 2011), p. 1.

69 See Marilyn Naidoo, *Contested Issues in Training Ministers in South Africa* (Stellenbosch: Sun Media, 2015), p. 63.

70 Williams quoted in Wayman, 'Rowan Williams: Theological Education is For Everyone'.

71 Boaventura De Sousa Santos, *Epistemologies of the South: Justice Against Epistemicide* (New York, Routledge, 2016), p. 12.
72 Naidoo, *Contested Issues*, p. 65.
73 Parker J. Palmer, 'The Community of Truth', in Chris Anderson and Lex Runciman (eds), *Open Questions: Readings for Critical Thinking and Writing* (New York: Bedford/ St Martin's, 2005), pp. 627–36.
74 Palmer, 'The Community of Truth', pp. 629–30.
75 bell hooks, *Teaching to Transgress: Education as the Practice of Freedom* (London: Routledge, 1994), p. 21.
76 Lavinia Byrne, *Women Before God* (London: SPCK, 1988), p. 7.
77 See Margaret Farley, 'Moral Imperatives for the Ordination of Women,' in Anne Marie Gardiner (ed.), *Women and Catholic Priesthood: An Expanded Vision* (New York: Paulist Press, 1976), pp. 40–1.

5

Distrusting Whiteness in Theological Education

I was a speaker at an online conference in 2021 entitled 'Dismantling Whiteness' that was organized by the Oxford Centre for Religion and Culture and focused on critical white theology. There was a significant amount of twitter backlash that myself and others received from those who were not in attendance at the conference but were offended by its title, '#Dismantling-Whiteness'. Some of the comments included the following:

> 'Self-hating whites are at it again.'[1]
> 'Leftist #woke racists.'[2]
> 'Come try and dismantle me, and you will be knocked the fuck out.'[3]
> 'You're going to Hell for race hustling.'[4]

Discussions on the topic of whiteness often lead to defensive, aggressive responses that expose the fragility of white identity politics and embedded racial prejudices. Theological education must not shy away from these topics or the rise of racism, the growth of interreligious intolerance, and the normalization of fascist politics that is on the rise in Europe. Racism is a plague that continues to spread across the UK, as is constantly made visible on social media platforms, where black politicians and black footballers are persistently at the receiving end of vile racist abuse. Take for example the racism directed at Diane Abbott, the first black woman Member of Parliament in the UK, who has been 'subjected to sustained and specific forms of gendered racism which intensified following the UK's decision to leave the European Union'.⁵ Diane Abbott described the abuse she has experienced:

> I've had death threats, I've had people tweeting that I should be hung if 'they could find a tree big enough to take the fat bitch's weight' ... I've had rape threats ... and n*gger, over and over and over again.⁶

Social media companies alone are not to blame for racist rhetoric (though they play a key role in giving racists a platform) – the ideology of whiteness that presents itself in the form of racism has been normalized in Britain and other parts of the world. Colonial and imperial ideologies that are built on the notion of white supremacy are embedded in British education systems, politics and belief systems, and continue to impact the lived experiences of people of colour in the UK. As white normativity and white hegemony dehumanize people of colour, this happens both explicitly and less visibly through epistemology and unconscious biases. Explicitly it is visible in the rhetoric of the most powerful people in the UK, noting the language of the current Prime Minister, Boris Johnson, who has referred to black people as 'piccaninnies' with 'watermelon smiles'. No matter what the context, this is not acceptable. This is a person leading a powerful nation, who says of Africa, in the light of Britain's imperial past, that 'The [African] continent may be a blot, but it is not a blot upon our conscience'. This is a person who further states that 'The problem is not that we were once in charge, but that we are not in charge anymore',⁷ adding, 'The best fate for Africa would be if the old colonial powers, or their citizens, scrambled once again in her direction; on the understanding that this time they will not be asked to feel guilty.'⁸ Such statements from the British Prime Minister are exceptionally dangerous and relevant when considering the role of theological education and formation in resisting systems of oppression inclusive of racism. Ideological racism and rhetoric from political leaders have enabled the normalization of racism and xenophobia, and it is therefore a necessity to address such realities in our classrooms, curricula and pedagogies, because it is also the case that students of colour have experienced racism in theological education institutes. Black and ethnic minority students have reported experiences of 'isolation', 'marginalization', explicit racism and persistent feelings of un-belonging.

Less explicit is the epistemological whiteness that permits what Nelson Maldonado-Torres refers to as 'epistemic racism' that has created a framework in which knowledge, meaning and rationality have been universalized and 'where certain people groups must be negated in order to legitimize the endurance of the Western intellectual tradition as a criterion for rationality and intellectual relevance'.[9] Such epistemic racism has silenced the epistemology of non-Western philosophy and theology, and in the case of women of colour, 'Epistemic indifference chimes acutely with the broader economy of political indifference to the embodied, material realities of having to live under the ongoing coloniality of gendered and sexualized forms of racism.'[10] Epistemic racism is therefore structural and systemic and it has a direct impact on the lived experiences of bodies that exist out of the boundaries of the white norm, where people of colour are dehumanized through the diminishing of their bodies, knowledge, experience and humanity. Christian theology is entangled with epistemic racism and colonialism, because racism and the ideology of whiteness have been embedded into theological education, as Willie James Jennings has described:

> The racial paterfamilias spirit haunts all Western institutes but its presence in educational spaces and especially the theology academy lives close to the surface, ready to reassert itself. That spirit lies so close to our institutionalizing practice because it was born of Christianity in its colonial form, moving and feeling itself in the power to dream a world well organized and running efficiently like a plantation where bodies are organic machines and profit begets more profit.[11]

The gaze of resistance in the face of racism must also then be turned on to the Christian faith, its missional history and theological education, all of which have throughout history permitted and legitimized violence against colonized bodies and black bodies. In order to do so, Christian theological education must be decolonized, because the ideology of whiteness is ingrained in Christian missional history; as Joseph Drexler-Dreis has remarked, 'Decolonization requires affirming the "difference" of the colonial difference, while undoing the coloniality of power that is attached to the colonial difference.'[12] It requires examining the way in which trust has been placed in dominant white theologies in order to address manifestations of the divine in history where God's reign has been used to delegitimize the bodies and experiences of colonized bodies.

Passive concern for racist oppression in our communities will therefore not be enough. Whiteness must be dismantled through participative struggles that require education on the realities of colonial Christianity and white imperial religiosity. Theological formation involves addressing how human beings relate to power in a world dominated by political arrangements, and questioning the role of God in the midst of such power dynamics. Theological education has been complicit in the dehumanization of students of colour; it has for the most part failed to acknowledge that 'white Christianity as organized religion supports the exploiter'[13] because it has been used to justify wars, crusades, apartheid and slavery. The Christianity of white supremacy has subjugated continents and divided and oppressed land and people. In agreement with Frederick Herzog, 'behind Auschwitz and Hiroshima lurks the face of the white God – whose infinite power men sought to imitate in acts of infinite violence.'[14] Yet despite these realities of history, the gospel has been embraced around the world in a multitude of languages, contexts and cultures; there has been a significant shift, 'from the West to the South', and as Felix Wilfred has remarked, 'a shift of Christianity from the rich and middle classes to the poor'.[15] Consequently, it is the case that 'Christianity can no longer be dominantly conceived from a Western perspective',[16] nor should the voices of the white middle classes control the narratives of Christian discourses. Yet it remains the case that for the most part Western perspectives dominate the academy, particularly in the UK context, and class divisions appear to be embedded in the dominant structures of theological learning. Those with the powers in theological education have too often neglected the theological truths from the majority world; they have pigeon-holed certain theologies as 'contextual' and created a hierarchy of knowledge(s), and in so doing they have failed to acknowledge that all theology is contextual. The study of World Christianity offers an opportunity to engage with lived and indigenous Christianity in the majority world as a process of decolonization. Yet despite studies in World Christianity offering a means by which Christianity can be situated in colonial and postcolonial contexts around the world, and enable a greater understanding of the complexities of Christianity, power and identity, many theological students do not engage with World Christianity. World Christianity is not a core module for those in training for ordination or ministerial formation in the UK.

This chapter will therefore aim to address what James Baldwin referred to as 'the white problem'[17] in dominant discourses of Christian theological education, because 'whiteness is just a metaphor for power.'[18] Whiteness has privileged the white, male, middle-class, heteronormative theological truth claims over and against those of black, womanist, mujerista, queer, Dalit and other liberationist theological epistemologies. This chapter therefore suggests that World Christianity can offer a critique of whiteness in theological education that leads to distrust in the dominant white epistemology. It therefore argues that World Christianity should be required as a core module in theological education and formation, and notes that there is a need to confront Christianity's history of colonialism, conquest, empire, racism and domination as a means of challenging the theological truth claims that have enabled those of us in the West to construct a world where whiteness dominates and where Christ is white. The teaching of World Christianity(s) enables students to reinterpret the impact of whiteness in different places and periods of history, including the present day, by exploring the role of empire and situating the colonial impact of whiteness, noting the ways in which knowledge has been racialized and the extent to which whiteness equates to power as a consequence of the lasting impact of empire and colonialism – because, as Joerg Rieger notes, empire affects everything, 'not just politics or economics but also culture, intellectual life, emotional sensitivities, personal relationships, and even our images of the sacred'.[19] This is visible in the ways in which the colonized people were seen as objects in need of civilizing and the indigenous epistemologies and religiosities were smeared, corrupted and stereotyped through racialized perceptions of the colonized. As Christine Hong writes:

> To press for movement toward decolonial and anticolonial teaching and learning in theological education, is to first acknowledge the crime of violence worked by white supremacy and Christian supremacy in theological education and on the lives of teachers and students as a colonial project.[20]

This chapter will also give focus to the need to decolonize theological education in order to address epistemic racism and enable dominant discourses of theology to be challenged by black theology, indigenous, postcolonial, indecent and liberationist theologies.

Christianity, colonialism and distrust in the 'heathen'

> I am verily persuaded 'till some scheme be concerted for the education of the children [of the Mohawks], this generous work will proceed very slowly. I mean such a scheme as will, by the Blessing of God, change their whole Habit of thinking and acting and tend to form them into the condition of a Civil Industrious people so that the principles of Virtue and Piety may be instilled into their minds in such a way, as will be

most likely to make the most lasting impression upon them, and withal introduce the English language among them instead of their own barbarous dialect.[21]

The narrative above depicts the ways in which British imperialism sought to colonialize bodies and minds. Education was often used as a means of instilling British values, virtues and notions of morality and decency throughout the Empire. The God of white Christianity was at the centre of such an education – often used in order to divinely justify the condemnation of the lived religiosities and practices of the colonialized communities. As Norman Etherington notes: 'although missions and the official Empire were quite different operations, they play related parts in a larger drama – the spread of modernization, globalization, and Western cultural hegemony.'[22] Christian education was often used to impose notions of 'morality' because the Christian religion, as presented by the Church of England, was deemed to be 'the true word', to be preached and planted throughout the colonized lands. By placing God at the centre of the Empire, it also enabled the British to justify acts of violence, greed and destruction under the guise of the Great Commission – where the British considered themselves the saviours of the 'heathens'. The English language was also deemed 'pure' and trustworthy in contrast to the 'barbarous dialect' of those whose land had been taken. Through polarized imagery, the British became emblematic of the decent, godly, trustworthy gentleman, in contrast to the ungodly, corrupt, untrustworthy 'savages'. Ngũgĩ Wa Thiong'o describes the lasting impact of such colonization of the mind on the colonialized peoples:

> It makes them see their past as one wasteland of non-achievement and it makes them want to distance themselves from that wasteland ... amidst this wasteland which it has created, imperialism presents itself as the cure and demands that the dependant sing hymns of praise with the constant refrain: 'Theft is Holy'.[23]

DISTRUSTING WHITENESS

Throughout the British Empire indigenous communities were considered 'pagan' obstacles to British hegemony, and the white saviour imaginary dominated the missions of the Church, often portraying the indigenous communities as ignorant, untrustworthy devil-worshippers. This is made apparent in the words of Alexander Whitaker, who described the missionary endeavours to the Native Americans in 1613:

> The principal and main ends were first to preach and baptize into the Christian Religion, and by propagation of that Gospel to recover out of the arms of the Devil, a number of poor and miserable souls, wrapped up unto death, in almost invincible ignorance.[24]

The beliefs and religiosities of the colonialized people under the British Empire were stigmatized and distorted. Hinduism, Islam and indigenous religious communities were portrayed by the British colonial powers as the religions of 'heathens', and the 'heathens' were depicted as being morally questionable and not to be trusted. As Russell Lawson remarks: 'During the reign of Elizabeth, the English turned from exploration to colonization, from bringing the Gospel to pagan peoples during voyages of discovery to settling among them and Christianizing them.'[25] Speaking of the role of the missionary in Africa, Valentin-Yves Mudimbe describes the missionary as 'an agent of a political empire, a representative of a civilization, and an envoy of God', intent upon 'the conversion of African minds and space'.[26] The relationship between missionaries and the indigenous people was complex and shaped by preconceived notions of righteousness and 'lofty aspirations and stern criticism of local cultural practices'.[27] The issue of unequal power dynamics and the thirst for control dictated the majority of missionary endeavours throughout the colonies, and this was most apparent in the missions that sought capitalist gain. The missionary efforts of the British Empire also enabled missionary organizations to make their fortunes through the dehumanization of the indigenous people.

The Church of England's Mission Society of the eighteenth century, known as the Society for the Propagation of the Gospel to Foreign Parts (SPG), spread the gospel throughout the British colonies while also enslaving millions of Africans and investing in sugar plantations in Barbados and elsewhere in the Caribbean. The transatlantic slave trade that across 350 years enslaved and trafficked over 12 million African people to the Americas and the Caribbean, controlled, diminished and dehumanized black bodies literally and theologically. Clerics benefited greatly from the slave trade: the SPG owned slaves in Codrington plantations in Barbados for almost 100 years – 40 per cent of the people enslaved in the plantations died within three years of arrival as a result of the brutality of their treatment. In Barbados there existed 'anti-conversion sentiment' in Protestant colonies as a result of the desire not to consider the enslaved people as 'free'. This was outlined in 1663 by William Blathwayt, on behalf of the Lords of Trade and Plantations in London, who states that 'the conversion of their slaves to Christianity would not only destroy their property but endanger the island, inasmuch as converted negroes grow more perverse and intractable than others.'[28] It was such sentiments that created an exclusive understanding of Christian theology and identity in which Christian identity became dependent upon ethnicity, creating what Katharine Gerbner refers to as 'Protestant Supremacy':

> Protestant Supremacy was the predecessor of White Supremacy, an ideology that emerged after the codification of racial slavery. I refer to 'Protestant' Supremacy, rather than 'Anglican' or 'Christian' Supremacy, because this ideology was present throughout the Protestant American colonies ... It was most likely to develop in places with an enslaved population that was larger than the free population ... They constructed a caste system based on Christian status, in which 'heathenish' slaves were afforded no rights or privileges while Catholics, Jews, and non-conforming Protestants

were viewed with suspicion and distrust, but granted more protections.[29]

James Perkinson, in agreement, highlights how 'Racialized rankings of others was and is an integral part of Western capital's ability to commandeer labour resources and raw materials around the globe.'[30] Distrust in the 'heathen' bodies of the indigenous and enslaved people was at the centre of the theology that permitted violence and subjugation. The theology of the missionaries was also forced to adapt to the dehumanization of black bodies for the sake of capital growth. British missions of the seventeenth and eighteenth century to enslaved people emphasized 'the beneficial aspects of slave conversion, arguing that Christian slaves would be more docile and harder working that their "heathen" counterparts ... missionaries suggested that race, rather than religion, was the defining feature of bondage'.[31] Consequently, a hierarchy of Christianity was permitted, where the Christian 'slave' was not seen as equal to the British Christians, and the Christian faith was taught in part as a means of developing a theology of subservience so that the enslaved might wholly obey their master. As Gerbner remarks, 'Regardless of their religious backgrounds, enslaved and free black men and women did not interpret the rite that marks Protestant conversion in the same way as Protestant missionaries.'[32] The lived Christianity of the black men and women was not accepted or trusted by the missionaries because it 'undermined the ideology of mastery and religious exclusivity' that was embedded in white Protestant missiology and theology. This was even more the case when enslaved people began to read the Bible and interpret Scripture in radically different ways from the colonial oppressors. Conversions to Christianity were seen throughout the British empire, but difficulties arose when Christianity was not understood in the same systematic way in which Christian doctrines were professed by the British.

The testimonies of their faith were isolated to the periphery of the Christian Church. This is a form of testimonial injustice shaped around notions of trust and distrust because it 'relies on prejudices against people belonging to particular social groups', where certain testimonies are distrusted based upon one's identity and, as Miranda Fricker remarks, the individual is 'wronged in her capacity as a knower ... and to be wronged in one's capacity as a knower is to be wronged in a capacity essential to human value'.[33] White Christianity therefore prevented the scriptural and doctrinal theologies developed by black bodies and indigenous bodies throughout the empire from being 'heard'. Consequently, God's revelation that was made apparent in black suffering and the bodies of the oppressed was not recognized as Christian truth. Deep-rooted preconceptions of the colonial other brought about an environment of distrust, where the idea of trust and trustworthiness was inextricably bound up with a 'pure' notion of the Christian faith and identity as presented by the British colonialists. Those who transgressed the boundaries of such rigid understandings of the Christian identity were often not trusted in their faith understandings and lived religiosity, particularly when their faith was understood or lived in ways that could be considered as rebelling against British imperialism or white supremacy. According to Robert Kawashima:

> Trust is also related to that cornerstone of civilization known as hospitality. For hospitality is none other than a discursive, even if unspoken, act of trust. To invite a stranger into one's home, or conversely, to accept an invitation to enter a stranger's home, is already, in effect, to give one's word to do no harm to the Other.[34]

The reality is, however, that missionary relationships with indigenous communities were for the most part not built on trust or hospitality – because there was no invite. This has significantly toxic implications for trust in mission.

Epistemic racism in theological education and the need for World Christianity

In a world where whiteness dominates, it is black bodies that are often scrutinized, while also being made invisible, because whiteness 'as a system of power, dictates how bodies are recognized, scrutinized, and evaluated in organizations vis-à-vis the white gaze'.[35] Institutionally, whiteness operates at the expense of black and ethnic bodies through a set of practices, and a culture that is deemed normative and is used to reinforce white supremacy. The womanist biblical scholar, Mitzi Smith, described her experience of the white male gaze in theological education:

> My gaze as a black woman was temporary, but the white gaze is inescapable. The white gaze to which black and brown scholars are subjected is pervasive, invading the classroom and transcending it. The white gaze requires that black and brown peoples constantly fortify themselves against attempts to diminish and discount their epistemological resources and constructions, especially when (or to preclude or mitigate) the decentering whiteness.[36]

The experiences of black bodies both within and outside theological education are often contested sites of struggle, existing in the midst of the dominant white Christianity that dictates the norm. As James Cone remarked, 'Black people did not need to go to seminary and study theology to know that white Christianity was fraudulent.' The norm also encourages a culture of silence in the face of such struggles that has significant theological implications, as highlighted by Cone in his discussion of white Christianity in *The Cross and the Lynching Tree*. Cone discusses the works of Ida Wells, noting how Wells addressed the understanding that the religiosity of white Christianity could not be trusted, because 'White Christianity was not genuine because it either openly supports slavery, segregation, and lynching as the will of God or it was silent about these evils.'[37] Wells challenged the failure of liberal white Christianity to either act or condemn the atrocities of slavery and segregation. She stated: 'Our American Christians are too busy saving the souls of white Christians from burning in hellfire to save the lives of black ones from present burning in fires kindled by white Christians.'[38] It is the same such white Christianity that denies the experiences of black students in education who experience racism and violence. A recurrent feature in black narratives of those in theological education is a feeling of 'un-belonging' and 'distrust'. For Anoop Nayak, 'The parameters of what it means to be Black, and subsequently what it means to be white, are marked out through a practice of differentiation.'[39] Such parameters are used to create environments of belonging, as Hong remarks:

> I was like many others, defined through the lens of white normativity ... I know what it's like to discover religious bias, racial bias, and patriarchy embedded under my skin through a lifetime of internalizing whiteness and the white framework of Christianity as normative.[40]

The dominant gaze of whiteness in theological education therefore creates a world where the powerful seek to master everything, through control of bodies and minds based upon normative constructions of being. Anyone who exists outside of the norm becomes alienated unless they adapt and deny aspects of their very being in the process. Many students and staff then end up policing themselves, in the knowledge that they are being watched, tested and reported on, thereby imposing oppression on their own bodies in order to 'be seen' in the way the powerful want them to 'be seen'.

Such notions of exclusion and marginalization are also apparent in the practice of epistemic racism in theological education. Theological education has been guilty of re-inscribing colonial and racial thinking in the process of removing or reducing the contributions of black and minority ethnic scholars.

This is an act of white supremacy, as Penelope Muzanenhamo and Rashedur Chowdhury have noted: 'The White supremacist construction of intellectual greatness as a property unique to the white race instructs individuals to value White people, their culture, and all phenomena connected to whiteness, over individuals of color and everything associated with them.'[41] The theologies of scholars from the majority world are often missing from reading lists and the lived Christianity and doctrinal and scriptural understandings from the majority world are silenced and/or marginalized. This is a form of epistemic racism in which white supremacist theology consciously and subconsciously distrusts the theologies of black and indigenous scholars. Colonialism offered the framework for permitting such exclusionary ways of knowing, noting that British imperialism sought to determine who is considered 'fully human' and therefore trustworthy. As Anthony Reddie says, 'the Church served as the primary institution that helped to define truth but also to provide the rationale for what it meant to be human ... Theological education and ministerial training are shaped by this framework.'[42] The white male Christian holds the power as 'knower' and the most worthy of trust, in contrast to the irrational and emotional woman and the wild, heathen, colonial subject. Through a process of structural and systemic inequality, such hegemonic Eurocentrism has determined what should be considered as 'legitimate' knowledge and who should be deemed worthy as being acceptable knowers in the Western world. This has led to the 'subaltern body being socially, politically and racially marginalized so that they can never express their ways of knowing and reasoning without being "Othered", oppressed and repressed, across time and space'.[43] Through the process of *othering*, indigenous thought and theology are barely recognized as theology; they are kept out of canons, often confined to the realm of culture studies or anthropology. Such epistemic injustice is noted by Muzanenhamo and Chowdhury, who describe the experiences of many black scholars: 'Black scholars are "outsiders within". This means that they are subject to "othering", and thus socially located as less powerful, less knowledgeable, less acceptable and, more broadly, rather untrustworthy in relation to white scholars.'[44] Epistemic racism is shaped by a hierarchy of knowledge that embeds epistemic injustice and dehumanizes individuals based upon their race, gender, ethnicity and religion. It is a way of knowing that cannot be trusted because it is based on prejudice and denies the experiences, testimonies and hermeneutics of marginalized individuals. This leads to the question of how such epistemic injustice can be resisted in theological education. In order to resist white supremacy there is a need to gain a greater understanding of how whiteness has impacted the Church, missions and theology, locally and globally.

The discipline of World Christianity is an acknowledgement that the local affects the global and a reminder of humanity's interconnectedness. As a field of study, it is interdisciplinary and intercontextual, in that it situates itself in the context of people's lived religiosities and takes seriously knowledge produced in and by communities and people from around the world. Dale Irvin notes that:

> World Christianity has its historical roots in the disciplines of missions, ecumenics, and world religions. It continues to pursue a threefold conversation, across borders of culture (historically the domain of mission studies), across borders of confession or communion (historically the domain of ecumenics), and across borders with other religious faiths (historically the domain of world religions).[45]

The study of lived Christianity around the world therefore enables the indigenous and marginalized communities to speak theological truths to discourses of power, thereby proposing 'new possibilities of knowing and constructing the world' in ways that go beyond Western rationality.[46] The study of World Christianity enables issues of epistemic struggle to be 'heard' in the classroom and curriculum and has the potential to dislodge structural inequalities in knowledge production and theology by engaging critically with issues of power, colonialism, mission and social change. As Miguel De La Torre writes, 'For white privilege to be maintained, white ignorance must be sustained'[47] because whiteness is 'about a false claim on innocence that depends on the demonization of blackness'.[48] Educating in resistance to such ignorance therefore enables a path to liberation, because the study of World Christianity offers a critical means by which the non-Western Christian theologies and religiosities can help to decolonize Christianity. In doing so, the hierarchies of the knowledge systems apparent within Christian theology can become exposed.

The study of World Christianity also enables the reclaiming and recentring of indigenous epistemologies. It offers a potential means of encouraging the student to engage with the complexities of the history of Christian mission and its entanglement with colonialism and slavery, which further calls for a decolonial engagement with World Christianity in which, as Raimundo Barreto and Roberto Sirvent have noted, there is 'an option for epistemic disobedience, the delinking from the hegemonic Western foundations of knowledge'.[49] Such an engagement with World Christianity will be necessary in order to address the systemic legacy of colonialism and its impact on Christianity, noting that racism is a propagation of whiteness that is a consequence of Eurocentric knowledge reinforced through the colonial 'matrix of power'.[50] As Walter Mignolo says, the 'task of decolonial thinking is the unveiling of epistemic silences of Western epistemology and affirming the epistemic rights of the racially devalued' as a means of allowing the silenced to build arguments to confront the dominant powers and sources of knowledge that have devalued and dehumanized the colonialized. Eurocentric epistemology justified not only racism but also patriarchy, heteronormativity and neo-liberalist capitalism. It for this reason that Reddie has questioned why it is

> that Christian theology has developed a penchant for observing in minute details many forms of theological abstraction, but has largely refused to observe the visceral and palpable

nature of racism within the body politic of white majority societies and the churches located within them.[51]

He further highlights that 'the embedded nature of whiteness has formed a world in which notions of manifest destiny and White exceptionalism have given rise to a toxic reality built on White supremacy'.[52] The challenge is therefore to tackle the systems and structures that strengthen and support whiteness, including academic and church structures, which have been complicit in the oppression of those who have had their rights, dignity and humanity denied.

In a world entrenched in the repercussions of empire, formation in theological education finds itself nestled in the realities of white supremacy, grave inequality, racial prejudice, homophobia and gender-based violence. Therefore educating those in theological education with the tools and knowledge to resist such structures of oppression is a theological imperative, because the impact of Christianity on black suffering cannot be denied – nor can the systemic shaming of the bodies that challenged the colonial norms with regards to gender and sexuality. Therefore whiteness in and through theological education must be dismantled. To do so, theological education will have to be epistemologically disobedient to Eurocentric Christianity if it is to dismantle whiteness. In agreement with Ngũgĩ Wa Thiong'o:

> [T]he biggest weapon wielded and actually daily unleashed by imperialism ... is the cultural bomb. The effect of the cultural bomb is to annihilate a people's belief in their names, in their languages, in their environment, in their heritage of struggle, in their unity, in their capacities and ultimately in themselves.[53]

This is why the study of World Christianity is so vital in theological education, because it enables a conscious awakening to the truths of imperialism and the conglomerates of power. It offers the student the opportunity to enter into dialogue with those who have been marginalized and oppressed by Eurocentric epistemologies, and through an engaged and intercultural dialoguing of learning, all aspects of life and religion as we know it can be transformed. The discipline of World Christianity enables the questioning of the role and purpose of the Christian Church, its contemporary missions and missional history, and an encounter with the variety of expressions of Christianity that can challenge the toxic theology of white Christianity that, as De La Torre has remarked, 'is based on fear not love'.[54]

Resisting whiteness with the lived Christianity of the oppressed

To make this point, I shall draw on some of my own research in the field of World Christianity that focused on the theology of the contemporary Dalit *devadāsīs* in South India, otherwise referred to as Dalit sacred sex workers. This ethnographic research focused on the lived religiosity of Dalit women in a South Indian village who had been dedicated to the goddess Yellamma in childhood, usually as a direct result of poverty or illness, and experienced multiple oppressions as a result of their caste, class, gender and economic status. The term 'Dalit' refers to those who exist outside of the Hindu caste system and are persecuted and marginalized for their socio-religious status. Dalit women in particular are the most persecuted, because in the South Indian context, 'Patriarchal structural violence is more ruinous under the hegemony of caste, as caste based atrocities including the rape of Dalit women often go unpunished.'[55] The struggles experienced by the Dalit *devadāsīs* are distinct from those of the gender-based oppression experienced by women around the world.[56] Their pain-pathos is rooted in casteism, racism, sexism and the collusion of Christian churches and colonial missionary agendas that have superimposed Western norms onto the bodies of the dedicated women.[57] The *devadāsīs* have become known as *devadasi devachi, bayko saarya gavachi*, meaning servant of god, but wife of the whole town. As a direct consequence of poverty, illness, caste and hereditary obligation, they have been dedicated to village goddesses from childhood. The women therefore exist today as outcaste and marginalized sacred 'prostitutes'. They have become objectified, as 'harlots', in need of reform and their profession and institution has been criminalized.[58]

The lived religiosity of Dalit sacred sex workers is one of religious hybridity and indecent lived religiosity. Many of the women I encountered had converted to Christianity and yet sustained their belief in and worship of local village goddesses. Their profound lived Christianity enabled an encounter with a subaltern religiosity that centres on the goddess who responds to the needs of the people at a given time and place, who was often worshipped alongside the *devi* Jesus in the brothels of the sacred sex workers. The religious hybridity of the Dalit *devadāsī* initiates a religious identity, shaped by the dedicated women's experience of both the goddess and Christ, where they simultaneously hold beliefs in both, and allow both Christ and the goddess to structure their meaning of life. Thereby they create a 'blurred' space of religious identity and 'borderless' spirituality in their love of Jesus and sustained belief in the ultimate powers of the goddess. As an oppressed community of Dalit women, the contemporary *devadāsīs* also experience multiple oppressions, including condemnation and judgement from local churches that described the beliefs of the dedicated women and their community with regard to the goddess as 'superstitious'. In so doing, the church as the dominant power degrades the Dalit religiosity and suppresses the goddess as mere 'superstition'. 'To ask what counts as religion is to pose a question about forms of knowledge as they intersect with relations of power. Whose ways of talking to gods and spirits are designated as religion and whose are stigmatized as superstition?'[59] In the religious context of the converted sacred sex workers, the Christian Church appears to hold the intellectual hegemony in the same way that the project of modernity during the Enlightenment period used colonialism and Christian mission to preach 'morality, new humanity, justice, and happiness'[60] at the expense of the indigenous belief systems of the colonialized. It does so by assigning the supremacy of Christianity over and against all other religious belief systems, so that the local village religiosity is stereotyped as ignorant superstition.

Despite attempts to control the religious behaviour of the Dalit village communities, inclusive of the converted *devadāsīs*, the religious praxis of the Dalit villagers remains transgressive in their understanding and worship of Jesus. Asked where Jesus is, one devadasi responded:

> 'He is with me now, next to me, just as he was when I would do bad things, he is with me when I have sex with people for the goddess, he is with me when I get called bad names and when I pray to him, he always answers.'[61]

The religious paradigm of the Dalit sacred sex workers also exposes the sexual lives of the oppressed, the role of the economy, caste hegemonies and the patriarchy of both society and theology. It also presents an alternative to the 'closed monotheism' of white Christian theology, where, as Reddie remarked, 'the "Christian God" is a jealous and competitive God who will not tolerate rivals and the "Other" who worship such God(s), – which in turn is conflated with White exceptionalism, privilege, and power.'[62] The hybrid god/ess of the Dalit sacred sex workers enables us to challenge the monotheistic God of white Christianity that has been used to justify white supremacy. The study of such lived Christianity also forces us to engage with the colonial past, where the Christian imperialist notions of morality gravely impacted and transformed the role of the *devadāsīs*. It further enables critical theological encounters with the indecent lives of the oppressed, where God is contemplated in brothels and questions are asked about the role of the Church in discussions on sex work. Because, as Frederick Herzog has remarked, 'God is found where human life is most threatened, where it has a hard time breaking through to triumph over the negativities that work against it.'⁶³ Problems arise, of course, when the Church insists on an exclusive religious belonging that refuses to acknowledge or incorporate the religious identity of such subaltern communities. As one dedicated *devadāsī* described:

> 'I am told to accept Christ, but Christ does not accept me. The church will not let me and my children be baptized, I am not welcome to come to church services, I am not welcome because I am prostitute, so the goddess Mathamma will release her wrath because I have accepted Christ, and the Church still does not welcome me because I am a sex worker, what hope is there for me?'⁶⁴

The study of World Christianity brings to the forefront such questioning and enables profound insights into the history of Christian missions and the lasting impact on the lived religiosity of the indigenous Christian communities where Christianity is lived as their own and decolonized in the process. Such narratives also expose the continued distrust that is apparent in the mission efforts of the Church, where the *devadāsī* is not trusted for her indecent 'prostitute' status and her lived expression of Christianity is not trusted as she maintains her faith in the local village goddess. Her epistemology is not considered rational or legitimate in contrast to that of the Church, which holds the authority on what should be deemed 'real' and 'trustworthy' Christianity.

Indigenous World Christianity(s) as transformative pedagogical methodology

In a previous role of mine, when I taught theology to those in training for ordination in the Church of England, I introduced such lived narratives of Christianity into a module on Missionary Movements. I did so as a means of conscious epistemic disobedience, used as an exemplification of what is possible when lived Christianity is liberated from whiteness, and as a means of outlining the colonial impact of Christianity in India. This enabled an intercultural pedagogy that addressed the matrix of power inclusive of the capitalism, racism, casteism, sexism and heteronormativity apparent in the social constructs of whiteness. The focus was on developing a transformative pedagogy that would enable whiteness to be addressed in a classroom of majority white ordinands preparing for ministry in majority white contexts. To be clear, dismantling whiteness requires addressing 'a set of normative cultural practices that is visible most clearly to those it definitely excludes and to those to whom it does violence. Those who are securely housed within its borders usually do not examine it.'[65] Therefore, this required making visible what to the majority in the room was invisible, because:

> The parameters of what it means to be Black, and subsequently what it means to be white, are marked out through a practice of differentiation. This process of demarcation secures blackness as a 'racial' and ethnic identity, while simultaneously permitting the mystique of whiteness as a de-racialized, un-thought-out category to continue.[66]

The same parameters have been applied to white Christianity, where imposed norms have dominated and created an epistemic hegemony that has made it possible to allow white Christianity to ignore the theological truth claims and experiences of Christians from the majority world. Teaching on the subject of Dalit hermeneutics and *devadāsī* Christianity therefore offered an opportunity to decentre the white dominant epistemic.

The students engaged theologically beyond the boundaries of the white norm in order to contemplate World Christianity, and in the process became conscious of the fact that Christianity is not the white man's religion. The indigenous Christianity of the oppressed instead presented the students with a lived Christianity that resisted white oppression, colonial norms and mission history. Marcella Althaus-Reid refers to this process as 'theologically pedagogic',[67] where the focus of theological education is on the praxis of liberation for the oppressed, so that those in dialogue become conscious of the unjust and dehumanizing aspects of the systems of oppression and seek to transform the world. Central to such a transformative pedagogy in World Christianity is the dismantling of colonialism in order to free 'subjugated knowledges', histories and lived religiosities, and deliberately explore sites of oppression, dehumanization and subjugation.[68] This requires of the student to 'learn to unlearn in order to relearn and rebuild',[69] because, for example, contemplating God in the brothels of the *devadāsīs* in South India challenges dominant structures of knowledge production; instead, knowledge stems from indecent spaces inclusive of the sexual and religious narratives of the oppressed. Narrating the lived theology of the *devadāsīs* also enables a decolonial expression of Christianity that situates the indigenous hybrid Christ at the centre of theological contemplations, in order to reimagine 'alternative ways of being in the world'.[70] Such narratives of subaltern religiosity were also the lens through which Scripture was reread and the students were able to engage with a liberating Dalit hermeneutics that challenged Eurocentric white hegemony.

The students had the opportunity to engage critically with the missional history of the Church and the role of colonialism in the lives of women, noting that during the British colonial rule of India, women were used as subjects in the debates over reform and independence: 'women became the site on which tradition was debated and reformulated.'[71] This had a significant impact on the role of the women dedicated to the temples and consequently students were able to engage with the historical identities of the women and the impact of colonialism on the indigenous populations. The indecent realities of the lived Christianity of the women were also not suppressed, despite these narratives challenging the colonial norm, because they involved worshipping Christ in brothels, alongside local village goddesses. Consequently, those in formational training were able to enter into dialogue with the sexual narratives of the oppressed. The pedagogical process relied on dialogue: the students were not taught a pre-prepared ideological construction or explanation of Christianity or the world views of the Dalit Christians through a Victorian missionary lens, but they were given the opportunity to discuss and contemplate the Christological beliefs of a subaltern community and make relevant such beliefs in their own understanding of God. For example, students highlighted the implications of understanding God as Dalit, as the Dalit Christians do, and therefore perceiving God as the 'outcast' and 'broken' God of the oppressed. This enabled the students to situate God in the brokenness of their own lives, as well as contemplate their own situatedness in the complex history of Christian Britain and her missions. The aim of such pedagogy was to enable transformative learning, where students were empowered in the process and made conscious of Christianity in the lives of the subaltern in order to critically examine normalized beliefs, values and knowledge. In doing so the epistemologies of the marginalized became central in contemplating God. In such transformative pedagogy, the learner also becomes conscious of the oppression of the marginalized and seeks out ways to engage in transformative action.

Central to such pedagogy were the lived narratives of the dedicated Dalit women – the students listened to the personal stories of the women and the Dalit Christian communities in the context of the South Indian village. The experiences of the women were narrated in their own words, their stories and experiences were not filtered through a Western, Eurocentric lens, and their beliefs about Jesus and their readings of Scripture therefore enabled the students to engage with the hermeneutics of a marginalized people. By engaging with such lived narratives of Christianity, the white Christ was deconstructed through an intersectional lens – as students grappled with issues of gender, race, caste, class and the role of colonialism and the Church. Students also became aware of their own interrelatedness with the Dalit Christian community, as Christians in solidarity.

The Dalit Christ also challenged the universalized notion of the *white* Christ. Engaging critically with the stories of World Christianity enabled learning to be both compelling and transformative, because students were able to witness the struggles of the global oppressed. Critical narrative as pedagogy can lead to transformative praxis and reconciliation, where whiteness is deconstructed in the process. This is possible through a process of de-centring, where knowledge is produced from the bodies and experiences of the marginalized.

Focusing on subaltern religiosity in the teaching of World Christianity therefore enabled a discourse that challenged the narratives of whiteness that had supported a missional history shaped by patronizing notions of charity, heathen and whore, and instead acknowledged that the missions of Europe 'baptized allegedly free barbarians and sovereigns to make them submissive Christians, dominated, colonials of a Christian Empire'.[72] Yet as Freire says, 'we would have to be naïve indeed to expect the elites to collaborate with us in their own destruction.'[73] This is why it is important to be subversive in order to dismantle the master's house with the master's tools – in other words, if we are to dismantle whiteness in and through theological education. It is not a simple task to dismantle whiteness in a majority white classroom, in a context in which the British Empire is often looked on with nostalgia and pride; a context in which white Christianity has been used to police such views and rely on white ignorance – an ignorance that is:

> not at all confined to the illiterate and uneducated but propagated at the highest levels of the land ...[74]

Theological education has been developed within a framework that relies on such ignorance – where patriarchal, heteronormative, white, middle-class norms have determined who and what is acceptable. The theologies that are born out of the bodies and experiences of those who have been silenced by such norms have the potential to destabilize power dynamics in and through theological education. The complexity of the lived religion of the colonized subject forces those who witness such religiosity to grapple with histories of oppression and notions of Christian belonging that critique whiteness and give agency and voice to the oppressed. Such narratives enable a pedagogy that encourages discussions on racism, sexism and sexuality that would otherwise be ignored. As James Cone has commented:

> Whites do not talk about racism because they do not have to talk about it. They have most of the power in the world – economic, political, social, cultural, intellectual and religious. There is little that Blacks and other people of color can do to change the power relations in the churches, seminaries and society.[75]

Teaching on subaltern Christianity in the majority world, and sharing narratives, scriptural hermeneutics, doctrinal understandings and expressions of faith, has the potential to disrupt dominant hegemonies by giving voice to the powerless. Yet the pedagogical process for such discussions is challenging, as Osei-Kofi has outlined:

> The desire to focus discussions on 'challenges' of being privileged becomes particularly tough when the majority of participants identify as part of the advantaged group in question, for example when the majority of faculty are White discussing issues of race, male when addressing sexism, cisgender when engaging with transphobia, or able-bodied when taking up disability studies ... it is imperative to try and move the dialogue in a direction that helps the group realize what is happening and how privilege is reproduced in the process being taken up.[76]

Central to such pedagogy is the methodology outlined by Paulo Freire, who notes, 'There is nothing more compelling than the facts of real life.' The facts of real life cannot be systematized into a banking model of education but instead they enable 'critical reflection, curiosity, demanding inquiry, uneasiness, and uncertainty'.[77] Becoming conscious of the theologies from the majority world and black theologies that resist whiteness enables a dialoguing that challenges whiteness in and through theological education. Failure to do so amounts to a theological education that cannot be trusted because it denies the lived Christianity of the oppressed and marginalized, and in agreement with Freire: 'If men are unable to perceive critically the themes of their time, and thus to intervene actively in reality, they are carried along in the wake of change.'[78] A theological education that does not acknowledge a need to address barriers to belonging, acts of racism and the persecution of people around the world is 'carrying along' without relevance or purpose.

Trust in resisting whiteness in dialogue

Addressing the topic of white privilege in the theological classroom can lead to difficult conversations. I recall one student saying, 'How can I be privileged? I am a single mum and rely on foodbanks to feed my children.' Such responses cannot be disregarded; the situatedness of the woman is relevant because, following Freire, 'all pedagogies are situated in place, in the spatially configured lived and interpretative experiences of the learner.'[79] To ignore the situated reality of the woman, who feels the struggles of class and gender inequality, is to prevent any pedagogy of solidarity in resisting whiteness. There is a need therefore to be trusting in the situatedness of those in dialogue, as Zachary Casey comments:

> When we are being pedagogical with one another, we are approaching the other with an attitude of inquiry that seeks to foster the other's self-appropriation of meaning; their reading of the world. In other words, being pedagogical means acting in such a way as to foster (political, partial, and

humanizing) learning, in ways that acknowledge the political nature of all human interaction and the various context(s) in which we live.[80]

Transformative dialogue requires mutual trust and the ability to reflect and think critically about one's faith and identity. According to Freire, this requires:

> thinking which discerns an indivisible solidarity between the world and people and admits of no dichotomy between them – thinking which perceives reality as process, as transformation, rather than as a static entity – thinking which does not separate itself from action, but constantly immerses itself in temporality without fear of the risks involved.[81]

Such critical thinking embraces difference; it does not see diversity as a cause for separation but rather acknowledges that dialogue and learning take place in community, and that without community liberation is not possible. Furthermore, it calls for action, noting, as Kwok Pui-Lan has highlighted, that 'action may take different forms, such as witnessing to the structural and social manifestations of injustice, political advocacy for policy changes, and caring for the poor through feeding programs and food pantries.'[82] Dialoguing that is shaped by pedagogy that offers the space for the lived experiences of those engaged challenges the ways in which existing models of dialogue have objectified women and other oppressed groups. The woman's narrative of class struggle is therefore extremely relevant when engaging with anti-racist pedagogy, because it is only by coming to terms with their own social location, their past, presence and background, and becoming conscious of these realities in the context of the world at large, that the individual is able to find a voice and situate the struggles of others with whom they engage. Such pedagogy for liberation requires a 'climate of mutual trust, which leads the dialoguers into ever closer partnership in the naming of the world'.[83] This is, therefore, a dialoguing of solidarity, where the power dynamics have been recognized and dialogue has moved beyond 'tolerance' to trust in the epistemologies and truth claims of all. Such dialogue enables critical and transformative movements for justice, where daily struggles can also become the starting point of dialogue. Central to such conversations is the requirement for a deeper understanding and appreciation of the socio-political location of the *other*. This is necessary for building trust, creating emotional space and bringing about a unified political solidarity.[84] Teaching on anti-racism invites students to open their minds in emotional spaces, think beyond the norm, be vulnerable within a community of learning, while recognizing and respecting the views, experiences and opinions of others. Theological education has the potential to offer a location in which the boundaries of race and class can be crossed, but only if all students (and staff) feel as though they belong. The epistemologies of sex workers expose the impacts of capitalism on the human body and the precariousness of social and political structures that often render women vulnerable.

Willie James Jennings' work is incredibly important in researching methodologies for creating such environments of trust and moving towards 'pedagogies of belonging' in theological education, 'over against the distorted imaginaries that foster pedagogical practices of insulation and exclusion'. Jennings suggests that the 'art of cultivating belonging' should be central to all theological education.[85] In order to create such environments there needs to be institutional change, where students and staff are free to be themselves and where those in more privileged positions are willing to sacrifice such privileges. This requires moving beyond attempted 'quick fixes' to racism, where, as Hong comments:

> I can recall countless times when white faculty persons or other persons in positions of influence become excited about antiracism and interreligious commitments for the first time. Usually, this person expends all their newfound energy focused on getting everything right and calling everything and every-

one out. In the end, they tire quickly and quit as soon as they make a faux pas, or offend the people with whom they are attempting to ally.[86]

Cultural, social and theological change will only occur if white people are willing to dismantle their own whiteness and put trust in the marginalized experiences and theologies of those who have been exploited and oppressed, as James Cone remarks:

> [W]hen whites undergo the true experience of conversion wherein they die to whiteness and are reborn anew in order to struggle against white oppression and for the liberation of the oppressed, there is a place for them in the black struggle of freedom ... But it must be made absolutely clear that it is the black community that decides both the authenticity of white conversion and also the place these converts will play in the black struggle of freedom.[87]

Authentic transformation demands trust that those joining in the struggle for change have become conscious of the ways in which whiteness operates and how whiteness, through globalized systems of oppression and exploitation, has crushed and destroyed the minds and bodies of entire nations and people. Body-politics of knowledge and geopolitics of people are exposed in the process of a dialogue shaped around such struggles, as dominant discourses of theology are challenged and interrogated. However, it is not without risk that educators engage in such pedagogical change, because those who seek transformation in traditional institutes of learning are often subject to discrediting techniques by those with power who seek to prevent change. In the words of bell hooks, 'it takes fierce commitment, a will to struggle, to let our work as teachers reflect progressive pedagogies.'[88]

Decolonizing the curriculum and disobedient epistemology

In *After Whiteness* Jennings argues for the need to journey towards inclusive and decolonial curricula in theological education. He refers to such a transformation as 'building the new Babel', 'enabling / a cacophony of voices that none of us can control'.[89] Building the New Babel requires taking a decolonial turn in theological education and critically examining the impact of colonialism on theological learning and formation. As Hong says, part of admitting our complicity as educators in spaces of oppression, white supremacy and Christian supremacy as hegemony includes 'conscious deprogramming from the belonging and unbelonging binary'.[90] It requires distrusting dominant ways of knowing in theology and becoming epistemologically disobedient. 'Epistemic disobedience' is a term coined by Mignolo, meaning 'to delink from the illusion of the zero point epistemology'. Mignolo's analysis is critical for understanding the need to decolonize theological education. He examines the way in which theology was the 'overarching conceptual and cosmological frame of knowledge-making' in the West and was displaced by secularization in the eighteenth century. He notes that secular philosophy and science became the dominant way of knowing, yet 'Both frames, theological and secular, bracketed their geo-historical foundation and, instead, made of theology and philosophy/science a frame of knowledge beyond geo-historical and body location.' In other words, both gave the impression of universal ways of knowing without locating the geopolitics or social location of how that knowing and reasoning came to be. Consequently, for Mignolo:

> Western imperial knowledge was cast in Western imperial language and was theo-politically and ego-politically founded. Such foundation legitimizes the assumptions and claims that knowledge was beyond bodies and place and that Christian theology and secular philosophy and science were the limits

of knowledge-making beyond and besides which all knowledge was lacking: folklore, myth, traditional knowledge, were invented to legitimize imperial epistemology.[91]

Dialoguing and trusting in the narratives of the oppressed in theological education enables us to come out of the closet that has normalized decency, racism, exploitation and sexism and trapped contemplations on God in a framework of oppression. Engaging with lived Christianity as expressed through the lens and bodies of those who have been labelled 'indecent', 'heathens', 'poor' and 'oppressed' challenges theological assumptions that normalize a 'pure' notion of Christianity and denies the horrors and indecency of the Christ of the cross. By engaging with the decolonial option in theological education we are able to make a conscious choice to shift our reasoning and ways of knowing and contemplating God to a position that trusts in the knowledge produced by the people who have been silenced by colonialism. Western theology supported by Eurocentric rationality has dehumanized people, minds and intellects. Such acts of dehumanization are sinful, they oppose the God of justice and therefore cannot be trusted. In the words of the Maori anthropologist Linda Tuhiwai Smith:

> [W]e were not 'fully human': some of us were not even considered partially human. Ideas about what counted as human in association with the power to define people as human or not human were already encoded in imperial and colonial discourses prior to the period of imperialism.[92]

Moving towards a decolonialized theological education requires becoming epistemologically disobedient and intentionally changing our curricula and interrogating oppressive conditions that have dehumanized people. This is not just about adding additional optional modules covering black theology or liberation theologies, but also about incorporating black, postcolonial, mujerista, womanist, queer, Dalit and other such dehumanized voices into all modules. Segregating theological voices into contextual theologies enables the continuation of white supremacy theology because the norm remains unchallenged, whereas decolonizing the curriculum challenges the dominant culture. Decolonizing the curriculum in theological education forces the dominant to recognize how they have maintained power; the dominant must therefore become conscious of their role in white supremacy and patriarchy – this is no doubt the reason why many scholars who maintain the most power will resist calls to decolonize the curriculum. Those with power have not had to defend their right to be on a reading list, or been questioned over the authenticity or rationality of their opinion; they have not had to make aspects of their identity invisible – gender, sexuality, culture, language and class, for example – in order to be accepted. When those in the dominant culture become aware of such realities, they can help to dismantle the norms that enable such power dynamics to oppress and create spaces of learning where marginalized voices are trusted.

It is for this reason that dialogue in theological education must also involve engaging with indecent stories of oppression – stories that enable us to engage with the ways power has been abused. As Althaus-Reid says:

> The sexual stories of the marginalised people are known but devalued. Incest and child abuse (and stories of domestic violence) have been silenced amongst wealthy people, but amongst the poor there is another kind of silence: the silence of secrecy has given way to the silence of impotence.[93]

The sexual stories of the oppressed enable us to engage with the hidden narratives of oppression that expose the indecency of power and abuse. Such stories bring about distrust in the hierarchal notions of purity within the Church and institutions that have silenced stories of child abuse, rape and violence against women. They also expose epistemologies that have been 'invisibilized' by the dominant hegemony of Western 'decency' and 'rationality'.

Theological education must then learn to understand that there exist certain power dynamics in the classroom, as well in the Church and society, all of which impact the experiences of the learner and educator. If educational institutes fail to address the politics of power and domination that penetrate the learning experiences of those in marginalized groups in particular, then they will house a culture of shame and embodied oppression. When educators create environments of learning that address issues of power imbalances and oppression, while taking seriously the embodied lived experiences of the student, they affirm the student in their wholeness and educate people to succeed. After all, if theological education is intentional about teaching about God's kin-dom, as educators we must have the courage to listen, witness and trust in the struggles and lived experiences of our students, while envisioning how learning can transform the world in light of the kin-dom of God. In order to transform pedagogies and curricula in theological education in ways that enable transformative and liberative praxis, educators can learn from the ways in which liberation theologians engage with aspects of life, Scripture and religion that are oppressive and seek to resist such oppression. Musa Dube, for example, reflects on 'growing up as a Christian', and remembers how she saw Jesus – with blonde hair and blue eyes. She remembers the 'colonization of the mind' she experienced as she understood the 'most godly to be white missionaries, and the most deviant to be Black Africans'.[94] In response to feeling marginalized by the dominant discourses of colonial Christianity, Dube looked to the Bible and began to reread it through an African feminist postcolonial lens. In doing so, she names her social location, and does so as a means of epistemic disobedience, highlighting that her epistemology is rooted not in imposed Western understandings of God but rather in her embodied experiences as an African womanist scholar. Rereading the Bible in a way that resists colonialism and acknowledges the social location of the reader enables a pathway out of epistemic and ontological colonization of the Bible. Dube provides a model of liberation theology where she brings her story and her narrative to the world of the Bible and theology. Take, for example, her rereading of the story of Rahab. She writes:

> As she walks away from the window I realize that I am her. I am Rahab. I am also leaning on a small window, stuck in a world divided by great walls – walls that too easily pretend that we have not touched and made love to one another and felt the passion of our humanness. Like Rahab, I am also standing at the window by a great wall that divides the powerful and the less powerful. I am standing in the shadow of death, where the powerful threaten to wipe out cities and they do.[95]

By reading her own story into the struggles of Rahab, Dube displays a model of epistemic decolonization. Through the use of embodied storytelling she liberates the text from the control of Western traditional interpretations, and brings to light the indecency of the sexual struggles of the oppressed and the impact of colonialism, power and the fear of death. This is a transformative pedagogical methodology because 'Narrative inquiry provides a space to illuminate the entanglements of what Darling-Hammond names as the (presumed) gap between "theoretically based knowledge" and "experience-based knowledge" – to show that theory needs practice, and practice is informed by theoretical investments.'[96] Dube decolonizes the Bible as she challenges the colonialist way of reading texts and understanding theology, where predetermined theological truths and interpretations are imposed; instead she challenges the power dynamics apparent within the narrative and in doing so highlights the injustices of the here and now. This enables the reader to listen to the story of Dube and Rahab and reconstruct knowledge of the text while also considering their own role in the narrative. Dube is a member of the Circle of Concerned African Women Theologians, a collective of womanist scholars who have challenged colonial and patriarchal practices within the Church, society and the Bible. The collective has taken what Mignolo refers to as a 'decolonial turn', where they have challenged colonial and dominant epistemologies through acts of epistemic disobedience. This is visible in the work of Mercy Amba Oduyoye, a founder of the collective. Oduyoye looks to folk stories, mythology and African proverbs in order to address the patriarchy of Church, society and Scripture and challenge issues of colonialism that have had a lasting impact on the lives of the colonialized. Through the use of folk stories and mythology, Oduyoye enables epistemologies that were distrusted by the colonial missionaries to become the trusted lens through which Christianity is understood. Noting that colonialism sought to erase indigenous knowledges through cultural domination,[97] Oduyoye and Dube present models of decolonial theologizing that offer alternative and transformative pedagogies through decolonial praxis. They enable the space for knowledges, stories and experiences that emerge from different social, economic and global contexts to enter dialogically into a Christian theologizing. Liberationist scholars, including Dube and Oduyoye, challenge the ways in which the colonial missionaries and Eurocentric epistemology silenced, erased, mocked and distrusted indigenous global epistemologies. Such strategies present an alternative to Eurocentrism in curriculum and teaching and disrupt Eurocentric epistemic privilege by resisting the norm.

Decolonizing as a method of trust

To be clear, decolonizing theological education is not about a denial or removal of Western or Eurocentric epistemologies, but rather a reassessing of theological truths that is demanded of theological education if it is to be trusted. While decolonial approaches have been taken up by some theological educators, they have not been normalized in theological education through research methods, curricula or pedagogies, and consequently dominant power structures remain deeply rooted in the vast majority of theological education institutes. To date, theological education for those in training for ministry within the UK has focused predominantly on additional training sessions that highlight inequality and racial bias, such as racism awareness training. Anthony Reddie has highlighted how problematic this is:

> First, in its operation as a stand-alone, non-assessed initiative, the work was always envisioned as an atypical form of educational provision separate from the substantive curriculum work of ministerial training and theological education. In the failure to integrate racism awareness into the substantive heart of ministerial training and theological education, the work of anti-racist educators, such as myself, was fatally undermined, as these initiatives were being perceived as barely tolerable encumbrances to the 'serious' and 'proper' work of ministerial formation.[98]

Having anti-racism training as stand-alone training fails to enable curricula that are anti-racist and resist domination. Furthermore, 'the incorporation of multiple ways of knowing (grafted onto the same hegemonic ontological foundation that is left unexamined) ... does not change ontological dominance.'[99] A commitment to dismantling racism in and through theological education therefore requires examining the history of colonialism, the role of Christian colonial missions, the deconstruction of knowledge as power, and the reclaiming of global knowledges that have been silenced and made invisible. This demands of the educator the need to put trust in diverse ways of knowing and enabling pedagogical encounters that encourage self-reflection and critical engagement and support students as knowledge producers. Trust is therefore a central component of a decolonial theological education: as the embodied experiences of students and multiple and interconnected ways of knowing God enter into dialogue with the curriculum in a way that encourages mutual love, they are 'affirmed in love, truth, honesty, justice, and caring warmth'.[100] The problem with simply adding anti-racism training is that trust is still placed in the dominant ways of knowing that have encouraged and enabled racism; as Cone has remarked, 'Commitment without analysis leads to romanticism and eventually to despair. Analysis without commitment leads to opportunism and eventually to a betrayal of one's people.'[101] Research and analysis of existing barriers to belonging alone will also not be enough; radical transformation will be dependent upon decolonial praxis in pedagogy, curriculum and the very structures that have housed racism throughout history and propagated an imperial Christianity that remains ingrained in theological education.

Notes

1 https://twitter.com/LeoKearse/status/1383374636855947273 (accessed 9.2.2022).
2 https://twitter.com/OutragedMary/status/1383400155433504768 (accessed 9.2.2022).
3 https://twitter.com/LordBotswana/status/1383497468885692418 (accessed 9.2.2022).
4 https://twitter.com/Whitejesus2021/status/1383687673089462275 (accessed 9.2.2022).
5 Lisa Amanda Palmer, 'Diane Abbott, Misogynoir and the Politics of Black British Feminism's Anticolonial Imperatives: "In Britain too, it's as if we Don't Exist"', *The Sociological Review* 68:3 (2020): 508–23, 510.
6 A. Dhrodia, 'Unsocial media: tracking Twitter abuse against women MPs' (2017), in *Medium*. Available at: https://medium.com/@AmnestyInsights/unsocial-media-tracking-twitter-abuse-against-womenmps-fc28aeca498a (accessed 10.9.2021).
7 https://www.spectator.co.uk/article/the-boris-archive-africa-is-a-mess-but-we-can-t-blame-colonialism (accessed 9.2.2022).
8 https://www.independent.co.uk/news/uk/politics/boris-johnson-colonialism-africa-british-empire-slavery-a9564541.html (accessed 9.2.2022).
9 Joseph Drexler-Dreis, *Decolonial Love: Salvation in Colonial Modernity* (New York: Fordham University Press, 2019), p. 36.
10 Palmer, 'Diane Abbott', 510.
11 Willie James Jennings, *After Whiteness: An Education in Belonging* (Grand Rapids, MI: Wm. B. Eerdmans, 2020), p. 88.

12 Drexler-Dreis, *Decolonial Love*, p. 42.

13 See Frederick Herzog, 'Theology of Liberation', in Joerg Rieger (ed.), *Theology from the Belly of the Whale: A Frederick Herzog Reader* (London: Bloomsbury, 1999), p. 82 (first published in *Continuum* 7:4 (Winter 1970)).

14 Frederick Herzog, 'God, Black or White?', in Rieger (ed.), *From the Belly of the Whale*, p. 67 (first published in *Review & Expositor* 67:3 (Summer 1970)).

15 Felix Wilfred, 'Christianity between Decline and Resurgence', in Jon Sobrino and Felix Wilfred (eds), *Christianity in Crisis?* (*Concilium* 2005/3, SCM Press 2005): 27–37, 31.

16 Raimundo C. Barreto Jr, *World Christianity as Public Religion* (Minneapolis, MN: Fortress Press, 2017), p. xv.

17 James Baldwin said, 'It's not the Negro problem ... it's the white problem. I'm only black because you *think* you're white.' Quoted in David Leeming, 'The White Problem', *PEN America: A Journal for Writers and Readers* 1:2 (Fall 2001). Emphasis original.

18 https://mediadiversified.org/2017/09/21/james-baldwin-i-am-not-your-negro-and-the-construction-of-race/ (accessed 9.2.2022).

19 Joerg Rieger, 'Empire, Deep Solidarity, and the Future of Resistance', in Jione Havea (ed.), *Religion and Power* (London: Lexington Books, 2021), p. 71.

20 Christine J. Hong, *Decolonial Futures: Intercultural and Interreligious Intelligence for Theological Education* (Maryland, NY: Lexington Books, 2021), p. 3.

21 John Ogilvie's Journal, New York State Library, quoted in Peter M. Doll, *Revolution, Religion, and National Identity: Imperial Anglicanism in British North America, 1745–1795* (Cranbury, NJ: Associated University Presses, 2000).

22 Norman Etherington, *Missions and Empire*: Oxford History of the British Empire Companion Series (Oxford, Oxford University Press, 2005), pp. 3–4.

23 Ngũgĩ Wa Thiong'o, *Decolonising the Mind: The Politics of Language in African Literature* (Oxford: James Currey, 2005), p. 3.

24 Alexander Whitaker, *Good News from Virginia* (London, 1613), p. 25. Quoted in Russell M. Lawson, 'Anglicans on the Frontier: The Great Commission and the Exploration and Colonization of North America', *Anglican and Episcopal History* 87:2 (2018): 180–204, 191.

25 Lawson, 'Anglicans on the Frontier', 185.

26 Valentin-Yves Mudimbe, *The Invention of Africa: Gnosis, Philosophy, and the Order of Knowledge* (Bloomington, IN: Indiana University Press, 1988).

27 Emma Wild-Wood, 'The Interpretations, Problems and Possibil-

ities of Missionary Sources in the History of Christianity in Africa', in *World Christianity: Methodological Considerations* (Leiden: Brill, 2020), p. 99.

28 See Katharine Gerbner, *Christian Slavery: Conversion and Race in the Protestant Atlantic World* (Philadelphia, PA: University of Pennsylvania Press, 2018), p. 2.

29 Ibid., pp. 2–3.

30 James W. Perkinson, *White Theology: Outing Supremacy in Modernity* (London: Palgrave Macmillan, 2004), p. 70.

31 Gerbner, *Christian Slavery*, p. 3.

32 Ibid., p. 10.

33 Miranda Fricker, *Epistemic Injustice: Power and the Ethics of Knowing* (Oxford: Oxford University Press, 2007), p. 44.

34 Robert S. Kawashima, 'Oaths, Vows, and Trust in the Bible', in Nina Caputo and Mitchell B. Hart (eds), *On the Word of a Jew: Religion, Reliability, and the Dynamics of Trust* (Bloomington, IN: Indiana University Press, 2019).

35 Veronica Caridad Rabelo, Kathrina J. Robotham, Courtney L. McCluney, '"Against a Sharp White Background": How Black Women Experience the White Gaze at Work', *Gender Work Organ* (2020): 1–19, 4.

36 Mitzi J. Smith, 'Teaching Before the White Gaze in Biblical Studies Classroom as a Black Woman', *Blog Series: Social Justice for Civic Engagement*, Wabash Center For Teaching and Learning in Theology and Religion, September 30 (2020): 2. Available at: https://www.wabashcenter.wabash.edu/2020/09/teaching-before-the-white-gaze-in-the-biblical-studies-classroom-as-a-black-woman/ (accessed 9.2.2022).

37 James Cone, *The Cross and the Lynching Tree* (New York: Orbis Books, 2011), p. 131.

38 Ibid., p. 132.

39 Anoop Nayak, 'Tales from the Darkside: Negotiating Whiteness in School Arenas', *International Studies in Sociology of Education* 7:1: 57–79, 64.

40 Hong, *Decolonial Futures*, p. 2.

41 Penelope Muzanenhamo and Rashedur Chowdhury, 'Epistemic Injustice and Hegemonic Ordeal in Management and Organisation Studies: Advancing Black Scholarship', *Human Relations* (2021): 1–24, 3.

42 Anthony Reddie, 'Critical Insights into *After Whiteness*', *Modern Theology* 37:4 (2021): 1016–26, 1017.

43 Shana Almeida, 'Race-Based Epistemologies: The Role of Race and Dominance in Knowledge Production', *Wagadu* 13 (2015): 81.

44 Muzanenhamo and Chowdhury, 'Epistemic Injustice', 2.

45 Dale Irvin, 'World Christianity: An Introduction', *Journal of World Christianity* 1:1 (2008): 1-26, 2.

46 Raimundo Barreto and Roberto Sirvent (eds), *Decolonial Christianities: Latinx and Latin American Perspectives* (Switzerland: Palgrave Macmillan, 2019), p. 4.

47 Miguel De La Torre, *Burying White Privilege: Resurrecting a Badass Christianity* (Grand Rapids, MI: Wm. B. Eerdmans, 2019), p. 45.

48 Jonathan Mirin, 'The Art of Whiteness in the Nonfiction of James Baldwin and Toni Morrison', in L. King and L. O. Scott, *James Baldwin and Toni Morrison: Comparative Critical and Theoretical Essays* (New York: Palgrave Macmillan), p. 223.

49 Barreto and Sirvent (eds), *Decolonial Christianities*, p. 4.

50 See Walter D. Mignolo, 'Epistemic Disobedience, Independent Thought and Decolonial Freedom', *Theory, Culture & Society* 26:7-8 (2009): 159-81, 161.

51 See Anthony Reddie, 'Reassessing the Inculcation of an Anti-Racist Ethic for Christian Ministry: From Racism Awareness to Deconstructing Whiteness', *Religions*, 11:497 (2020): 1-17, 5.

52 Ibid., 6.

53 Ngũgĩ Wa Thiong'o, *Decolonising the Mind*, p. 3.

54 De La Torre, *Burying White Privilege*, p. 37.

55 Eve Parker, *Theologising with the Sacred 'Prostitutes' of South India* (Leiden: Brill, 2021), p. 12.

56 It is important to note my own 'respective distinctiveness' as a white British woman, yet having witnessed the multifaceted plight of Dalit women during my time working in India, including the gendered violence and sexual degradation experienced, I seek to allow the voices and experiences of the Dalit women's pain-pathos to speak for themselves.

57 Parker, *Theologising with the Sacred 'Prostitutes'*, p. 2.

58 Ibid., p. 23.

59 Lucinda Ramberg, *Given to the Goddess: South Indian Devadasis and the Sexuality of Religion* (Durham, NC: Duke University Press, 2014), p. 5.

60 See Chris Sugden, *Seeking the Asian Face of Jesus: A Critical and Comparative Study: The Practice and Theology of Christian Social Witness in Indonesia and India 1974-1996* (New Delhi: Regnum, 1997), p. 389.

61 Mathamma Kanagarathinam, interview, Nagalapuram, Andhra Pradesh, 12.12.2014.

62 Reddie, 'Reassessing the Inculcation', 7.

63 Herzog, 'God: Black or White?', p. 72.

64 Bama, interview, Madurai, Tamilnadu, 11.11.2014.
65 Ruth Frankenberg, *White Women, Race Matters: The Social Construction of Whiteness* (Minneapolis, MN: University of Minnesota Press, 1994), pp. 228–9.
66 Nayak, 'Tales from the Darkside', 64.
67 Marcella Althaus-Reid, *The Queer God* (London: Routledge, 2003), p. 169.
68 Ada María Isasi-Díaz and Eduardo Mendieta (eds), *Decolonizing Epistemologies: Latina/o Theology and Philosophy* (New York: Fordham University Press, 2012), p. 7.
69 Walter Mignolo, 'Decolonizing Western Epistemology', in Isasi-Díaz and Mendieta (eds), *Decolonizing Epistemologies*, p. 7.
70 Barreto and Sirvent (eds), *Decolonial Christianities*, p. 10.
71 Lata Mani, 'Contentious Traditions: The Debate on Sati in Colonial India', in Kumkum Sangari et al. (eds), *Recasting Women: Essays in Colonial History* (Delhi: Kali for Women, 1989), pp. 117–18.
72 Enrique Dussel, 'Epistemological Decolonization of Theology', in Barreto and Sirvent (eds), *Decolonial Christianities*, p. 33.
73 Paulo Freire, *Pedagogy of the Oppressed*, quoted in Stephen Nathan Haymes, *Race, Culture, and the City: A Pedagogy for Black Urban Struggle* (New York: State University of New York Press, 1995), p. 136.
74 Charles W. Mills, *Black Rights/White Wrongs: The Critique of Racial Liberalism* (New York: Oxford University Press, 2017), p. 49.
75 James H. Cone, 'Theology's Great Sin: Silence in the Face of White Supremacy', *Black Theology: An International Journal* 2:2 (2004): 139–52, 144.
76 N. Osei-Kofi, 'Feminist Approaches to Social Justice Education: The Role of Faculty Development', *Feminist Formations* 30:3 (2018): 160–71, 150.
77 Ira Shor and Paulo Freire, *A Pedagogy for Liberation: Dialogues on Transforming Education* (London: Bergin & Garvey, 1987), p. 8.
78 Paulo Freire, *Education for Critical Consciousness* (New York: Continuum, 1974), p. 6.
79 Haymes, *Race, Culture, and the City*, p. 2.
80 Zachary A. Casey, *A Pedagogy of Anticapitalist Antiracism: Whiteness, Neoliberalism and Resistance in Education* (New York: State University of New York Press, 2016), p. 18.
81 Paulo Freire, *Pedagogy of the Oppressed* (New York: Continuum, 2000), p. 81.
82 Kwok Pui-Lan, *Globalization, Gender, and Peacebuilding: The future of interfaith dialogue* (Mahwah, NJ: Paulist Press, 2012), pp. 22–3.
83 Freire, *Pedagogy of the Oppressed*, p. 91.

84 bell hooks, *Teaching to Transgress: Education as the Practice of Freedom* (New York: Routledge, 1994), p. 132.
85 Jennings, *After Whiteness*, p. 10.
86 Hong, *Decolonial Futures*, p. 31.
87 James H. Cone, *God of the Oppressed* (Maryknoll, NY: Orbis Books, 1997), p. 242.
88 hooks, *Teaching to Transgress*, p. 143.
89 Jennings, *After Whiteness*, pp. 99–100.
90 Hong, *Decolonial Futures*, p. 45.
91 Mignolo, 'Epistemic Disobedience', 176–7.
92 Linda Tuhiwai Smith, *Decolonizing Methodologies: Research and Indigenous Peoples* (London: Zed Books, 1999), p. 25.
93 Marcella Althaus-Reid, *Indecent Theology: Theological Perversions in Sex, Gender and Politics* (London: Routledge, 2000), p. 136.
94 Melissa D. Browning, 'Listening to Musa Dube's Postcolonial Feminist Theology', *Journal of Race, Ethnicity, and Religion* 2:11 (2011): 1–27, 5.
95 Musa W. Dube, 'Rahab is Hanging Out a Red Ribbon: One African Woman's Perspective on the Future of Feminist New Testament Scholarship', in K. O. Wicker, A. S. Miller and M. W. Dube (eds), *Feminist New Testament Studies: Religion/Culture/Critique* (New York: Palgrave Macmillan, 2005), pp. 177–202.
96 Shenila Khoja-Moolji, 'Pedagogical (Re)Encounters: Enacting a Decolonial Praxis in Teacher Professional Development in Pakistan', *Comparative Education Review* 61:S1 (2017): 146–70, 153.
97 See Mercy Amba Oduyoye, *Hearing and Knowing: Theological Reflections on Christianity in Africa* (Eugene, OR: Wipf & Stock, 1986).
98 Reddie, 'Reassessing the Inculcation', 4.
99 V. Andreotti, S. Stein, C. Ahenakew and D. Hunt, 'Mapping Interpretations of Decolonization in the Context of Higher Education', *Decolonization: Indigeneity, Education and Society* 4:1(2015): 21–40, 27.
100 Mercy Amba Oduyoye, 'The African Experience of God through the Eyes of an Akan Woman', *CrossCurrents* 47:4 (1997/1998): 493–504, 499.
101 James Cone, *For My People: Black Theology and the Black Church* (Maryknoll, NY: Orbis Books, 1984), p. 96.

6

Towards a Pedagogy of Trust

People are dialogue, I say,
if not their words would touch nothing.
Ernesto Cardenal[1]

I am because we are, we are because I am ...[2]

Why must it take the body of a dead black man on the streets of Minneapolis in the USA, or the murdered body of a woman, buried in the woods at the hands of a police officer, to make us realize that there are issues of power, trust, racism, misogyny and inequality in police institutions around the world? Why must it take the uncovering of the bodies of dead children under Catholic mission schools, or the rise of abuse cases in the Church of England and other denominations, to make us realize that there are issues of power, trust, violence, spiritual abuse, colonialism and inequality in our Church institutions? Why must it take starving children in Ethiopia, sinking nations in the Pacific, deforestation, the melting of icebergs to make us realize that there are issues of power, trust, greed, capitalism, climate injustice and inequality in our neo-liberal global economic systems? Why must it take foodbanks, homelessness, lack of funding for healthcare, geographical disparities and a staggering divide between the rich and poor to make us realize that the ruling classes are not on our side? The very structures, systems and institutions that we have been told to put our trust in have failed us, and have failed those most commonly on the margins, and yet many of us continue to show such systems deference. It should not take the murdered bodies of women and black men and abused children to make us realize that there are significant problems with trust and power in society and the establishments that rule. If the voices of the marginalized are not being heard in these institutions of power then why should we put our trust in these institutions? Why should they maintain power if they cannot be trusted? Why is it that deference is expected by the ruling classes and the ruling establishments when they have failed to put trust in the narratives and struggles of those they have marginalized and oppressed? Such global imbalances of power and trust bring about significant questions for theological education and formation today, because theological education has been complicit in validating systems of injustices` and perpetuating the conditions of coloniality, inequality and domination.

Education offers a means by which we can address such questions of power and trust, particularly when pedagogy aims to create environments that are humanizing and engaged with the social and political realities of the world. For Paulo Freire, for education to enable liberation from systems of oppression and cultures of impunity, a pedagogy shaped by dialogue is critical because it enables the conscious awakening of both the educator and students. Critical consciousness is a 'means of freeing people from the bondage of the culture of silence, and the dialogue between teachers and students is the way of promoting their critical consciousness'.[3] In pursuit of an alternative theological education, dialogue will be vital; a dialoguing that enables hope in the midst of struggle. However, in agreement with Roberto Goizueta, 'before there can be a genuine dialogue or conversation among different social groups (racial, cultural, gender, class, etc.), these must be recognized as equal partners in the dialogue.'[4] The power dynamics of dialogue in education will therefore need to be exposed, because theological formation through dialogue is dangerous if those with power have the ability to silence, shame and oppress the theological truth claims of their partners in dialogue. This requires addressing the neo-liberal paradigm that has mastered control of academic spaces of learning and the embedded individualism whereby human relations have been dominated by greed and competition. It is within such a framework that theological formation has often failed to emphasize the interconnected presence of God's kin-dom. The term 'kin-dom' is important to explain here in greater detail because it embodies the lived solidarity that a theological education shaped by hope, justice and transformation must strive for. As a term, it was used by the mujerista ethicist and theologian Ada María Isasi-Díaz in order to challenge the hierarchal and elitist theology of the 'Kingdom'. She writes: 'Kin-dom of God as a metaphor includes the meaning that "kingdom" had for Jesus and his community while neither endorsing nor sustaining the oppressive understandings that have been added to it throughout history.'[5] The kin-dom establishes a true dialogical relationship that is focused on the community not on the individual alone, that rejects 'present oppressive systems and institutions', is praxis focused and encourages liberation, justice and solidarity and embraces diversity.[6] A theological education that embeds the values of the kin-dom encourages a dialogue of mutuality, respect and reciprocity. 'Theological education has the potential to be the seedbed for the renewal of churches, their ministries, mission, and commitment to Christian unity.'[7] It is for this reason that Namsoon Kang called for 'a transformative theological education that seriously takes up and challenges the issues of "power and knowledge"'.[8] This is needed more than ever as the economic injustices and global equalities become even more apparent in the context of a global pandemic. Pedagogy that is shaped by the kin-dom will witness the lived experiences of the marginalized and all people present and affirm the collective experiences of all, thereby enabling the unmasking and interrogating of forces of oppression and the dismantling of structures of inequality. This final chapter will focus on how we can develop such an alternative culture within theological education, where people are equal partners in dialogue shaped by a kin-dom theology where community and the desire for an alternative justice-driven world that resists systems and structures of oppression are central. In this way it educates for hope with a vision of recognition, acceptance, love, trust and respect in the embodied experiences of all those in dialogue.

Embodying the kin-dom in education: an act of interconnected love

When students come to the classroom, all come with their own stories, experiences, politics, religious upbringings, traumas, sexualities, life situations and ways of reading and understanding Scripture and God. None of these realities are left at the door when they enter a space of learning and formation. As theological educators we make a choice as to whether to ignore such personal realities or embrace and celebrate the diversity of being. Teaching theology in a way that celebrates theological and hermeneutical diversity makes the space to allow all voices to be heard and respected. Osvaldo Vena makes this point:

> By upholding diversity we recognize the contextual nature of all truth and the ontological and epistemological value of context. We become aware of the ideology of the dominant culture, which sees itself as universal and tends to view diversity as a problem to be overcome either by negating it or by isolating and bracketing it.[9]

In our diversity, we each have our own stories and identities and these stories are not static but fluid and may be subject to change as we enter into dialogue with others. Yet such dialogue is not without risk, particularly when those who enter the classroom fear the differences of 'others'. It is by acknowledging our interconnectedness that such fear can be overcome and the realities of society can be addressed, noting, as Boaventura de Sousa Santos has described, that:

> We live in a time when the most appalling social injustices and most unjust human suffering no longer seem to generate the moral indignation and the political will necessary both

to combat them effectively and to create a more just and fair society.[10]

An interconnected theological education acknowledges global injustices and prevents the homogenization of theological thought, while enabling the diverse contexts of theology apparent in Christianity around the world to speak truth to power. The role of the educator in enabling such critical engagement is vital in giving students the tools to engage and the space to do so without the fear of consequences. bell hooks has referred to such educators as 'progressive educators':

> Progressive educators discussing issues of imperialism, race, gender, class, and sexuality heightened everyone's awareness of the importance of these concerns (even those individuals who did not agree with our perspective). That awareness has created the conditions for concrete change, even if those conditions are not yet known to everyone.[11]

Such teaching takes courage and vulnerability on behalf of the educator, who risks marginalizing themselves from fellow educators who refuse to acknowledge the struggles of others, the embodied experiences of students and global epistemologies. Parker Palmer captures the courage of transformative and progressive teaching:

> The courage to teach is the courage to keep one's heart open in those very moments when the heart is asked to hold more than it is able so that teacher and students can be woven into the fabric of community that learning and living, require.[12]

Recognition of the embodied experiences of the student is a loving act, as the educator trusts in the lived experiences of the student and the knowledge that the student brings to the classroom:

> Love in the classroom prepares teachers and students to open our minds and hearts. It is the foundation on which every

learning community can be created. Teachers need not fear that practicing love in the classroom will lead to favouritism. Love will always move us away from domination in all its forms. Love will always challenge and change us. This is the heart of the matter.[13]

Education that is built on trust and love requires openness about one's own situated reality, and a conscious reckoning with our own social, political and economic identities, so that we may become conscious of the lens through which we perceive the world around us. For those of us in the West, this question brings about a confessional reckoning with narratives of power, privilege and persecution. We are forced to acknowledge that we speak in a context of complex power relations that demand an understanding of history, place and society, where we are met with the realities of the atrocities of empire, racism and xenophobia. This requires asking critical questions about the mission of the Church, while acknowledging that our missional history has been rooted in the complexities of the legacies of war, slavery and occupation. It requires acknowledging the context of today, one of global inequality where we are capable of drowning out the cries of the poor, the plight of the refugees and those who suffer the most from climate change. This has become increasingly necessary as we educate in the context of a global pandemic where the struggles of the students become even more relevant to their learning experience. While the global pandemic has put a spotlight on the viciousness of capitalist greed, made apparent in the global vaccine warfare, and exacerbated existing inequalities, it has also brought to light existing barriers to belonging in education. Students with disabilities and those with existing health concerns have become more vulnerable in physical classrooms; the digital divide has also left many without access to the internet and left behind those who lack knowledge of digital technologies. There is a need to recognize that we are part of an interconnected struggle; and in the midst of a global pandemic, such struggles have become increasingly relevant. The failure to be in solidarity with those who have been most affected leads to an education that focuses on individualism. According to Emile Durkheim: 'The lack of solidarity and integration in modern society springs from an excessive individualism – from what he termed "egoism" and "anomie" which arise when private interests and greeds burst forth beyond social regulation and group control.'[14] Taking a decolonial turn in theological education will challenge such individualism because 'decolonising pedagogy centred on multiplicity is one that accepts the "cacophony of voices" ... what it centres are identities defined in their own terms, an otherness premised on political, ideological, epistemological multiplicity.'[15] Decolonialization is therefore an act of the kin-dom on earth being brought into realization.

A lived theology of the kin-dom is shaped by such multiplicity, where the diversity of God's people is realized and embraced, where the love of neighbour is embodied through the act of solidarity because 'solidarity is the creation of a community united in the work of positively transforming the world, better understood as "the unfolding of the kin-dom of God".' This becomes apparent in Isasi-Díaz's understanding of the kindom, where she argues that we must live and work to embody 'a being with others' where:

> solidarity entails a conscious moral and political decision *by the oppressors* to identify with the poor and oppressed in liberating praxis in order to transform the structures that perpetuate poverty and oppression, and by *the oppressed* to become moral agents in their own historical process of liberation (in great part by speaking truth to power).[16]

A pedagogy rooted in the values of the kin-dom of God is revealed in human relations with one another and the world around us, where education is committed to living in love of such relations and therefore a commitment to the liberation of the oppressed. The implications of such lived solidarity for theological education is pedagogy that develops:

as a conversation across lines of class, ethnicity, and gender, resulting in a raised awareness (conscientization) of (1) the factors that contribute to oppression, (2) each party's involvement in perpetuating oppressive structures, and (3) the need for joint action in order to liberate both the oppressor and the oppressed.[17]

This is a theological education of hope and kinship where, to quote Ana Maria Araújo Freire, 'Hope is a revolutionary transformer, either through knowledge or through radical ethics, but it loses strength, brilliance, and political clarity without fraternal love.'[18] The notion of fraternal love resonates with a pedagogy of solidarity. Such love demands a fraternal honesty where we are willing and able to challenge those with whom we are in communion about the powers and privileges they hold. It also requires offering one another support in the struggle for liberation, noting that in the fight to bring about God's kin-dom of justice, the injustices of the world can be so overwhelming that as individuals we can feel helpless. It is for this reason that solidarity is so vital in the call for transformation, and why education can be the tool through which those involved in the struggle can 'get organized' and offer the means through which our interconnected hope for transformation can be realized.

This means calling on theological education institutes in the West to address the form of Christianity that has at times been used throughout the history of the Church to deny the 'Jesus of history', the Jesus who, as Anthony Reddie argues, 'comes to us as the radical ethnic other living as he did as a Galilean Jew'.[19] In doing so, theological education would offer a challenge to the aspects of history and the contemporary Church and her mission by which Jesus 'becomes a symbolic Englishman who reaffirms empire, colonialism and British superiority'.[20] This is how white supremacy operates in theological education and why an interconnected theological education requires a decolonizing of theology and missiology. Students must be freed from the homogenous theologies of the ruling elites in order to encounter and contemplate Christ as the radical rebel who engages in the lived struggles of the oppressed. An interconnected theological education would give focus to the curriculum as a tool of liberation, noting that the curriculum provides bodies of knowledge to students with the intention of equipping them to help bring about God's kin-dom on earth. If voices of the kin-dom are missing from the curriculum, the student is being equipped to fail. An interconnected theological education therefore addresses such silencing of voices and the history of colonialism while acknowledging embedded colonial norms where whiteness and patriarchy continue to oppress the colonialized. Such a theological education then challenges cultures of dehumanization by giving focus to the indigenous theology and theologies of liberation born out of struggles and resistance. Producing a theological education that challenges notions of mission imposed from a position of privilege, power and possession would enable a systematic means by which injustices could be addressed and the means by which the struggle for change could be greater realized. It also demands of those of in the West the need to understand that, in being interconnected with our global sisters and brothers, we must confess to our sins and theologically apologize for the atrocities of empire and the ways in which the sins of our imperial past continue to impact the colonialized. This requires an apology, a lived apology, because an apology is an acknowledgement of responsibility; it is praxis, because it is an act of self-reflection and the intention and promise to change, to cease to be oppressive. How are the oppressed to trust in an education that justified their oppression throughout history if there has been no apology? A liberal theological education that adds seats to tables and does additional anti-racist training will therefore not be enough. As Frederick Herzog says:

> Liberal theology needs to make way for liberated theology, a theology in which the initiative and power of God's liberation unite the theologian more fully with the lot of the disadvantaged. Liberated theology will probably find that its first reward in engaging society is conflict and not applause.[21]

A liberated theological education will no doubt lead to conflict with those who have maintained the power. However, in hopeful agreement with bell hooks: 'Through the cultivation of awareness, through the decolonization of our minds, we have the tools to break the dominator model of human social engagement and the will to imagine new and different ways that people might come together.'[22] A theological education that can be trusted in its repentance for the sins of racism, xenophobia and misogyny is one that lives out an apology as transformative pedagogy that educates for the liberation of the oppressed.

Deconstructing 'trustworthiness' in dialogue

Contemplating the role of trust in dialogue is complex, because trust is relational and often impacted by social constructs of power and vulnerability. According to Trudy Govier, 'Trust is an attitude based on beliefs and expectation about what others are likely to do … When we trust we are vulnerable but we accept our vulnerability.'[23] Determining who we trust can be dependent upon who we deem to be most like ourselves, which can be influenced by social categories such as ethnicity, religion and class status. This is a type of trust that creates moral communities based upon who individuals or groups assume to be most like themselves.[24] For example, in the case of religious groups, religious leaders are often accepted as 'bearers and interpreters of true knowledge and therefore granted significant authority, which is undermined by sovereign power'.[25] Trust can also be assumed and determined by dominant hegemonies; for example, in most religions, men are deemed more trustworthy than women. Within Christianity, women have been informed by the Church fathers, inclusive of Tertullian, that we are 'the gate of hell … the temptress of the forbidden tree … the first deserter of the divine law … the devil's doorway'.[26] Biblical imagery depicting women as whores, sinners and temptresses has been used to deem women untrustworthy sinners and therefore not worthy of authority. Therefore in contrast to trust is distrust:

> When we distrust, we fear that others may act in ways that are immoral or harmful to us; we are vulnerable to them and take the risk seriously; we do not see them as well-motivated persons of integrity, and we interpret their further actions and statements consistently with these negative expectations.[27]

Distrust is often associated with difference and has been used as a mechanism for racial stereotyping in order to justify discrimination and xenophobia.[28] This is apparent in Sandra Smith's sociological study of race and trust, which finds that the social construct of 'race is the most important determinant of trust'.[29] Distrust is often granted to opinions that risk dismantling the dominant belief system or ideology, and therefore may act as a challenge to cultures and systems that are oppressive to the views and beliefs of the minority.

A recent study into the experience of Muslim students in higher education institutes in the UK, for example, found that British Muslim students there have experienced racism that has been 'reinforced by a narrative of suspicion, rooted in a presumed alignment between Islam and violent extremism'. Consequently, Muslim students reportedly felt that they were subjected to 'heightened surveillance that presumes them to be suspicious on account of their faith'.[30] Social and political prejudices have a significant impact on lived experiences of trustworthiness and therefore impact one's sense of belonging and self-worth. Stereotypes are often used as a means of reinforcing such prejudices and to 'monitor' the behaviour of minority and oppressed groups. As Mathew Guest notes, this is made visible by the interventions of existing power structures, inclusive of government and university management, 'that reinforce a general perception that freedom of speech and freedom of religion are being infringed', particularly for Muslims in higher education.[31] In bell hooks' work on *Teaching to Transgress*, she notes that:

Any attempt on the part of the individual students to critique the bourgeois biases that shape pedagogical process, particularly as they relate to epistemological perspectives (the points from which information is shared) will, in most cases, no doubt be viewed as negative and disruptive.[32]

Trustworthiness of epistemologies is therefore maintained through the censorship of opinions and dialogue. It is impacted by gender, ethnicity, sexuality, class and caste. This is visible in the way in which white, male and middle/upper-class Christianity dominates in many spheres of dialoguing, and has been normalized as a result of colonialism. Trust in knowledge must therefore be understood in relation to power, because as we discern what truths we believe and disbelieve, our insights are shaped by certain contexts, languages and epistemologies. It is the power-holders who determine the way in which truths or knowledges are taught, discerned and accepted, and they 'assume that their self-interests speak for God'.[33]

Those in dialogue must trust others and in doing so be respectful and loving and willing to be challenged by new knowledge. Yet in order to have trust in dialogue, spaces of dialogue must address existing power imbalances so as to prevent what Marianne Moyaert has referred to as 'testimonial injustice'. She notes that 'Testimonial injustice is about not accrediting the appropriate credibility to someone's testimonial activity, not because the speaker has nothing meaningful to say or contribute to the conversation but because she is simply not recognized as a credible source of knowledge.'[34] The centrality of trust in contexts of testimony and authority is vital in situating unequal power dynamics, because integrity has been assumed and granted to white, male and middle/upper-class people as a consequence of the dominance of colonialism that has sought to control knowledge and world views. This has come at the expense of the faith truths, beliefs and perspectives offered by women, people of colour, indigenous communities and the working class, whose testimonies have often been ignored or marginalized by the dominant discourses that have been deemed more trustworthy as a consequence of the way in which imperialism has enabled knowledge and religion to be constructed and controlled. Further, critique must therefore be applied to the hegemony of knowledge and to the political and religious framework of trust that has been used to maintain such knowledge through imposed norms.

Difficulties in dialoguing often arise as a consequence of exclusivist truth claims that can lead to prejudice, intolerance and ultimately violence. Trusting the person(s) we are in dialogue with also requires trusting truth claims that will be different from our own. It requires the dismantling of oppressive power dynamics, which are often determined by race, caste, class, gender and sexuality. For Paulo Freire, in order to achieve liberative dialogue those involved must be 'ideologically committed to equality, to the abolition of privilege'.[35] Freire talks of the need to be cautious of the ruling oppressive class when they are inclined to join the struggle for liberation, noting that they:

> always bring with them the marks of their origin: their prejudices and their deformations, which include a lack of confidence in the people's ability to think, to want, and to know ... They talk about the people, but they do not trust them; and trusting the people is the indispensable precondition for revolutionary change.[36]

Such trust is consciously reserved for the dominant groups who do not want revolutionary change because change would impact their own position and privileges. This is how colonialism operates. It divides nations and peoples into trustworthy and untrustworthy, deserving and undeserving, worthy and unworthy; and religion plays an important role in maintaining this status quo when it is used as an instrument against the oppressed people. Education involves self-criticism and the need to interrogate our own assumptions, especially when we are in positions of privilege.

Dialogue as kin-dom pedagogy

> True dialogue cannot exist unless the dialoguers engage in critical thinking – thinking which discerns an indivisible solidarity between the world and the people and admits of no dichotomy between them – thinking which perceives reality as process, as transformation, rather than as a static entity – thinking which does not separate itself from action, but constantly immerses itself in temporality without fear of the risks involved.[37]

When we enter into dialogue, we must ask of ourselves the question, 'Where do we speak from?'[38] For those of us who speak from positions of privilege, it requires being conscious of such privileges and challenging the cultures of impunity that enable these privileges to oppress. It demands of us the need to reflect critically on our own religious identity and traditions in order to enable an engaged and transformative dialogue that focuses on the needs of the oppressed. In doing so, our trust is placed in the truths and experiences of those who have been marginalized. The power dynamics of dialogue and learning can reinforce oppressive values and beliefs such as racism, sexism, homophobia, religious marginalization and classism. This is particularly the case when dialoguing takes place in a context or manner in which the power dynamics are not equal, which can lead to exacerbated intolerance and further injustice and oppression. This is most visible when taking into consideration the marginalization of minority faith perspectives, women, people of colour, LGBTQI+ voices and the role that colonialism plays in constructing and shaping norms that ultimately determine whose truth claim is of more value. Even when dialoguing takes place among people of the same faith, people do not all 'share the same hope or speak the same language'.[39] The hope and language of the oppressor differ greatly from those of the oppressed, and prejudices can dominate discourse, leading to the marginalization of the beliefs and experiences of already subjugated communities. Trustworthiness is often determined by implicitly held attitudes towards the 'other', and this impacts dialogue and pedagogy as well as the ways we attain and comprehend knowledge and truth. Our implicitly and explicitly held beliefs regarding trustworthiness have been impacted by accepted norms that have been strongly influenced by dominant powers. These in turn have created trustworthiness in their image. The most obvious example of this is the pervasive depiction of the Christian God as a white man, which, as the psychologist Steven O. Roberts notes, 'has important consequences for who we think should and should not be in charge'.[40] Christians are told of the importance of putting our trust in God; if such dominant imagery and ideology is left unchallenged, is it any wonder why so much trust has been put in the hands of white men at the expense of all others?

A dialoguing that does not address such issues can lead to the internalization of imposed norms, in which people are socialized to accept dominant structures of authority and belief, and may ultimately result in self-loathing, fear, spiritual subjugation and silencing. Dialogue therefore not only serves to liberate the oppressed but also the oppressor, in that dialogue may enable consciousness in their oppressive stance. According to Nilan Yu, 'For the disadvantaged, an important step toward empowerment and liberation is achievement of critical consciousness: the recognition of inequality and oppression that shape their lived experience.'[41] The individual who is oppressed has to trust in their own embodied experience in order to resist the imposed oppression. This requires a learning process in which all parties must be vulnerable in order to enable their own bodily experiences and socio-political positioning to be exposed as a means of uncovering and challenging the power dynamics present. Such a dialoguing would challenge oppressive structures of cultural exchange and dominance. By 'founding itself upon love, humility, and faith, dialogue becomes a horizontal relationship of which mutual trust between the dialogues is the logical consequence'.[42] As bell hooks states:

To engage in dialogue is one of the simplest ways we can begin as teachers, scholars, and critical thinkers to cross boundaries, the barriers that may or may not be erected by race, class, professional standing, and a host of other differences.[43]

A pedagogy that educates for freedom in the light of the kin-dom engages in dialogue and values student knowledge and experience, enriches and enables critique, encourages a reciprocal teacher-student relationship and participates in reflection and praxis.

Trust is a central component of honest and transformative dialogue; when people enter into dialogue with one another they are humanized and transformed in the process, because they encounter other women and men, and in so doing they come to discover more about themselves. As Freire remarks, 'Dialogue is thus an essential necessity ... and requires an intense faith in humankind, faith in their power to make and remake, to create and re-create, faith in their vocation to be more fully human.'[44] Dialogue in pedagogy gives value to the embodied experiences of the student, their social location and their complex subjectivity. Through dialogue we become more aware of our own being and self, especially when the purpose and intention of dialogue is to gain new knowledge and engage critically, openly and truthfully. Dialogical pedagogy is a 'form of communication between teachers and students, or between students themselves, through which experiences, understanding and attitudes about the curriculum content are exchanged'.[45] Dialogue is also vital when students read texts, because they must be able to engage critically and dialogically with the reading resources made available to them, not simply memorize or repeat material but rather reflect and engage for the sake of self-enhancement. However, in educating for the kin-dom on earth such self-enhancement cannot be disconnected from the struggles of the impoverished and marginalized. A pedagogy that focuses on liberation in the light of the kin-dom is therefore dialogue as dialectical relationship that involves self and social transformation. It is therefore educating for God's kindom on earth, where, to quote Peter McLaren:

> Being critically conscious is not a precondition for social justice action but critical consciousness is an outcome of acting justly. We act in and on the world and then reflect on our actions in an attempt to effect a deeper, more critical change in our society. We make society, as society makes us. What takes priority in all of this is ethics – the purpose of creating a more just society absent of needless suffering.[46]

Entering the storm with Jesus – emotion in pedagogy

In Mark 6.45–56 we hear of how the disciples found themselves stuck in a boat in the middle of the lake struggling against the wind and waves (6.48). This passage has often been used to highlight the importance of faith in Jesus and the miraculous act of Jesus walking on water (6.49), but are we perhaps neglecting to consider the personal storm of Jesus – which appears to be a significant aspect of this text and offers us an insight into the role of emotion in pedagogy? According to Dean Deppe, 'even though one section is dominated by miracles and the other with teaching on discipleship, in reality Mark employs the three sea journeys for didactic purposes.'[47] While the story narrates the miraculous act of Jesus, it also exposes the emotions and struggles of both Jesus and the disciples and the role of hope, solidarity, trust and dialogue in the midst of such struggle. By the time Jesus walks on water, the disciples already know of Jesus' miraculous capabilities – they have just witnessed him feeding thousands of people having started out with just five loaves and two fish. They have also witnessed him heal the blind, the paralysed and those unable to speak, and by this point he has already commanded storms to respond to his voice. But we also know that Jesus has just recently been informed about the brutal murder of John the Baptist, who was arrested, imprisoned and violently beheaded and whose head was served on a platter (6.14–29). Yet what we do not know is how Jesus felt: did he cry and if so how, did he grieve, what was his response to the loss of a loved one?

Matthew 14.13 tells us that on hearing the news of John Jesus withdrew on a boat to a deserted place by himself – but before he could simply be alone the crowds heard he was there and followed, so he never got the chance to grieve. Emotions are often portrayed as feminine, particularly in Greco-Roman texts. Philo, for example, argued for the mastery of passions as an act of masculinity.[48] Susanna Asikainen comments that for Agamemnon, 'crying is acceptable for men of lower classes, whose masculinity is marginalized, but not for hegemonically masculine, elite men.' She also remarks on how, for Seneca, 'being consumed by sorrow is womanish (muliebre)'.[49] Yet in Mark's Gospel in particular, Jesus seems to challenge such portrayals of masculinity. He is described as showing anger in Mark 1.41 and in Mark 3.5; in Gethsemane, 'He took with him Peter and James and John, and began to be distressed and agitated' (Mark 14.33); and in Mark 3.5, 'He looked around at them with anger; he was grieved at their hardness of heart and said to the man ...' Such emotions show the humanity of Jesus and the centrality of emotion in his teaching and dialogue, where he also appears to challenge hegemonic masculinity 'since control over emotions was an important ideal for masculinity'.[50] Noting that masculinity is socially constructed and influenced by culture, colonialism, economy, religion and politics, this has had significant consequences for how men believe they must act toward one another and towards women. The Church and dominant discourses of theology have often promoted toxic constructs of masculinity, where men dominate and where women are portrayed as irrational and overly emotional. Lovemore Togarasei highlights the ways in which Jesus often challenges hegemonic masculinity in his associations with women, commenting:

> Jesus also broke many cultural taboos concerning women that would lead his contemporaries to consider him unmanly. He

forgave a woman who was a sinner (Luke 7.36–50) allowing her to touch and kiss him. He also allowed a haemorrhaging woman to touch him (Luke 8.43–48). Against cultural taboos that forbade men from speaking to women in public … He accepted women as disciples (Luke 8.3) and allowed Mary to sit at the position of a student as he allowed her the choice of intellectual and spiritual development (10.39). Jesus' breaking of these taboos shows that his manhood was not defined simply by culture and tradition but transcended these.[51]

The emotions of Jesus and the disciples offer important insights into transformative learning, because emotion in learning enables a deeper and more profound learning to occur for both the students and the educator. Emotions, inclusive of anger, guilt and sadness, are valid ways of knowing because 'it is within the intrapersonal where emotions and feelings are experienced which can then move into empathic connections at the interpersonal level.'[52] Emotions therefore play a significant role in transformative pedagogy. As bell hooks has commented, 'emotional awareness can serve as a force to bind us together in community and enable us to transcend difference', and 'enable us to be bound together in heavenly solidarity'.[53] In Mark 6.45–46 the emotions of Jesus are seemingly apparent in his actions and appearance: after Jesus had sought solitude and prayed, he walked out into the lake where the disciples were in a boat battling the wind and waves, but when they saw him they thought he was a ghost. This gives the reader an insight into how Jesus looked at this moment in time to the disciples, as ghosts 'are described as being as pale as death or as black as ash, having the image of their mortal body either in life or often at the time of their gruesome death'.[54] It suggests an image of Jesus grieving and therefore a solemn figure alone in the water. The disciples react in fear, again revealing emotion; in Greco-Roman tradition, ghosts 'that appeared at night were typically the haunting sort, the kind that would inspire fear – a common motif in ancient ghost stories'.[55] Yet in Greco-Roman mythology ghosts could not walk on water, as water was considered a barrier to ghosts. The text therefore reveals Jesus crossing the boundaries of the living and the dead; he also crosses the boundaries of normalized structures of power and tradition: he displays his divinity in his ability to walk on water and his humanity in his grief, and as an educator he also situates himself in the struggles of his disciples.

'Then he got into the boat with them and the wind ceased. And they were utterly astounded, for they did not understand about the loaves, but their hearts were hardened' (Mark 6.51–52). Jesus displays a love of his students and a willingness to challenge them on their inability to open their hearts and think critically to become conscious of the world around them. The hardening of hearts also suggests that Jesus is challenging the disciples for their repressed emotions; according to Mark Hathaway, 'While blocked or repressed emotions impede our ability to respond, experiencing and refocusing emotions may serve as a source of energy to bring about change.'[56] For Freire, critical dialogue 'founds itself upon love, humility, and faith, where dialogue becomes a horizontal relationship of which mutual trust between the dialoguers is the logical consequence'.[57] There is a tendency within dominant discourses of theological education in the West to 'harden hearts' in relation to diverse theologies and ways of knowing and experiencing God, particularly when those ways of knowing are not deemed credible by Western epistemology and rationality. Marcella Althaus-Reid notes, 'we find quasi-anthropological compulsion of the West for classifying a theory of understanding of God as theology into neat, closed compartments or systems'.[58] The teaching methods of Jesus often bring about discomfort as he challenges the dominant ways of knowing through storytelling, action and questioning. His teaching is always embodied and allows for 'unsettling emotions to surface in the learning encounter', where those present in Scripture as well as readers of Scripture are able to learn in ways that enable us to imagine new possibilities. As Maxine Greene comments, 'imagining things being otherwise may be a first step toward acting on the belief that they can be changed.'[59] It is through our emotions that we critically engage in theological dialogue for the sake of learning, because 'we can learn from our shame, our anger, happiness, if we allow ourselves to hear what they are saying, to explore where they come from and where they lead.'[60] A pedagogy that enables the space for emotional dialogue is transformative because we can learn from our emotions and grow together.

Teaching theology is an emotional experience that requires encountering unexpected storms and struggles and stepping into the unknown in order to face the waves of the contexts in which we find ourselves. The motif apparent in the text is the willingness of Jesus to meet the students in their own context and enable them to wrestle with the unknown, despite being in the midst of his own personal struggles. Jesus makes himself vulnerable in the process. It is by learning from emotion that we can better engage in conversation with others and ourselves. To quote Hannah Arendt: 'I am both the one who asks and the one who answers ... [where] thinking thus become dialectical and critical as we engage in questioning and answering.'[61] Authentic dialogue in learning requires taking a risk, in that trust is necessary when the educator and learner enter the context of the other and expose their vulnerabilities in the process. It is through engaging in the struggles of those we are in dialogue with that the hearts of the educator and learner will cease to be hardened.

Trust in the struggle for a pedagogy of solidarity

> What are the words you do not have yet? What do you need to say? What are the tyrannies you swallow day by day and attempt to make your own, until you will sicken and die of them, still in silence? We have been socialized to respect fear more than our own need for language.[62]

Allan Aubrey Boesak argues that:

> Christians in the struggle see social justice as the 'essential truth of the struggle' ... Christians choose to join the struggle because they join God in God's struggle for justice and dignity, for the humanization of the world. It is embracing the restlessness that longs for a different world, a new humanity, recreated tomorrow.[63]

To join in the struggle is to be in solidarity, a solidarity that allows the space for both commonalities and differences and enables dialogue and discussions across social divides. Solidarity involves acknowledging our responsibilities to others, while being conscious of the well-being of those who struggle and making the space to honour their experiences, voices and knowledge. Solidarity in education therefore affirms the voices of those in the classroom, particularly those who have been marginalized by dominant power dynamics, in order to enable students to become more fully themselves. Vijay Prashad remarks on how 'The most profound bonds are built in the heat of the struggle, especially when one demonstrates to the collective that one is prepared to share the burden of others' misery.'[64] For the educator to be in solidarity with the students they must be willing to witness the invisible power dynamics and enable the student to be free to challenge perspectives inclusive of those held by the educator. This means being deliberately inclusive in the classroom, which may demand of the educator the need to teach outside their own comfort zone while promoting student engagement and belonging and being in solidarity with those students who have experienced the oppression of marginalization.

Struggle and solidarity are central to theologies of liberation. James Cone, for example, notes that he begins and ends his 'theological reflection in the social context of black people's struggle for justice'.[65] He argues that in Christ's struggle on the cross, God's salvation as liberation is revealed and realized in the lives of 'all who are struggling for survival and dignity in a world bent on denying their humanity'.[66] It is in putting trust in the struggles of the oppressed and seeking solidarity that education can be the site for the disruption of oppression and help to bring about liberation. The womanist theologian Shawn Copeland highlights the role of the cross in bringing about solidarity in the struggles of resistance:

> The enslaved Africans sang because they saw on the rugged wooden planks One who had endured what was their daily portion. The cross was treasured because it enthroned the One who went all the way with them and for them. The enslaved African sang because they saw the results of the cross – triumph over the principalities and powers of death, triumph over evil in this world.[67]

A pedagogy that is shaped by the solidarity and the struggles of the cross seeks to alleviate the suffering of others, even when this means sacrificing personal powers because 'Sacrifice is a necessary part of struggle, but so too is fellowship.'[68] It takes courage to unlearn dominant epistemologies that have silenced epistemologies from the majority world, the working class, women, queer bodies and disabled bodies. It also takes courage, trust and faith to teach in ways that privilege the voices of the oppressed and to enter into critical dialogue. In the words of Freire:

> It is not easy to have faith. Above all, it is not easy due to the demands faith places on whoever experiences it. It demands a stand for freedom, which implies respect for the freedom of others, in an ethical sense, in the sense of humility, coherence, and tolerance.[69]

Prashad states that 'To struggle against prejudices and foes is the best crucible to create the trust and love necessary for the production of solidarity.'[70] The intersectional struggles that we encounter in the classroom, inclusive of classism, sexism, racism and ableism, call on the educator to display a praxis of love because 'To craft solidarity is to negotiate across historically produced divides to combat congealed centers of power that benefit from political disunity.'[71] Therefore, in agreement with Prashad, 'The effort to build solidarity must be directed not just to education but to the entire array of things called struggle.'[72] To build solidarity we must be willing to listen, because to listen is to enter into trusting dialogue. Listening to stories of struggle and embodied journeys of faith enables theological education not only to focus on the kingdom to come, but to start with where the world is at, to understand the world around us in order to change it, and to work towards the kin-dom in the here and now. Ira Shor makes the case that 'The teacher needs to model an active, skeptical learner in the classroom who invites students to be curious and critical and creative.'[73] The teacher that educates for the sake of the kin-dom works to know their students and encourages students to study themselves as well as literature and the world around them. Knowledge is then remade in the classroom as the student engages through critical inquiry.

The challenge of a pedagogy of solidarity shaped by struggle is also to encourage the students to resist the systems and structures of power and temptation that prevent prophetic voices of resistance within the Church and society. In speaking out against the temptation of power, Saul Alinsky uses the example of:

> the priest who wants to be a bishop and bootlicks and politicks his way up, justifying it with the rationale, 'After I get to be bishop I'll use my office for Christian reformation' ... Unfortunately, one changes in many ways on the road to the bishopric ... and then one says, 'I'll wait until I'm a cardinal and then I can be more effective' ... and so it goes on.[74]

For Alinsky, this is 'where men speak of moral principles but act on power principles'; these are not the people who are willing to leave everything to walk in the path of Christ (Luke 5.11). The challenge will be to organize the voices and cast out the nets into the institutes that develop the next generations of religious leaders, in order to call on students in theological education to be engaged in the lives of the poor, inclusive of contexts of community activism and social movements of liberation. As Joe Kincheloe says:

> Students need to move beyond simply knowing about critical, multicultural practice. They must also move toward an embodied and corporeal understanding of such practice and an effective investment in such practice at the level of everyday life such that they are able to deflect the invasive power of capital ... and put ideology-critique at its center of gravity.[75]

In acknowledging our interconnectedness as human beings today, we are called on to be in solidarity with those to whom we are connected and who struggle. Our theological education must then enable the space for communal protest and activism in order to be in true solidarity with such struggle and work towards transformation. It must be radical if it is to be prophetic; it must not be afraid to confront, to listen and to see the world unveiled.

> Everything which is a source of solidarity is moral, everything which forces man to take account of other men is moral, everything which forces him to regulate his conduct through something other than the striving of his ego is moral, and morality is as solid as these ties are numerous and strong.[76]

As teaching in solidarity requires a theology shaped by dialogue, this is not a dialoguing of religious elites in a room, but one of solidarity that promotes an understanding of self and others. Such a dialoguing requires an acknowledgment of the Church's embedded 'whiteness' and its role in empire, and demands an interrogation of our theological learning processes and pedagogies that are too often dominated by Eurocentrism. Theological education, as with mission, has the potential to dehumanize if it is not rooted in lived experience and the struggles of the marginalized. Then it must help in the process of understanding and experiencing the interconnections of these different realities and experiences. A pedagogy of solidarity in theological education would enable space for the messy and complex, if it is to be truthful to the lives of the oppressed, born out of the lived experiences of struggle. Such pedagogy is practical because it requires relocating and contemplating God in spaces of oppression, and must therefore be liberative because it demands of us the need to know the suffering of the oppressed and act in the here and now for their brokenness to be transformed. A pedagogy of solidarity cultivates in students the desire to radically transform the world, and not be afraid of getting lost in the uncertainty of what that may mean, so students may enter into the reality of those whose side the Church is called to take, in order to know the truths of their suffering better so that they can help to transform the suppressive system. This also requires unlearning the normative and opening our minds to the unknown.

Love and justice are central to a pedagogy of solidarity, because love demands courage and commitment; it is 'an act of freedom'.[77] The solidarity of Christ on the cross and the hope of the resurrection should be the foundation on which theological education is rooted, because, as Sharon Welch comments, this is 'the hope for the power of solidarity to transform reality, a hope that human identity is found in relation to others, in participation in the formation of a community that transcends us now and after death'.[78] Such hope is founded in the participatory struggle of the cross, that acknowledges not just the promise of life after death, but the need for life before death, a fullness of life for all. It is for this reason that Christianity is a radical faith; its Scriptures speak of resistance and revolution, and its disciples are called on to be countercultural, to use the resources available to them, cast their nets into the unknown, work within the systems in order to change them, and to educate with a transformative message of freedom from earthly empires. Such a faith demands a radical theological education that is rooted in the lived experiences of the oppressed and marginalized, just as Paul's letter to the Christians of Corinth notes:

God chose what is foolish in the world to shame the wise; God chose what is weak in the world to shame the strong; God chose what is low and despised in the world, things that are not, to reduce to nothing things that are, so that no one might boast in the presence of God. (1 Cor. 1.27–29)

The 'foolish', 'weak', 'low' and 'despised' must embrace a potential Kairos moment in theological education and collectively shame the dominant structures of power in order to help bring about a pedagogy of liberation.

Ubuntu as trust in a pedagogy of liberation

'Umuntu ngumuntu ngabantu' (I am because you are, you are because I am)[79]

[T]he politics of solidarity, decency, and integrity has been swallowed whole by the politics of vulgarity. By overwhelming levels of abusive power, craven cowardice, untamed voraciousness, unrepentant racism, shameless bigotry, and unending violence. And it is backed up by an imperialistic, fundamentalist religion that has turned the revolutionary Savior from Galilee into the fascist Butcher of Nazareth.[80]

The African philosophy of Ubuntu places emphasis on 'being human through other people'. Ubuntu is opposite to vengeance, opposite to confrontation, opposite to retribution. Ubuntu 'values life, dignity, compassion, humaneness, harmony and reconciliation'.[81] Ubuntu has been defined as living in the knowledge of our interconnected humanity, as 'affirm[ing] one's humanity by recognizing the humanity of others and, on that basis, establish[ing] humane relations with them'.[82] Togetherness, solidarity, interdependence, social justice, compassion, respect and inclusion encapsulate the philosophy of Ubuntu. John Mbiti describes Ubuntu in a way that captures the extent to which as a philosophy it adheres to the values of the kin-dom, noting that the individual cannot exist alone but as part of a community, 'including ... past generations and his contemporaries ... whatever happens to the whole group happens to the individual. The individual can only say: "I am because we are; and since we are therefore I am".'[83] In the search for a pedagogy of liberation, the philosophy of Ubuntu therefore encourages respect, cooperation and dialogue among students and educators. It challenges cultures of impunity that fail to address barriers to belonging for students who have been marginalized, and calls for epistemic disobedience to the Eurocentric epistemology that has fed into the ideology of individualism and greed made apparent in neo-liberal capitalism. It works towards bringing about a better world that gives focus to social justice, inclusion and transformation; it is a philosophy that recognizes the self and others in active participation with one another.

Ubuntu, as with other indigenous knowledge, has been for the most part dismissed in Eurocentric epistemology:

> [D]espite *Ubuntu* philosophy being a significant and a powerful education instrument that has been used for many centuries by indigenous African communities to educate, guide and maintain positive human interactions and relationships among African indigenous people, it has been excluded and oppressed in formal educational arenas in favour of Western philosophies.[84]

Embracing Ubuntu will therefore encourage addressing epistemic injustice in the curriculum and focusing on the realities of injustice and barriers to belonging in theological education, because Ubuntu presents us with a philosophy of radical trust that is rooted in the desire to transform systems that oppose the sacred bonds we hold with one another in our interconnectedness. Ubuntu is therefore the opposite of colonial Christianity and imperialism that sought to separate, divide and conquer through a desire to transform the colonialized. Moyo notes that:

> To engage Ubuntu with an approach of decoloniality is to question the hegemonic understandings rooted in the Eurocentric epistemic perspective that attends to 'universalized' notions of Eurocentric modernity, where institutions and societies are founded on individualistic mental frames and hierarchies, or the hierarchization of human value.[85]

To live and teach by the philosophy of Ubuntu is therefore to embrace the inclusion and respect of all; it decolonizes the mind by acknowledging indigenous ways of knowing. As a pedagogical method, Ubuntu therefore 'has a capacity to promote values of co-existence and social cohesion among students from diverse backgrounds'.[86] To live Ubuntu is to resist oppression by becoming conscious of that which prevents the community from surviving as one, and becoming conscious of the systems of oppression that have forced people into the margins, inclusive of racism, sexism and patriarchy. To grasp the full breadth of these realities means gaining a conscious and deliberate understanding, and making a decision, not only as individuals but as a community, in resistance against the structures of oppression that deny the fullness of life to those we are in community with, 'not only politically but socially; not only psychologically but theologically as well'.[87] Social justice therefore becomes embedded within pedagogy, as Sylvan Blignaut and Oscar Koopman have remarked:

> If teacher educators do not undertake this important task of focusing critically on social justice, their students will run the risk of perpetuating racism, stereotypes, and existing inequalities and thereby reproduce the old prevailing hegemony and the existing social order characterized by inequity and injustice.[88]

Teaching with the values of Ubuntu philosophy unlearns oppressive teaching and learns to listen, appreciate and value the experience of all students, thereby creating cultures of empowerment and affirmation. Students do not compete with one another as individuals in opposition but instead grow together in dialogue as equal partners where trust is vital for formational growth. Ubuntu pedagogy rejects exclusivist teaching and education and therefore challenges colonial, capitalist and patriarchal intersecting forces of oppression that have distrusted indigenous epistemologies and the experiences and voices of the marginalized. This is a pedagogy that challenges dichotomous understandings of good and bad, pure and impure, decent and indecent, and will enable a radical transformation in education, because:

> African moral order never defined rigid frontiers of good and evil. Good and evil exist in the same continuum ... This is a guarantee against any exaggerated sense of moral superiority which goodness by itself may entail. The notion of perfection, therefore, is alien to African thought. Perfection in itself constitutes a temptation to danger, an invitation to arrogance and self-glorification.[89]

Becoming conscious of the dangers of individual greed and the demand for power and domination enables the kin-dom to be witnessed because, as Miguel de la Torre says, 'One can only cringe when witnessing self-proclaimed religious leaders swap their prophetic voice for satisfying porridge at the emperor's banquet table.'[90] We need, then, to work towards a theological education that enables critical thinking, distrust in systems of power, and trust in the struggles of those we are in community with in order to uncover the relations of domination. In agreement with Boesak, 'There is such a thing as a Kairos moment: a God-given moment that calls for discernment, decision, and bold actions of faith.'[91] We are in a potential Kairos moment in theological education today, not just in my own context in the UK, but also in many other parts of the world, where we must take up Boesak's call to discern and act boldly. We must learn to distrust white supremacy theology, unlearn oppressive patriarchal, heteronormative, white, Western theologies that have been normalized, and relearn through a pedagogy of Ubuntu.

Those who possess the power have come to the assumption that they possess all truths and that their truths are the only ones that are trustworthy. A culture of deference has enabled such a system of knowledge and education to continue. Yet the truth is that everyone holds part of the truth. As Freire remarks:

> I believe that those who are weak are those who think they possess the truth and are thus intolerant; those who are strong are those who say: 'Perhaps I have part of the truth, but I don't have the whole truth. You have part of the truth. Let's seek it together.'[92]

A theological education that 'seeks truths' together would be a theological education that is a shaped by a dialogue of mutual respect, where a curriculum is developed that enables multiple truths to be heard. Such a process is vital if theological education is to enable students to flourish and to bring about social transformation. A pedagogy of Ubuntu would enable a relearning that is shaped by an affirmation of our humanness in the humanness of the other. Such pedagogy requires consciousness, as Boesak describes:

> consciousness that my humanity is bound to the humanity of the other, that my humanity is validated by the humanity of the other, that I can only be what I ought to be when the other is what they ought to be.[93]

Such pedagogy in theological education brings about a relearning shaped by solidarity, because solidarity is to negotiate across historically produced divides to combat congealed centres of power that benefit from disunity, and to join in the struggle of the oppressed. To join in the struggle is to be in solidarity, a solidarity that allows space for both commonalities and differences and enables dialogue and discussions across social divides; and 'The most profound bonds are built in the heat of the struggle, especially when one demonstrates to the collective that one is prepared to share the burden of other's misery.'[94] Participating in a pedagogy of liberation shaped by the philosophy of Ubuntu places value on the sharing of the ideas, knowledge, experiences and struggles of one another, and enables the space to understand oneself and others in cooperation and respect, with love and compassion.

Conclusion

> The liberal, then, is one who sees 'both sides' of the issue and shies away from 'extremism' in any form. He wants to change the heart of the racist without ceasing to be his friend; he wants progress without conflict ... He wants change without risk, victory without blood.[95]

Paulo Freire stated that 'without a vision for tomorrow hope is impossible.' The embodied narratives of students feeling marginalized, silenced, oppressed and downtrodden in and through theological education demand of those in theological education to have a vision for change. A theological education that can be trusted by those who have been marginalized by cultures of oppression requires those with power to be prepared to give it up; it necessitates critical engagements with the dominant discourses of theology. As the revolution of the oppressed will not be possible without the people, it can only be achieved with the people, people of all faiths united against the oppressor. A theological education that seeks to transform the world in the light of the kin-dom of God must work towards liberation for the downtrodden and therefore demands that together in solidarity we address the power dynamics, we trust and value each other, we refuse to accept systems and cultures of marginalization, and that, ultimately, we seek to transform the world. As Christine Hong says, 'Lasting communal and personal change does not suddenly occur without effort. For the work of anticolonial teaching and learning and the furthering of intercultural and intelligence, strategy is essential.'[96] Unbinding and exposing oppressive frameworks will take work, because while we have become skilled at deconstructing aspects of education that oppose the values of the kin-dom, the task ahead is to reconstruct in the light of the kin-dom of God.

Notes

1 Ernesto Cardenal, *Cosmic Canticle* (St Paul, MN: Curbstone Press, 1993), p. 27.

2 'I am because we are' embodies the philosophy of Ubuntu, and is a well-known proverb in South Africa that speaks to humanity's interconnectedness and responsibility to one another. See Betty Press, *I am Because We are: African Wisdom in Image and Proverb* (Jackson, MS: University Press of Mississippi, 2013).

3 Yi-Haung Shih, 'Rethinking Paulo Freire's Dialogic Pedagogy and its Implications for Teachers' Training', *Journal of Education and Learning* 7:4 (2018): 230–35, 231.

4 See Roberto S. Goizueta, *Caminemos con Jesús: Toward a Hispanic/ Latino Theology of Accompaniment* (New York: Orbis Books, 1995).

5 Ada María Isasi-Díaz, 'Kin-dom of God: A Mujerista Proposal', in Benjamin Valentin (ed.), *In Our Own Voices: Latino/a Renditions of Theology* (Maryknoll, NY: Orbis, 2010): pp. 171–89, pp. 182–3.

6 Ibid., pp. 178–9.

7 Dietrich Werner et al., 'Introduction', in Dietrich Werner, David Esterline, Namsoon Kang, Joshva Raja (eds), *Handbook of Theological Education in World Christianity: Theological Perspectives, Regional Surveys, Ecumenical Trends* (Oxford: Regnum Books, 2010), p. xxv.

8 Namsoon Kang, 'From Colonial to Postcolonial Theological Education: Envisioning Postcolonial Theological Education, Dilemmas and Possibilities', in Dietrich Werner et al. (eds), *Handbook of Theological Education in World Christianity*, p. 31.

9 See Osvaldo D. Vena, 'My Hermeneutical Journey and Daily Journey into Hermeneutics: Meaning Making and Biblical Interpretation in the North American Diaspora', in Fernando F. Segovia (ed.), *Interpreting Beyond Borders* (Sheffield: Sheffield Academic Press, 2000), p. 104.

10 Boaventura de Sousa Santos, *If God Were a Human Rights Activist* (Stanford, CA: Stanford University Press, 2015), p. xiv.
11 bell hooks, *Teaching Community: A Pedagogy of Hope* (New York: Routledge, 2003), p. 8.
12 Parker Palmer, *The Courage to Teach: Exploring the Inner Landscape of a Teacher's Life* (San Francisco, CA: John Wiley & Sons, 2007), p. 12.
13 hooks, *Teaching Community*, p. 137.
14 Daniel H. Hargreaves, 'A Sociological Critique of Individualism in Education', *British Journal of Educational Studies* 28:3 (1980): 187–98, 190.
15 Carol Azumah Dennis, 'Decolonising Education: A Pedagogic Intervention', in Gurminder K. Bhambra, Dalia Gebrial and Kerem Nişancıoğlu (eds), *Decolonising the University* (London: Pluto Press, 2018), p. 197.
16 Ruben Rosario Rodriguez, *Racism and God-talk: A Latino/a Perspective* (New York: New York University Press, 2008), pp. 224–5. Emphasis original.
17 Ibid., p. 225.
18 Ana Maria Araújo Freire, 'Foreword', in Peter McLaren, *Che Guevara, Paulo Freire, and the Pedagogy of Revolution* (Oxford: Rowman & Littlefield Publishers, 2000), p. xvi.
19 Anthony Reddie, *Theologising Brexit: A Liberationist and Postcolonial Critique* (Abingdon: Routledge, 2019), p. 60.
20 Ibid.
21 See Frederick Herzog, 'Theology of Liberation', in Joerg Rieger (ed.), *Theology from the Belly of the Whale: A Frederick Herzog Reader* (London: Bloomsbury, 1999), p. 89 (first published in *Continuum* 7:4 (Winter 1970)).
22 hooks, *Teaching Community*, p. 35.
23 Trudy Govier, 'Trust, Distrust, and Feminist Theory,' *Hypatia* 7:1 (Winter 1992): 16–33, 17.
24 See Sandra Susan Smith, 'Race and Trust', *Annual Review of Sociology*, 36 (August 2010): 453–75, 463.
25 Steven G. Ogden, *The Church, Authority, and Foucault: Imagining the Church as Open Space of Freedom* (Abingdon: Routledge, 2017), p. 28.
26 Tertullian, *On the Apparel of Women*, pp. 1, 1–2.
27 Govier, 'Trust, Distrust, and Feminist Theory', 17–18.
28 See Nelani Lombaard and Luzelle Naude, 'Breaking the Cycle: Black Adolescents' Experiences of Being Stereotyped during Identity Development', *Journal of Psychology in Africa* 27:2 (2017): 185–90, 185.

29 Sandra Susan Smith, 'Race and Trust', *Annual Review of Sociology* 36 (2010): 453–75, 470.

30 See Mathew Guest, 'The Limits of Inclusivity: Islamophobia in Higher Education', openDemocracy, 14 July 2020, available at: https://www.opendemocracy.net/en/transformation/limits-inclusivity-islamophobia-higher-education/ (accessed 9.2.2022).

31 See Mathew Guest et al., *Islam and Muslims on UK University Campuses: Perceptions and Challenges* (Durham: Durham University; London: SOAS; Coventry: Coventry University; and Lancaster: Lancaster University, 2020), p. 10.

32 bell hooks, *Teaching to Transgress: Education as the Practice of Freedom* (New York: Routledge, 1994), p. 184.

33 Rosemary Radford Ruether, 'Women and Interfaith Relations: Toward a Transnational Feminism', in Catherine Cornille and Jillian Maxey (eds), *Women and Interreligious Dialogue* (Eugene, OR: Cascade Books, 2013), p. 13.

34 Marianne Moyaert, 'Interreligious Hermeneutics, Prejudice, and the Problem of Testimonial Injustice', *Religious Education* 114:5 (2019): 609–23, 616.

35 Paulo Freire, *Pedagogy of Freedom: Ethics, Democracy and Civic Courage* (Lanham, MD: Rowman & Littlefield, 1998), p. x.

36 Paulo Freire, *Pedagogy of the Oppressed* (New York: Continuum, 2000), p. 60.

37 Ibid., p. 64.

38 Moyaert, 'Interreligious Hermeneutics', 612.

39 James Baldwin, *Dark Days* (London: Penguin Books, 1985), p. 38.

40 Melissa De Witte, 'Who people believe rules in heaven influences their beliefs about who rules on earth, Stanford scholars find', *Stanford News*, 31 January 2020, available at: https://news.stanford.edu/2020/01/31/consequences-perceiving-god-white-man/ (accessed 9.2.2022).

41 See Nilan Yu, 'Consciousness-Raising and Critical Practice', in Nilan Yu (ed.), *Consciousness-Raising: Critical Pedagogy and Practice for Social Change* (London: Routledge, 2018), p. 1.

42 Freire, *Pedagogy of the Oppressed*, p. 91.

43 hooks, *Teaching to Transgress*, p. 130.

44 Freire, *Pedagogy of the Oppressed*, p. 62.

45 Vučina Zorić, 'Sokratova dijaloška metoda', *Život i škola* 54:20 (2008): 27–40, 27.

46 Peter McLaren, 'Liberation Theology and Adult Education', *Dialogues in Social Justice: An Adult Education Journal* 6:2 (2021): 3–7, 7.

47 Dean B. Deppe, *The Theological Intentions of Mark's Literary Devices* (Eugene, OR: Wipf & Stock, 2015), p. 138.

48 Susanna Asikainen, *Jesus and Other Men: Ideal Masculinities in the Synoptic Gospels* (Leiden: Brill, 2018), p. 137.
49 Ibid., p. 138.
50 Ibid., p. 153.
51 Lovemore Togarasei, 'Christianity and Hegemonic Masculinities: Transforming Botswana Hegemonic Masculinity Using the Jesus of Luke', *Scriptura* 112 (2013): 9.
52 Jude Walker, 'In Support of Teacher Transformation: Emotions as Pedagogy', *Adult Education Research Conference* (2018): 3.
53 hooks, *Teaching Community*, p. 114.
54 Jason Robert Combs, 'A Ghost on the Water? Understanding an Absurdity in Mark 6:49–50, *Journal of Biblical Literature* 127:2 (2008): 345–58, 352.
55 Ibid.
56 Mark D. Hathaway, 'Activating Hope in the Midst of Crisis: Emotions, Transformative Learning, and "The Work that Reconnects"', *Journal of Transformative Education* 15:4 (2017): 296–314, 297.
57 Freire, *Pedagogy of the Oppressed*, p. 64.
58 Marcella Althaus-Reid, 'Gustavo Gutiérrez Goes to Disneyland: Theme Park Theologies and the Diaspora of the Discourse of the Popular Theologian in Liberation Theology', in Segovia (ed.), *Interpreting Beyond Borders*, p. 45.
59 Maxine Greene, *Releasing the Imagination: Essays on Education, the Arts, and Social Change* (San Francisco, CA: Jossey-Bass, 1995), p. 2.
60 Walker, 'In Support of Teacher Transformation', 6.
61 Hannah Arendt, 'History of Political Theory', in *The Library of Congress, The Hannah Arendt Papers*, 1955. Quoted in Walker, 'In Support of Teacher Transformation', 7.
62 Audre Lorde, *Sister Outsider: Essays and Speeches* (Berkeley, CA: Crossing Press, 1984), p. 41.
63 Allan Aubrey Boesak, *Selfless Revolutionaries: Biko, Black Consciousness, Black Theology, and a Global Ethic of Solidarity and Resistance* (Eugene, OR: Cascade Book, 2021), p. 278.
64 Vijay Prashad, *The Karma of Brown Folk* (Minneapolis, MN: University of Minnesota Press, 2000), p. 198.
65 James H. Cone, *The Cross and the Lynching Tree* (New York: Orbis Books, 2011), p. 151.
66 Ibid.
67 Shawn Copeland, '"Wading through Many Sorrows": Towards a Theology of Suffering in Womanist Perspective', in Emilie M. Townes (ed.), *A Troubling in My Soul: Womanist Perspectives on Evil and Suffering* (Maryknoll, NY: Orbis Books, 1993), pp. 109–29.

68 Prashad, *Karma*, p. 198.
69 Paulo Freire, *Pedagogy of the Heart* (London: Bloomsbury, 2021), p. 58.
70 Prashad, *Karma*, p. 198.
71 Ibid.
72 Ibid.
73 Ira Shor, quoted in Ira Shor and Paulo Freire (eds), *A Pedagogy for Liberation: Dialogues on Transforming Education* (London: Bergin & Garvey, 1987), p. 8.
74 See Saul D. Alinsky, *Rules for Radicals: A Pragmatic Primer for Realistic Radicals* (New York: Vintage Books, 1989), p. 13.
75 Joe L. Kincheloe, Foreword, in McLaren, *Che Guevara*, p. xii.
76 Emile Durkheim, *The Division of Labour in Society*, trans. W. D. Wells (New York: The Free Press, 1964), p. 398.
77 Freire, *Pedagogy of the Oppressed*, p. 70.
78 Sharon Welch, *Communities of Resistance and Solidarity: A Feminist Theology of Liberation* (Maryknoll, NY: Orbis, 1985), p. 45.
79 Beatrice Dedaa Okyere-Manu, 'Who is Umuntu in Umuntu Ngumuntu Ngabantu? Interrogating Moral Issues Facing Ndau Women in Polygyny', *South African Journal of Philosophy* 37:2 (2018): 207–16, 207.
80 See Boesak, *Selfless Revolutionaries*, p. 209.
81 Jacob Mugumbate and Andrew Nyanguru, 'Exploring African Philosophy: The Value of Ubuntu in Social Work', *African Journal of Social Work* 3:1 (2013): 82–100, 85.
82 Mogobe B. Ramose, 'The Philosophy of Ubuntu and Ubuntu as a Philosophy', in P. H. Coetzee and A. P. J. Roux (eds), *Philosophy from Africa: A Text with Readings*, 2nd edn (London: Oxford University Press, 2002), p. 231.
83 John S. Mbiti, *African Religions and Philosophy*, 2nd edn (Oxford: Heinemann Educational, 1989), p. 106.
84 See Nomalungelo I. Ngubane and Manyane Makua, 'Intersection of *Ubuntu* Pedagogy and Social Justice: Transforming South African Higher Education', *Transformation in Higher Education* 6:a113 (2021): 1–8, 2.
85 See Otrude Nontobeko Moyo, *Africanity and Ubuntu as Decolonizing Discourse* (Cham, Switzerland: Palgrave Macmillan, 2021), p. 49.
86 Ngubane and Makua, 'Intersection of *Ubuntu* Pedagogy', 2.
87 Allan Boesak, 'A Theology of Freedom, Not of Absolutes: Learning, Unlearning, and Re-learning: Towards a More Complete Liberation', Lecture Six, 30 October 2021, 3.

88 Sylvan E. Blignaut and Oscar Koopman, 'Towards an Embodied Critical Pedagogy of Discomfort as a Decolonial Teaching', *Alternations* 31 (2020): 81–96, 82.

89 Adbul Karim Bangura, 'Ubuntugogy: An African Educational Paradigm that Transcends Pedagogy, Andragogy, Ergonagy and Heutagogy', *Journal of Third World Studies* 22:2 (2005): 13–53, 19–20.

90 Miguel De La Torre, *Burying White Privilege: Resurrecting a Badass Christianity* (Grand Rapids, MI: Wm. B. Eerdmans, 2019), p. 5.

91 Boesak, 'A Theology of Freedom', 8.

92 Antonio Faundez and Paulo Freire, *Learning to Question: A Pedagogy of Liberation* (Geneva: WCC Publications, 1989), p. 20.

93 Boesak, 'A Theology of Freedom', 4.

94 Prashad, *Karma*, p. 198.

95 James H. Cone, *Black Theology and Black Power* (San Francisco: Harper & Row, 1989), p. 27.

96 Christine J. Hong, *Decolonial Futures: Intercultural and Interreligious Intelligence for Theological Education* (Maryland, NY: Lexington Books, 2021), p. 49.

Index of Bible References

Old Testament

Genesis
16.1–16   68–73

Judges
16.5   76–7
19.1–29   37–46

Esther
4.13–17   98
5.2   100

New Testament

Matthew
14.13–21   50
15.22–36   50
15.23–27   12–18

Mark
6.45–56   179–83
12.13–17   79

Luke
5.11   186
7.14.18   80
7.36–50   50, 78–80
18.1–8   104–5, 113–14

1 Corinthians
1.27   189

Index of Names and Subjects

Abram 68–9, 71–3
abuse xvii, 7, 18, 23, 30–9, 40–5, 59, 60–8, 86, 91–2, 120–1, 152, 163–4
African xvi, xvii, 5, 30, 34, 67–9, 121, 127–8, 153–5, 185, 189, 190, 192
Althaus-Reid, Marcella 26, 47, 52, 83, 93, 97, 116, 142, 152, 161–2, 182, 198
Anglican xviii, 20, 22, 128
anti-colonial 16, 75, 125, 157, 195
anti-racism 148, 156
  anti-racist 147, 156, 171
Archbishop of Canterbury 64, 65

Bishop Macrorie vii
Blue, Ellen 109–10, 118
Boesak, Allan 72, 83, 98, 100, 118, 183, 192–3, 198–200
British Empire 6, 20, 127, 129, 144

Canaanite 12–17, 25

Church of England vii, xviii, 18–19, 22, 42, 44, 54–5, 57, 59–64, 66, 95–6, 98, 126, 140, 163
Church of Ireland 85, 88, 115
Church Times xiii, 28, 82, 116
colonial vii, viii, ix, x, xiii, xiv, xvii, xix, 1–2, 5–6, 8, 12, 16, 19–22, 24, 29, 33–4, 40, 43, 67, 121–7, 129–30, 132–3, 135–7, 139, 141–4, 151, 153–6, 170–1, 174, 176, 180, 190–2
  colonialized 30, 33, 48, 67, 139, 171
concubine 37–40, 43–5, 68
Cone, James 15–16, 80, 84, 131, 145, 149, 157, 159, 161–2, 184, 198, 200
Cooper, Thia 11, 26, 52, 53
Covid-19 24, 62
curricula xiii, xix, xx, 2–4, 10, 14, 25, 30, 49, 56, 66, 85–6, 89, 101, 103,

INDEX OF NAMES AND SUBJECTS

106–7, 109, 122, 150–1, 153, 155–6
curriculum xx, 1–3, 11–12, 24–5, 87, 103, 106–9, 113, 134, 150, 152, 155–7, 171, 178, 190, 193

Dalit 30, 124, 137–9, 141–4, 151
De La Torre, Miguel 15, 27, 55, 81, 101, 117, 122, 135, 137, 160, 192, 200
decolonial 12, 43, 125, 135, 142, 150–1, 155–7, 169, 191
decolonizing 150, 152, 155, 170
dehumanize 121, 187
Delilah 76–8
dialogue 8, 10–11, 14, 24, 48–9, 74–5, 94, 103–4, 107, 110–11, 136, 142–9, 152, 156, 163–6, 172, 174–87, 190, 192–4
dialogical 25, 29, 32, 112, 155, 165, 178
disabled xiv, 3, 9–10, 19, 23, 30, 73–5, 185
discernment 92, 95, 192
discrimination 21, 44, 58, 173
dismembered 38, 40–1, 45, 47
diversity 5, 8, 23, 49, 61, 92, 97, 100, 103, 110, 112–13, 147, 165–6
doctrine xviii, 22, 103, 112,

Dube, Musa 46, 52, 108, 118, 153–5, 162

ecclesiastical viii, 58, 76
embodied xviii, 2, 20, 22–3, 31, 36, 70–1, 73, 91, 93–4, 102, 106, 110, 112–13, 122, 153–56, 166–7, 169, 177–8, 172, 186–7, 194
embodying 166
empowerment 101, 177, 192
emotion 56, 92, 179–83
engendered xix, 109, 111–12, 133
engendering 85, 87, 94, 106–8, 110, 113
epistemic racism 122, 125, 131–4
Eurocentric viii, ix, xii, xvii, 1, 6, 10, 20, 33–4, 41, 72, 107, 111, 135–7, 142–3, 151, 155, 190–1
Esther 98–100

Faith in the City 64, 82
Fāgogo 29, 58
Fanon, Frantz xviii, xxiii, 54, 81
feminist pedagogy xx, 101, 103–4, 109
flourishing xx, 3–4, 8, 24–5, 47, 55, 93, 97, 115
formation ix, xi, xii, xx, 4, 11–12, 14, 18, 20, 43, 45, 49, 55, 57, 59, 60, 64, 66–7, 86–93, 96, 103,

106–7, 110, 121, 123–4, 136, 150, 156, 164–6, 188
formational xi, xii, 10, 92, 103, 142, 192
Forrest, Ian xv, xxii, 58, 60, 81, 83
France-Williams, A. D. A. 19, 27, 60, 82
Freire, Paulo vii, xxi, 2, 5, 7, 11, 25–6, 33, 51, 53, 74, 83, 144–7, 161, 164, 175, 178, 182, 185, 193–9
Fricker, Miranda 130, 159

Gafney, Wilda 36
gaze viii, xi, xx, 4, 6, 43, 54–63, 67, 69, 71–2, 74–9, 91, 97, 105–6, 123, 131–2
gender violence xix, 70
Gonzalez, Justo 108, 118

Hagar 67–73
hermeneutics xx, 32, 36, 87, 98, 103, 110, 134, 141–3, 145
Herzog, Frederick 80, 123, 158, 171, 196
Herzog, William R. 84, 104, 117, 139
Heteronormativity viii, 1, 3, 4, 7, 135, 141
Hong, Christine xiii, xviii, xx, 16, 27, 57, 81, 83, 125, 132, 148, 150, 158–9, 162, 195
hooks, bell 14, 26, 94, 101, 108, 110, 113, 116–19, 149, 162, 167, 172–3, 177, 181, 196–8
Hull, John 73–4, 83

Isasi-Díaz, Ada María xxi, 51, 107, 118, 161, 165, 195
indecent 31, 42–5, 57, 76, 78, 80, 90, 125, 138–40, 142, 151, 192
indigenous x, 6, 10, 13, 25, 30, 32–4, 43, 124–5, 127, 129–30, 133–5, 139–42, 155, 171, 174, 190–2
interconnected xx, 156, 165–8, 170–1, 189
intercultural xviii, 137, 141, 195
interdisciplinary 111, 134
intersectional 35, 63, 69, 104, 106, 143, 185
Isherwood, Lisa 85, 115

Jennings, Willie James viii, xxi, 18, 20, 27, 46, 52, 122, 148, 150, 157, 162

Kennerley, Ginnie 88, 90, 115
Kin-dom xix, 153, 165–6, 169–71, 178, 186, 190, 192, 194–5
Kirkbride, Alice 59

Levite 37–8, 40, 44–5, 47
LGBTQI+ xiii, xiv, 5, 10, 23, 56, 60, 62, 73, 75, 77, 85, 89, 93, 95, 97, 106

INDEX OF NAMES AND SUBJECTS

liberation theology 64, 153, 74

McLaren, Peter 179, 196–7
Mignolo, Walter ix, xviii, xxi, xxiii, 135, 150, 155, 160–2
Mills, Charles ix, xxi, 161
missiology xvi, 129, 170
Mordecai 99
Morrison, Toni 4, 25–6, 160
Mud Flower Collective 7, 97

Nash, Sally 91–2, 116
Ndebele, Njabulo vii, xxi

Oduyoye, Mercy Amba 155, 162

Pacific 29–30, 163
Pharisee 50, 78, 80, 187
postcolonial xix, xx, 124, 125, 151, 153
Pui-Lan, Kwok 52, 147, 161

racism xi, xix, 2–7, 14–16, 18–19, 21, 23, 30, 35, 39, 41, 47–8, 57, 70, 72, 120–5, 131–7, 141, 145–6, 148, 151, 156–7, 163, 168, 172, 173, 176, 185, 189, 191
Rahab 154
rape 30, 37–9, 41–4, 61, 88, 121, 137, 152
Reddie, Anthony xvii, xxiii, 5, 20, 22, 26–8, 133, 135, 139, 156, 160, 162, 170, 196
Resistance 7, 24–5, 30, 36, 43, 69, 100, 110, 123, 135, 171, 185–6, 188, 191
revolution xiv, 24, 97, 188, 194
Rieger, Joerg 125, 158, 196
Robinson-Brown, Jarel 73, 77, 83–4

same-sex 40, 61
Samoa 29, 48
sexism xix, 2–3, 5, 7, 14–16, 35, 40, 48, 57, 97, 137, 141, 145, 151, 176, 185, 191
shame viii, x, xv, 16, 30, 41, 54–5, 61–2, 67, 77–9, 87–94, 153, 164, 183, 189
Smith, Linda T. 48, 151, 162
Smith, Mitzi 131, 159
Society for the Propagation of the Gospel to Foreign Parts 128
spiritualities 30, 57
Stoddart, Eric 55, 71, 88, 84
storytelling 12, 34–5, 109, 113, 154
subaltern 133, 138, 140, 142–5

Tamez, Elsa 44, 52, 115
temptress 85, 87, 89, 91, 94, 98, 172
testimony 35–8, 40, 45, 76, 113, 174

transformative pedagogy 87,
  100, 105–6, 110, 141–3,
  172, 181
trustworthy xiv–xx, 11, 16,
  55–60, 66–7, 75–6, 80,
  102–3, 105, 126, 133,
  140, 172, 175, 193
torture 30, 36–8, 40–1, 43,
  59
Trible, Phyllis 38, 52, 68,
  71, 82–3
Tutu, Desmond xvii

Ubuntu xvii, xx, 189–95
un-belonging xix, 5, 19, 46,
  56, 85, 93–6, 108, 110,
  122, 132

Weems, Renita J 34, 51, 68,
  69, 82
Wells, Ida 131–2
widow 103–6, 113–14

whiteness xviii, xx, 5, 9–10,
  18, 20–3, 25, 30, 74,
  120–5, 131–6, 141, 144–6,
  149–50, 171, 187
white supremacy viii, 5 121,
  123, 125, 128, 130–1,
  133–4, 136, 139, 150,
  152, 170, 193
Williams, Delores 71
Williams, Rowan xi, xxi, 86,
  93, 111, 115–16, 118
woke 50, 120
womanist 4, 7, 34–6, 39,
  124, 131, 151, 153–4, 185
working class 5, 13–14, 18,
  30, 32, 42, 56, 60, 62–6,
  71, 76, 89, 101, 174, 185
World Christianity xx, 124,
  131, 134–7, 140–1, 144
worship 18, 36, 93, 138–9,
  142

Trust + power — x, xvi,

Trust in clergy / the church — xiii – xiv — how translatable is this to IME 2?
+ is it culture or process or both?

formation — shaping of minds — xi

Situates herself — xvii

Tokenism in diversity — 8

Personhood — 18-19

"Bleeding women" (women's voices)
Page 35, 46.

formation as becoming self — 48.